THE RIDDLE OF CHRISTIAN MYSTICAL EXPERIENCE

LOUVAIN THEOLOGICAL & PASTORAL MONOGRAPHS
29

THE RIDDLE OF CHRISTIAN MYSTICAL EXPERIENCE

The Role of the Humanity of Jesus

Paul Mommaers

PEETERS PRESS
LOUVAIN

© 2003, Peeters, Bondgenotenlaan 153, 3000 Leuven, Belgium

ISBN 90-429-1232-4 (Peeters Leuven)
D. 2003/0602/8

TABLE OF CONTENTS

FOREWORD

This is a book that was asking to be written. Admittedly the immediate request came only in 1997, when the Master of Campion Hall in Oxford came and asked me to give the Martin D'Arcy Lectures for the year 1998, leaving the choice of topic open to me. But over many years, and from different directions, there had been hints and nudges, question marks and dots at the end of sentences...

Anyone who engages in the study of the writings of the great mystics, whether French, English, Spanish, or — more especially in my case — Flemish, is faced by a recurring puzzle or "riddle" that is latent or explicit in much of what they are saying. On the one hand their mystical experiences seem to lift them to realms that surpass the human and the corporeal; on the other, the real bodily presence of Jesus Christ is constantly present in their thoughts and lives. How do they resolve this apparent paradox? Is it possible for them to be lost in imageless contemplation while fixing their attention on Christ, the image of God? Leaving aside dogmatic or moral considerations, why should someone engulfed in the divinity be drawn simultaneously to follow the humanity of Christ? If a person is raised to the height of mystical experience can he or she continue to experience the lowly pleasure and pain of a human body? Is there indeed a solution to this many-sided question or should one posit an insoluble conundrum? And do these writings provide a single solution or are there variations and degrees of success — or failure — in their attempts to satisfy their readers?

However, these doubts and queries, that grew as I went deeper into the careful study of the mystics, had been preceded by earlier questions that had left me equally dissatisfied. As a young theology student I had had the good fortune to spend a semester in Edinburgh. There I met among my fellow students a brilliant Indian woman, as intelligent as she was attractive. Little wonder that I was fascinated and that we spent many hours in discussions! Although she had been educated in a Catholic school — "I loved the sisters!" — and was working at that time on her PhD thesis on Yeats, she came from a deeply rooted Hindu tradition. She was the one who first brought home to me the great question that must confront all inter-religious dialogue: in what sense is the role of Jesus Christ unique? Surely this Palestinian, a man of flesh and blood, has to be put on a par with the other great mystical teachers who have brought such wisdom and truth to other parts of the world. If mystical experience is not a monopoly of Christians, how essential to it is the bodily presence of Christ? These may seem abstract questions, but they took on concrete reality when, in the shadow of Arthur's seat, my Indian friend looked me in the eyes and asked, "Can't we together go beyond such figures as Jesus and Krishna and Buddha?" The words that burned into my mind, "to go beyond", have now of course become common-place in inter-religious dialogue, but at that moment they seemed irresistible.

The questions that had come home to me with such force in Edinburgh gathered fresh force when I visited India some years later and was able to spend some time in a Brahmin household, privileged to take part in their prayer rituals. There spread out on a simple dais I could see images of Hindu gods and among them a picture of Jesus Christ. What was I to make of the fraternal company He was keeping, apparently waiting to disappear into the imageless beyond? Was I to feel at home there, I a Jesuit, a member of the "Company" of Jesus?

However in recent years, I have found that the questions I was asking were being reinforced by reflections that came from a very different quarter. The twentieth century witnessed the gradual emergence and growth of a new-found interest for what is sometimes called "spirituality", a term that covers a wide gamut of phenomena, from the scholarly publications that were the glory of the French Jesuits (culminating in their great *Dictionnaire de Spiritualité*) through the range of devotional and spiritual writings that brought new life to many Catholic publishers, and on to the outer reaches of esoteric interests, that have found an ever more ravenous public. I myself became interested in the links between Western mysticism, in particular Jan van Ruusbroec, and the great Buddhist tradition. The fruit of this interest was a book written in collaboration with a Buddhist scholar putting side by side the two traditions.

Common strands in this variegated world of spirituality are the longing to "go beyond" and the importance given to personal experience. For many of these spiritual traditions the goal and culmination is presented as a "feeling", a particular type of satisfaction, which is some times presented as ecstatic and which normally is described as pleasurable. What room was there here for the humanity of Christ? If a spirituality could be considered successful in so far as it took the person out of oneself, if the supreme good to be hoped for was a ravishing feeling of great joy, what did this have to do with the Risen, let alone the crucified, Lord Jesus Christ? Again, if mysticism was essentially directed to the good of the individual person, how could it escape the stain of egoism? What link could there possibly be with one's fellow human beings, in particular with those most destitute and in need of help?

These were the questions with which I began my reflections with a view to writing this book. Now that it is written I cannot pretend to have answered them all, but at least I have the feeling and the hope that thanks to this book some of my readers may be able to see ahead of me to possible solutions.

My sincere thanks are due to those who have helped me bring this book into the world. In the first place to Dr Joseph Munitiz, SJ, the then Master of Campion Hall, who both invited me to give the Martin D'Arcy Lectures and then helped me with great patience to transform the spoken lectures into a legible book. As for articulating my conclusions and expressing them in appropriate English I owe a great debt to Dr Elisabeth Dutton, whose sharp-sighted sense for fluent clarity has been invaluable. I also wish to express my thanks to several colleagues at the University of Antwerp (UFSIA), especially Dr Walter Van Herck, who read through the text and offered me that most valuable of scholarly gifts, a critical understanding. I remember with gratitude the company I enjoyed during several months at Campion Hall, Oxford: there I found brisk intellects ready to give "without counting the cost" (as some mystics say). Last, but not least, I am grateful to Professor Terrence Merrigan of the Katholieke Universiteit, Leuven. As director of the series "Theological and Pastoral Monographs" he both read my text with great care and sympathy and then made it welcome.

CHAPTER I

THE IMAGE AND THE IDOL

Plotinus describes the contemplative who has reached his goal as follows: "He is like one who, having penetrated the inner sanctuary, leaves the temple images behind him… for there his converse was not with image, not with trace, but with the very truth in view of which all the rest is but of secondary concern."

And Ruusbroec tells his reader that "all encumbrance from images" has to be driven out from the person who "wants to become spiritual": "In possessing God with affection, man will be freed of images inside, since God is a spirit and no man can make a proper image of him. In possessing God … man must enter into a bare imagelessness which is God."

It looks then as if the master contemplatives from different traditions stand for an utterly imageless experience as the final point of the spiritual path. And this going beyond all images seems to imply that representations of the divine are just stepping stones to be left behind, not to say "encumbrances" to be got rid of.

Perhaps we would agree with this purifying view of the spiritual path. Apparently the idea of the Absolute — of ultimate Reality as utterly detached from everything relative — is engrained in us.[1]

---

[1] Even with the present-day scientific notion of seeing reality in a purely objective way, this very old spiritual tendency seems to be at work. Charles Taylor "claims, then, that the motivating power of the secular and naturalistic drive to extend objective knowledge as far as possible, *and even farther*, receives its deepest energy from the traditional drive to spiritual purity." See Fergus Kerr, *Theology after Wittgenstein* (Oxford: Basil Blackwell, 1986) 25-26.

In addition, the trend in spirituality nowadays seems to be to sheer "not-knowing" (a considerable step further than the *Cloud of Unknowing*): the apophatic experience ("Dionysian" style) and imageless meditation ("Buddhist" style) are in vogue.

However, such a stern view of contemplation would not find favour with Plotinus or Ruusbroec. In the passage from the *Enneads* quoted above, the dots refer to a significant parenthesis: "though these (= images) become once more first objects of regard when he leaves the holies." Obviously, Plotinus sees the person "whose ascent is achieved" coming down again to the images he left behind. And we should not presume that he fails to appreciate representations of the divine. Far from being empty signs pointing to the Void, they are filled with Reality, the All is present in them:

> I think therefore, that those ancient sages, who sought to secure the presence of divine beings by the erection of shrines and statues, showed insight into the nature of the All; they perceived that, though this Soul is everywhere tractable, its presence will be secured all the more readily when an appropriate receptacle is elaborated, a place especially capable of receiving some portion or phase of it, something reproducing it, or representing it and serving like a mirror to catch an image of it.

And Ruusbroec too, in the passage quoted above, has a parenthesis of similar import:

> Yet in his (spiritual) practice man should concentrate on good images, such as the passion of our Lord and all things that may rouse him to higher devotion.[2]

---

[2] Quotations are from Plotinus, *The Enneads*, trans. Stephen MacKenna (London: Faber & Faber, 1969) 624, 270 (*Ennead* VI, 9,11 and IV, 3,11). Ruusbroec's passages (slightly touched up) are from *The Sparkling Stone*, contained in *Opera omnia, X: Vanden blinkenden steen, Vanden vier becoringhen, Vanden kerstenen ghelove, Brieven*, eds. Guido de Baere, Thom Mertens, Hilde Noë,

The passages just quoted indicate clearly enough the topic of this book. It can be summarized in the following questions: Is it the case that full-fledged contemplatives are gifted with an imageless experience that does away once and for all with all images or necessarily reduces them to inane substitutes? And if, on the contrary, the images do not need to disappear from the full-grown experience, then how can the imageless go together with the imaged? To put this in a more general way, how does immediacy relate to mediation?

In the Christian spiritual tradition the issue of the value of images is all the more crucial as contemplation is supposed to focus on

with an introduction by Paul Mommaers, English translation by André Lefevere, Latin translation by Laurentius Surius, Studiën en tekstuitgaven van *Ons Geestelijk Erf* 20, 10 (Tielt: Lannoo; Leiden: E.J. Brill, 1991) 36-41 and 38-40. The text was also published in the series Corpus Christianorum: Continuatio Mediaevalis 110 (Tielt: Lannoo; Turnhout: Brepols, 1991). In the context of this chapter it is worth remembering the report by Porphyry of Plotinus' reluctance to have himself portrayed: "Plotinus, the philosopher our contemporary, seemed ashamed of being in the body ... He showed, too, an unconquerable reluctance to sit to a painter or a sculptor, and when Amelius persisted in urging him to allow of a portrait being made he asked him, 'Is it not enough to carry about this image in which nature has enclosed us? Do you really think I must also consent to leave, as a desirable spectacle to posterity, an image of the image?'" (See Plotinus, *The Enneads*, trans. Stephen MacKenna, 1). However, this rejection of the portrait does not imply Plotinus' denial of the (ontological) value of the image. Here is a significant reflection: "We may be told that an image (*eidôlon*) need not be thus closely attached to its archetype, that we know images (*eikona*) holding in the absence of their archetype and that a warmed object may retain its heat when the fire is withdrawn. To begin with the image and archetype: if we are reminded of an artist's picture (*eikona*) we observe that here the image was produced by the artist, not by its subject; even in the case of a self-portrait, the picture is no 'image (*eikona*) of the archetype', since it is not produced by the painter's body, the original (*to eidos*) represented: the reproduction is due to the effective laying on of the colours. Nor is there strictly any such making of image (*eikonos kai tou indalmatos*) as we see in water or in mirrors or in a shadow; in these cases the original is the cause of the image, which, at once, springs from it and cannot exist apart from it" (*Ennead* VI, 4,10).

the figure of Christ.[3] He is "the image of the invisible God"
(Colossians 2,9), the "stamp of God's very being" (Hebrews 1,3).
He is "the one mediator between God and men, Christ Jesus, himself man" (1 Timothy 2,5). Moreover, this "mediator of a new
covenant" (Hebrews 9,15;12,14), being himself man, is God's
perceptible image: "For it is in Christ that the complete being of
the Godhead dwells embodied" (Col. 2,9).[4]

However, the believer's view of Christ as the unique and adequate image of God — "Anyone who has seen me has seen the
Father" (John 14,9) — does not alter the fact that, as this particular man, the Godman belongs to the realm of the imaginable. That
is why the issue of the contemplative's images sharpens into a crucial Christological riddle. Is Jesus himself only a "temple image"
or even an "encumbrance"? Does the most conducive of images
turn in the contemplative's experience into the most subtle of
idols? And anyway, even if Jesus appears to be the right "Door",
what happens to him in the experience of those who have passed
through it? And what about this "Way", when the contemplative

[3] Contemplation, even in its most advanced mystical stages, is the awareness
of salvation and union with God. It is always secondary to "simple" faith. It is
nothing more (and nothing less!) than "illumined" faith. If then Christ is the key
figure of the Christian religion, he is also the central "object" of contemplation.
And the difficulty caused by the figure of the Godman in contemplation is the
reflection of the basic paradox of the common Christian faith making itself felt in
personal prayer. By concentrating attention upon Jesus Christ, the contemplative
undertakes a disconcerting spiritual exercise, and in this mental struggling consists his particular awareness of what is general knowledge: "Christ nailed to the
Cross ... a stumbling-block ... and folly" (1 Cor. 1,23).

[4] Obviously, "embodied" (*somatikos*) does not mean that the invisible and
untouchable One is reduced to a mere body. In order to grasp the meaning of this
divine corporality, we may think of the way in which the human spirit dwells in
the body — making "le corps" into "la chair," as French philosophers put it —
or God's spirit dwells in the temple. See John 2,21: "But the temple he was
speaking of was his body."

traveller has reached his goal, the Ultimate? Will he retrace his steps? Why should he?

In the first place we need to get a right perspective on the significance of the concept of image. The material available here is overwhelming, yet it seems possible to distinguish the most important pieces of the puzzle and thus to grasp what is one of the contemplative tradition's most urgent problems.

This hopeful outlook is not meant to suggest that we can expect plain sailing. Nowadays the age-old sense of "image" is not evident anymore. Plunged as we are into a "culture of the visual", we are used to considering images as self-sufficient phenomena. An image just points at other images, or its "sense" (a word that is, of course, going out of fashion) lies in itself: an image is an image and there is no need to look for some real thing beyond it. In this way, then, we have entered a "virtual" world, the realm of visual appearance which is, as we are about to see, far from the traditional world of the image.

In addition to this general shift in our view of images, there is a particular line of thinking that is quite influential and may hamper us as we try to appreciate the long-standing sense of the image. In its sophisticated way, philosophical "deconstruction" appears to go well together with our "culture of the visual." Here all signs are exposed as empty. It is the most tenacious of illusions to consider them as actually representing the reality they seem to signify. Instead, then, of being a substantiation of the real thing that shows itself in them, an image is nothing more than a substitute that refers to other substitutes. Our human world on the whole is a world of signs generating signs, an indefinite web of substitutes for a presence that is never there.[5]

---

[5] Here is a striking passage from Jacques Derrida himself commenting on the description by J.J. Rousseau of his having recourse to supplements in the absence

Image as an Anthropological Concept

Primarily "image", as used here, is not a psychological term connected to the imaginative way of knowing, which proceeds by using mental or physical images in order to have a certain kind of perception. By the same token it does not point in the first instance at the mental procedure of contemplative persons who, as the phrase goes, "empty their mind of all images" in order to "see" God.

Basically "image" conveys an anthropological view that originates mainly from the Bible and denotes the nature of the human being as a whole. According to the Creation narrative,[6] man and woman are seen as really, ontologically related to God. So much so that they appear as the actual and perceptible representation of the Unseen, in the pregnant sense of the divine Being essentially present in the human.[7]

Obviously, since the image-maker is the Creator who freely gives shape to his image, there is an indelible difference between the Artist and his work, a distance that remains forever. God has made man and woman "to the image of Himself," as Ruusbroec

of his "Maman" ("How often I kissed my bed, recalling that she had slept in it …"): "Through this sequence of supplements there emerges a law: that of an endless linked series, ineluctably multiplying the supplementary mediations that produce the sense of the very thing that they defer: the impression of the thing itself, of immediate presence, or originary perception. Immediacy is derived. Everything begins with the intermediary …" Quoted in Jonathan Culler, *On Deconstruction: Theory and Criticism after Structuralism* (London: Routledge and Kegan Paul, 1983) 105.

[6] Genesis 1, 26-27 (=P) and Genesis 2, 7 (=J).

[7] In no way, then, can the sense of "image of God" when applied to man and woman, boil down to their just being a "shadow" of the Divine, in a manner comparable to that by which those living their empty existence in Hades or Sheol, are the insubstantial "shades" of their former real selves.

consistently puts it. Yet, this transcendence of the LORD does not alter his special[8] immanence in the human, so much so that "if God is anthropomorphic, man is theomorphic."[9]

The key passage of the second Creation narrative (*Genesis* 2,7) deserves particular attention here: "Then the Lord God formed a man (*adam*) from the dust of the ground (*adaman*) and breathed into his nostrils the breath of life. Thus the man became a living creature." This unique, life-giving face-to-face between God and man shows that the human creature shares indeed in the Maker's own way of being. Is not "Life" the most biblical definition of the indefinable One? God *is* Life, unceasingly generating itself and inexhaustibly communicating itself.[10] Thus man and woman are God's image because of their sharing in that same Life.

[8] Only man and woman are God's "image," all other creatures are God's "vestiges," *vestigia Dei*.

[9] Paul Ricoeur comments on *Genesis* 1, 26-27 as follows: "L'homme est créé en forme des 'Elohim', c'est-à-dire selon un modèle céleste qui l'arrache à la sphère du visible; ainsi, si Dieu est anthropomorphe, l'homme est théomorphe." And J. Blenkinsop comments on *Ezekiel* 1, 26-28: "L'humanité est à l'image de Dieu, Dieu est à l'image de l'humanité — une compénétration mystérieuse." Both quotations from Paul Ricoeur and André LaCocque, *Penser La Bible* (Paris: Seuil 1998) 26.

[10] Ruusbroec likes to speak of God as "a living eternal something" (*een levende eewich yet*), as the One who "lives in us and we in Him." He sees God as "a common outflowing." And he calls the link between God and man "the living life which is hidden in us" (*dat levende leven*). See Jan van Ruusbroec, *Werken*, naar het standaardhandschrift van Groenendaal uitgegeven door het Ruusbroecgenootschap te Antwerpen, 4 vols. (Tielt: Lannoo, 1944-1948²). See IV, 51, 12-21; III, 211, 29. See also *Opera omnia*, III: *Die geestelike brulocht*, ed. Joseph Alaerts, with an introduction by Paul Mommaers, trans. Helen Rolfson, directed by Guido de Baere, Studiën en tekstuitgaven van *Ons Geestelijk Erf* 20, 3 (Tielt: Lannoo; Turnhout: Brepols, 1988) b1088. The text was also published in the series Corpus Christianorum: Continuatio Mediaevalis 103 (Tielt: Lannoo; Turnhout: Brepols, 1988). The *Opera omnia* is the critical edition of the original Middle Dutch text, arranged synoptically with an English translation and

In this way the sense of image is significantly enriched. Far from being just a static, thinglike entity, an object for the senses, the image appears as being fundamentally a spiritual and personal reality, a subject. The human image of God shares in the LORD's hiddenness, freedom and "extroversion."[11] This emphasis on the inner liveliness of the God-like image implies that man does not resemble his Creator because he might "look like" him. In order to have man represent him, God does not make him into a sort of portrait but enables him to *act* in a God-like manner.[12]

To stress the spiritual liveliness of God's image does not mean that one should bypass the bodily aspect of the resemblance — think of the upright stature of human beings; see Ezekiel's vision (1,26-28). The Bible never loses sight of the body which is, as Wittgenstein puts it, "the best picture of the soul." It never considers the soul an ethereal substance enclosed in the body, for, as several mystics say, "the body is in the soul, not the soul in the body."

Connected with the theme of God being Life, and humanity really sharing in it, is the prohibition of images that appears so

the sixteenth-century Latin edition by Laurentius Surius. The complete *Opera omnia* will run to ten volumes, four of which were in print when this study was being drafted. (See bibliography). These will be cited here. As for Ruusbroec's other works, quotations will be taken from *Werken*, I-IV, a complete and thoroughly reliable edition of the Middle-Dutch text published by the Ruusbroecgenootschap.

[11] As André LaCocque puts it (*Penser la Bible*, 28): "L'être humain est *imago Dei* parce que tout en lui est appel à entrer en communication avec le modèle divin, lui-même totalement 'extraverti'. Dieu est la référence ultime de l'être humain tendu vers Autrui. C'est pourquoi l'imago est immédiatement mise en relation avec la vie sexuelle (1,27 cfr. 2,7.21), c'est-à-dire avec la communication par excellence."

[12] Not all resemblance is just "put before the eyes," as Aristotle said. Our rather spontaneous association of resembling and being in the image of (as a portrait or a snapshot is in the likeness or image of someone) is misleading. There is no way of catching a likeness of God.

strongly in the Old Testament.[13] Why is Israel not allowed to produce any image of Yahweh? The main reason ties in with the view of God as Life. Only the living human person can represent the living God. Compared to this image, that freely moves of itself, all other images are lifeless things. As such they would misrepresent God's self-revelation:

> On the day when the LORD spoke to you out of the fire on Horeb, you saw no figure of any kind; so take good care not to fall into the degrading practice of making figures carved in relief, in the form of a man or a woman, or of any animal on earth or bird that flies in the air, or of any reptile on the ground or fish in the nature under the earth.[14]

By its sheer being as a visible object — something that, as we say so suggestively, "falls under" our categories — the non-human image carries the risk of presenting a degrading portrait of the formless Life. Instead of being the mobile image that should represent in the first instance God's personal life force, it appears as a motionless idol that rigidifies the divine. This is the almost irresistible "temptation" the Bible is concerned with when it so rigorously prohibits "making figures."

However, here again we ought not jump to the conclusion that Scripture tends to spiritualize the human's encounter with God. In this case, too, there is no question of any dichotomic opposition between visible and invisible, material and spiritual, as if persons were supposed to meet the invisible One directly in a purified,

---

[13] For recent (also iconographical) research on the historical background of this ban, see Karel van der Toorn (ed.), *The Image and the Book. Iconic Cults, Aniconism, and the Rise of Book Religion in Israel and the Near East* (Leuven: Peeters, 1997) 73-95, where it is shown that there had been a long-standing worship of images in Israel. Most striking is the question, addressed by Herbert Niehr, whether there was indeed a cult statue of Yahweh in the first temple.

[14] *Deuteronomy* 4,15-19.

imageless way. The prohibition does not target the image as such but its reductive nature.[15]

At this point two more biblical views concerning God's self-manifestation deserve attention as they help to focus the prohibition of images.[16] In fact the founding revelation is not completely imageless, although at the same time it may appear as an immediate contact between God and man. A few lines before the prohibition passage in Deuteronomy already quoted, one finds the words: "When the LORD spoke to you from the fire you heard a voice speaking, but you saw no figure; there was only a voice" (4,12). Undoubtedly, this is a genuine biblical teaching: hearing God's word is far better than seeing his image.[17]

In brief, words, as fleeting invisible signs, are most suited for persons to "show" their inner core. And in this way the biblical view of the immediate character of Moses knowing God makes sense. To speak to each other is the most direct form of self-revelation, as appears from *Numbers*:

[15] See Pierre Miquel, "Images (culte des)," in *Dictionnaire de spiritualité* VII/2 (1971)1506-1507.

[16] I am borrowing here from Hans Urs von Balthasar, *Herrlichkeit. Eine Theologische Aesthetik* (Einsiedeln: Johannes-Verlag, 1961-1969) Band III, 2, Teil 1, pp. 38-40, and Band III, 2, Teil 2, pp. 253-258; 267-274.

[17] This theme will play an important role in the Christian tradition as well. From Paul's *fides ex auditu*, "faith is awakened by the message" (*Romans*, 10,17), theologians again and again point to the priority of listening to the *word* of God. And contemplatives refer to their hearing his *voice*. Geert Grote (+ 1384) deserves to be mentioned here. He is the sole medieval author who explicitly reflects upon the issue of images in contemplation, and he pays special attention to the word taking precedence over the image. See Gerardo Groote, *Il trattato "de quattuor generibus meditabilium,"* introduced, edited and translated, and annotated by Ilario Tolomio, Publicazzioni dell'Istituto di Storia della Filosofia e del Centro per Ricerche di Filosofia Medioevale: Nuova Serie 18 (Padova: Editrice Antenore, 1975) line 439 ff.

> If he were your prophet and nothing more, I would make myself
> known to him in a vision, I would speak to him in a dream... With
> him I speak face to face, openly and not in riddles (12,6-8).

This understandable preference of the Old Testament for the *word* puts the prohibition of images in the right perspective.[18] The chosen people should not lay themselves open to the temptation of staring at opaque figures. Following the example of Moses they ought to listen to the expressive word of God.

And yet, there is still something more to the biblical view of images. The same passage from *Numbers* (12,8) that highlights God's speaking face to face with Moses continues as follows: "He shall see the very form of the LORD." Is this recognition of God's "form" in flat contradiction with the rejection of every divine "figure"? The answer is to be found in what the Bible calls the *kabod* of God, and this draws attention once again to the unique reality of life, particularly of a person's life.[19]

---

[18] André LaCocque confirms this view, perhaps more in depth, by linking the prohibition of any representation of God (*Exodus* 20,1-5) with the revelation of the divine Name: "And if [the Israelites] ask me his name, what shall I say? God answered, 'I AM'; that is who I am. Tell them that I AM has sent you to them" (*Ex.* 3,13-14). That God reveals his name means that he is a personal God who may be invoked, who enters an I-thou relationship. Consequently, this iconophobia does not imply that God wants to remain incognito. Paradoxically, the revelation of the Name is given by an aniconic God who wants to be accessible and known. The mediation of the visible representation is replaced by the immediacy of the inimaginable personal dialogue. However, this immediacy that removes the danger of objectifying the divine carries the risk of degrading the relationship by treating God with too much familiarity. That is why the first two commandments rejecting rivals and idols (Ex. 20,2-6) are followed by the third one that indicates the right way of dialoguing with the divine "You": "You shall not make wrong use of the name of the LORD your God; the LORD will not leave unpunished the man who misuses his name" (*Ex.* 20,7). See LaCocque, *Penser la Bible*, 318-319.

[19] Von Balthasar, *Herrlichkeit*, III, 2, 1, pp. 31-36, who first draws attention to a general, biological and anthropological, phenomenon. All living creatures

For the human being, *kabod* means the radiation of one's powerfulness, which makes one appear as actually present. However, the term not only refers to this emanation, but also points to the source of radiation within. *Kabod* then designates at once the "I" and its "prestige", that is, its commanding regard. When it refers to God, *kabod* analogously means that the divine Person presents to the human person his very Self together with, or rather *in* a fascinating radiation. And this is where the sense of God's "form" shown to Moses becomes clear. As a person, God can take shape; he can, so to say, body himself forth without becoming a "figure." Thus the Bible enriches the concept of "image" with a specific meaning derived from the way in which persons "show" themselves to each other.[20]

In the context of mystical experience two specifications deserve mention here. First one notes that even if the Bible makes a distinction between the perceptible form and the unseen core of the person, in no way does it separate them. To experience the other person's radiation does not mean that one comes into contact only with an emanation while being kept away from the inner, proper self. By nature persons are such that in their self-manifestation

appear to each other as powerful: they attract one another or keep the other at a distance. This mutual influence is particularly evident between persons. In this case, the one also senses, *in* the other's manifest power, the secret source of that power. By way of illustration, there is the impact, at once sensible and spiritual, of one person gazing at another.

[20] There is in the Old Testament a shift towards the recognition of God manifesting himself in his image as well as in his word. In place of the exclusive preference for the *word* with a corresponding rigorous rejection of the *image*, there appears a blending of both. This tendency culminates in the New Testament when the Word will be seen: "Our theme is the word of life. This life was made visible; we have seen it" (1 John, 1,2). And the Father will manifest himself in voice and image: "This testimony to me was given by the Father who sent me, although you never heard his voice, or saw his form" (John, 5,37).

mediation and immediacy go together. Scripture shows how personal encounter is a compound phenomenon. And as we will see in chapter 5, this same idea is at the centre of Ruusbroec's description of mystical union with God.

The second point to be noticed concerns the way in which God shows his form to a human person. The word "show" turns out to be quite equivocal here. Obviously the Unseen does not hold before this person's sensible or/and spiritual eye a picture-like representation, a figure, that allows one to gain an idea of God. God's form affects the human being as a whole. The person's consciousness in its entirety is touched, and touched in the strong sense of the word: God strictly impresses his form into the conscious stuff of the body-heart-mind complex. It is, then, by the quality of this influence that he makes himself known. In brief, without presenting any figure, God represents himself in the human person who, far from looking at God's image, feels his form.

As for the mystic's way of knowing God, it will become clear that the impression of the divine form belongs to the passive aspect of contemplation. Ruusbroec has a suggestive word here: *overvormen:* "God enkindles His fire in our heart. For that fire makes one with itself and like to itself all the things it can master and *transform*" (*overvormen*: give a new form to it). On the other hand, the image as a means to attain a view of God belongs to the active (or the preparatory) aspect of contemplation. Here again the word used by Ruusbroec is expressive enough: *vore nemen*, "hold before" one's eye. As quoted above, "in his practice man should concentrate (*vore nemen*) on good images."[21]

---

[21] Quotations from *Opera Omnia*, III, b214-216 and X, 38-39.

Image as a Psychological Concept

It is time now to pay attention to the sense of "image" with which we are nowadays (still) most familiar. From the image that represents something else by somehow being it (I am my father's image), we shift to the image that represents by resembling the original (I have an image of my father). This is a clear shift, but a tricky one. For traditionally both concepts — the ontological and the psychological — mostly interact, particularly in mystical writings. Take, for example, the expression "to go beyond the image": this may refer to a psychological movement — in contemplation one lets go of all images so as to reach a state of imageless emptiness. But the same expression may also point to an ontological shift: by being united with his Image, one will be united with the invisible God as well. Again, in Christian contemplation a person may make use of an image of Jesus (meditating on his Passion etc.) in order to come to realize how Christ is being impressed upon him: by looking at the "son of man" he may become aware of the Son living in him.[22]

---

[22] Recent research on the sense of "image" in the Middle Ages brings to the fore the proper reality of the image and its function. See *L'image. Fonctions et usages des images dans l'Occident médiéval*, Actes du 6e "International Workshop on Medieval Societies," Centre Ettore Majorana, Erice, Sicile, 17-23 octobre 1992, sous la direction de J. Baschet et J.-Cl. Schmitt (Paris: Le Léopard d'Or, 1996). The need is felt "to speak not only of what [an image] represents but of what it is, and for what it serves," or "to get across the density of the thing, its being an object" (pp. 10-11). Here again the distance from our "culture of the visual" appears: this "objectalité" of the image is precisely one of its traditional characteristics that is now vanishing. For two striking examples of this medieval view, consider how Aquinas himself supported "le culte de lâtrie pour l'image" (p. 53; see also p. 42, note 10: "imago autem repraesentat rem magis determinate [quam vestigium] secundum omnes suas partes et dispositionem

At this point there is no need to focus on the difference between mental images (I call the beloved to mind) and quasi-material ones (I see her in this snapshot). Let us first indicate why the image as a means of being in touch with the imaged comes into existence.

The origin seems to lie in the experience of absence and the desire for the absent thing to be present (again). Absent, then, does not mean inexistent but imperceptible. Absence is always about a lack of perception: something real that ought to be tangibly here and is not (anymore).

Apparently, two inherent features of the human condition bring to the fore the experience of absence. There is, on the one hand, the confrontation with death or with any other separation forced on us and, on the other hand, a sense of the sacred. As for the former, it is, more precisely, the shock of seeing the particular person one has known alive being now lifeless. Face to face with the corpse — is it just a thing or still a human body? — one encounters the paradox of presence going together with absence and gradually evaporating. Thus the question arises as to the possibility of a form of presence that might somehow fit with this irrevocable absence. Can the one who has disappeared still appear? Is there a way of perceiving the imperceptible? The solution to this existential crux is the image as representation.

There is plenty of evidence for death playing a key role here. A few reminders may suffice. As for the etymology of "image",

---

partium, ex quibus etiam aliquid de interioribus rei percipi potest.") And notice the "tight, even ontological, link between the seal [of a person] and that person himself" (p. 285). Nowadays this ontological link can still be felt in the "contiguity" that connects certain things with the person they represent without resembling him. Thus I can cherish my deceased father's pen as an irreplaceable relic. The essential study of the medieval view on image, imagination and the "failure of imagining" is, obviously, Johan Huizinga's *Herfsttij der Middeleeuwen* (Baarn: H. D. Tjeenk Willink & Zoon, 1921²). See especially chapters VI, IX, X.

the Latin term *imago* originates with a funeral rite of the Romans.[23] And the Greek word *eidôlon* first referred to the dead person's "shade" before it came to mean portrait.[24] In the history of the visual arts the Egyptian funeral portrait plays a major role.[25] And two literary pieces of evidence deserve attention here. In the *Wisdom of Solomon* the author first describes how death, image-making and idolatry are connected (14, 15-16). Then he goes on to expose the very real representative power of certain images (14, 17-20):

[23] See Régis Debray, *Vie et mort de l'image: Une histoire du regard en Occident,* Bibliothèque des idées (Paris: Gallimard, 1992) 27-28. Pascal Quignard gives the following details: "Le mot français image remonte à un vieux rite funéraire romain. *Imago* voulait dire à l'origine la tête de mort du mort découpée, placée sous le foyer, puis surmodelée et enfourchée sur un bâton, puis posée sur le toit, puis le masque de cire empreint sur son visage, puis la peinture à la cire qui représente ses traits placée sur les bandeaux de la tête momifiée." See his *Vie secrète* (Paris: Gallimard, 1998) 113. Pliny complains that in his days "the painting of portraits that used to transmit through the ages extremely correct likenesses of persons, has entirely gone out ... Consequently nobody's likeness lives (*nullius effigie vivente*)." And then he tells about the old days: "In the halls of our ancestors it was otherwise; portraits were the objects displayed to be looked at, not statues by foreign artists, nor bronzes nor marbles, but wax models of faces were set out each on a separate side-board, to furnish likenesses to be carried in procession at a funeral in the clan, and always when some member of it passed away the entire company of his house that had ever existed was present." See Pliny, *Natural History*, trans. H. Rackham, Loeb Classical Gallery 394, Pliny in Ten Volumes, vol. IX (London: Heinemann, 1968) 371-373.

[24] Debray, *Vie et mort de l'image*, 28-29, quoting from Euripides' *Alcestis*, verses 348-354, where the widower Admetos says: "... Stolen is life's joy with thee. Fashioned by craftsmens' cunning hands, thy form Imaged, shall lie as sleeping on a bed, Falling whereon, and clasping with mine hands, Calling thy name, in fancy shall mine arms Hold my beloved, though I hold her not: A drear delight, I wot: yet shall I lift the burden from my soul." See Euripides, *Alcestis*, transl. Arthur S. Way, Loeb Classical Gallery 12, Euripides in Four Volumes, vol. IV (London: Heinemann, 1964) 433-435.

Some father, overwhelmed with untimely grief for the child suddenly taken from him, made an image of the child and honoured thenceforth as a god what was once a dead human being, handing on to his household the observance of rites and ceremonies. Then this impious custom, established by the passage of time, was observed as a law. Or again graven images came to be worshipped at the command of despotic princes. When men could not do honour to such a prince before his face because he lived far away, they made a likeness of that distant face, and produced a visible image of the king they sought to honour, eager to pay court to the absent prince as though he were present. Then the cult grows in fervour as those to whom the king is unknown are spurred on by ambitious craftsmen. In his desire, it may be, to please the monarch, a craftsman skillfully distorts the likeness into an ideal form, and the common people, beguiled by the beauty of the workmanship, take for an object of worship him whom lately they honoured as a man.

And Pliny tells us a touching story about the invention of modeling portraits from clay. Here the significance of image-making originates with the inevitable absence of the beloved.

(It) was first invented by Butades, a potter of Sicyon, at Corinth. He did this owing to his daughter, who was in love with a young man; and she, when he was going abroad, drew in outline on the wall the shadow of his face thrown by a lamp. Her father pressed clay on this and made a relief, which he hardened by exposure to fire with the rest of his pottery.[26]

To close this discussion of absence as the root cause explanation of the representative image, it is worth making a big leap forward. In the Prologue to her *Mirror of Simple Souls*, a major mystical

---

[25] It is a way of preserving the deceased that resembles mummification. Its aim is to represent the human being as he or she was, as if going on to be alive, and to preserve for eternity this image of earthly life. See Pierre Miquel, "Icône, II: Théologie de l'icône," *Dictionnaire de spiritualité* VII/2 (1971) 1232.

[26] Pliny, *Natural History*, IX:371-373.

work, Marguerite Porete (+1310) describes the source of this book and its purpose as follows: "And for the sake of my memory of Him, He gave me this book, which makes present in some fashion His love itself." And here is how she illustrates this conviction:

> Thus listen with humility to a little exemplum of love in the world and listen to it as a parallel to divine love. *Exemplum.* Once upon a time, there was a maiden, daughter of a king, of great heart and nobility and also of noble character; and she lived in a far off land. So it happened that this maiden heard tell of the great gentle courtesy and nobility of the king, Alexander, and very soon her will loved him because of the great renown of his gentility. But this maiden was so far from this great lord, in whom she had fixed her love, from herself, that she was able neither to see him nor to have him. Thus she was inconsolable in herself, for no love except this one would be sufficient for her. When she saw that this faraway love, who was so close within her, was so far outside her, she thought to herself that she would comfort her melancholy by imagining some figure for her love, by whom she was continually wounded in heart. And so she had an image painted which would represent the semblance of the king she loved, an image as close as possible to that which presented itself to her in her love for him and in the affection of the love which captured her. And by means of this image with her other habits she dreamed of the king.[27]

[27] Marguerite Porete, *The Mirror of Simple Souls*, transl. Ellen L. Babinsky, The Classics of Western Spirituality (New York: Paulist Press, 1993). Marguerite clearly relativizes the presence which is brought about by this God-given "image": "To have His image does not alter the fact that I am in a strange land and far from the palace where the very noble friends of this Lord dwell." Here is the original text of this last passage: "Mais non obstant que j'aye son ymage, n'est il pas que je ne soie en estrange pais et loing du palais." See Margaretae Porete, *Le Mirouer des Simples Ames*, ed. Romana Guarnieri, *Speculum simplicium animarum*, cura et studio Paul Verdeyen, Corpus Christianorum, Continuatio Medievalis 69 (Turnhout: Brepols, 1986) line 40-42.

The second feature of the human condition in which the image as representation has its root, is the experience of the sacred. Here the urge to give shape to presence-in-absence manifests itself even more forcefully. So much so that, more than in the case of death, the image tends to be considered as sharing in the substance of its divine original. Students (especially historians) of religion are familiar with this phenomenon. Whenever people are endowed with a sense of the sacred — be it as adepts of a cosmic or of an acosmic religion — they appear to take for granted that certain images literally incarnate the divine. The unseen is seen as actually revealing itself in the image by *being* it. Consequently, the person who looks at the image in the right way does not just perceive a sign that turns his or her thoughts towards the signified. The image itself affects the person who as a whole reacts to this influential presence.

Obviously, the image thus invested with the divine — "materialising" it — provokes veneration. This does not imply, however, that it turns necessarily into an object of adoration. As a rule, the basic assumption here is not that the figure is simply identical with the figured. The sweeping statement that all ("primitive") image worship is idolatry does not do justice to well-established cultural findings.[28]

---

[28] Mircea Eliade makes this point quite clear: "L'adoration d'un objet cosmique ou tellurique pour lui-même ne se rencontre jamais dans l'histoire des religions. Un objet sacré, quelles qu'en soient la forme et la substance, est sacré parce qu'il révèle la réalité ultime ou parce qu'il y participe. Tout objet religieux incarne toujours quelque chose: le sacré. Il l'incarne par sa faculté d'être — comme le ciel, le soleil, la lune, la terre –, ou par sa forme (c'est-à-dire par symbole), ou encore par une hiérophanie." (Quoted by Pierre Miquel, "Images (culte des)," 1504). For the way in which cultivated people in the Greek-Roman world — among others Plotinus — revered religious images, see ibid., 1505.

Phenomenology of the Image

The phenomenon of the human production of images and the use made of them as a means of cognition has been reflected upon for ages. Mental images in particular have been the object — but one may ask if they are anything like an object — of ceaseless searching. It will serve our purpose to have a look at some present-day insights.[29]

In the first place we have to abandon the opinion, welcomed by common sense as well as by sophisticated minds, that the mental image is a thing in the mind: an inward picture that represents an outer object.[30] In this view one takes for granted that we "have" mental contents which are associated in an almost mechanical manner with the corresponding objects. The problem with this static impression of our way of knowing is that it overlooks the fact that we "do" something by means of these inner images. We focus our attention on the things beyond them, and it is of these things we become aware: "When I produce within me the image of Peter, it is Peter who is the object of my actual consciousness."[31] Instead of just being psychic existents — countless stars on an inner sky — mental images appear as a function of consciousness. By the same token the *act* of, say, imagining overshadows the alleged depicting image, and this mental operation comes to be regarded as one of

---

[29] My main source here is Jean-Paul Sartre's *L'Imaginaire* (Paris: Gallimard, 1986).

[30] Sartre here speaks of our "twofold mistake": "We thought, without even being aware of it, that the image was *in* consciousness and the object of the image *in* the image. We considered consciousness as a place populated by small simulacra and these simulacra were the images." He calls this the "illusion of immanence" (ibid., p. 17).

[31] Ibid., p. 15.

our genuine forms of consciousness, a distinctive — not an isolated — way of being aware of something.[32]

Looking ahead to the discussion of the use of mental images in contemplation, we can retain from Sartre's analysis what appears to be its main point: imagining is, in the very first place, an act, the act of *intending*.[33] To imagine is, just as much as to perceive, a psychic movement by which we reach out to an object. However, whereas perception attains the object as actually present, imagination reaches it as absent. In both cases though, consciousness appears primarily as the awareness of what is beyond and not of what is within. In order, then, to become conscious of an image as image, as a thing in me, a second act of consciousness is needed. The object-directed movement has to be followed by a *reflective* one that brings about the self-awareness of "I have an image."[34]

[32] Iris Murdoch to some extent agrees with this view when she denies the necessity of a "present mental content," while pointing at our "pictorial activity": "Thinking and feeling imagery is not like an internal picture show. Yet it is not unlike it either. Nor does the fact that we use metaphors in talking or writing imply that these, or any metaphorical pictures are privately present. To say I think (doubt, imagine etc.) need not imply a present mental content. Yet it is not true that there is no significant inward pictorial activity, or that we must philosophically obliterate 'consciousness'." See her *Metaphysics as a Guide to Morals* (Harmondsworth: Penguin, 1993) 328.

[33] Obviously, Sartre here assumes the current phenomenological view of human consciousness as "intentionality." On this intending in the case of the image, see *L'Imaginaire*, 22, 28, 41-42, 115-116, 121.

[34] See, for instance, Sartre, *L'Imaginaire*, 137-138: we should not "confondre la conscience réfléchissante et la conscience irréfléchie." In his previous work, *Esquisse d'une théorie des émotions* (Paris: Hermann, 1960), Sartre had shown already that emotion is also a way of intending an object. Emotion is not in the first place a "state of consciousness," that is, the reflective awareness of, for instance, "I am frightened." A person who is frightened is frightened of or by something. Emotion is then a particular way of "apprehending" — a significant word indeed: to become aware of reality is always frightening — the world.

One more insight of Sartre's into our imagining consciousness deserves attention here. The fact that by producing an image we intend an object implies that we have already some knowledge of it. Far from being a mental scrabbling about for something, imagining is a determinate intending. I want to realize the knowledge I already have of the object — a knowledge that is as yet empty, speculative — by changing it into an intuition. When I imagine Peter, says Sartre, I intend him "being fair, tall, with a tip tilted or a hooked nose, etc."[35]

L'Imaginaire makes captivating philosophical reading and, needless to say, Sartre does not bother about the role of the image in contemplation. It comes then as a surprise that mystics from different ages in describing their particular brand of awareness — the Invisible "showing" himself to them — often appear to agree with the modern phenomenologist. There is in the first place the mystic's definition of contemplative consciousness as "intending," intending the "divine object."[36] Ruusbroec for one continually underlines the act of what he calls *gode meynen*, "to intend God," presenting it as a matter of the first importance at each and every stage of the contemplative way.[37] However, we should not fail to

---

[35] Sartre, *L'Imaginaire*, 115-116. See also p. 28: "L'intention est au centre de la conscience: c'est elle qui vise l'objet, c'est-à-dire qui le constitue pour ce qu'il est. Le savoir qui est indissolublement lié à l'intention, précise que l'objet est tel ou tel, ajoute synthétiquement des déterminations."

[36] So Ruusbroec: "Even though the eyes be clear and the sight keen, clarity of sight without its lovely, delightful object (*voerworp*) brings little or no enjoyment or profit" (*Opera Omnia* III, b138-139). It goes without saying that people like Ruusbroec know better than anybody else that God is not an object. By using the word "object," they want to point out that what matters is not their own feeling but *something* felt. See Paul Mommaers, Jan Van Bragt, *Mysticism Buddhist and Christian: Encounters with Jan van Ruusbroec*, Nanzan Studies in Religion and Culture (New York: Crossroad, 1995) 18.

[37] *Meynen* is cognate with "to mean," and it is often accompanied by *minnen*, "to love." We shall dwell on this point in chapter 5.

notice that this *meynen* as such is not a contemplative phenomenon. To intend something is just a characteristic of the human mind, and that is why every Christian is supposed to intend God, always and in everything she does. And so, among the things one can do "with an eye on God," there is contemplation. Or rather, next to effectively loving one's fellow-human, there is prayer, which in some cases may blossom into contemplative experience.

What does one do then, "for God's sake," in prayer? Traditionally two terms with the same etymological root come together here, namely "attention" and "intention."[38] In prayer one intends

---

[38] Evidently, "attention" is a complicated subject. For our purposes, the article of R. Vernay, "Attention," in *Dictionnaire de spiritualité* I (1937) 1058-1077, is very helpful. It contains plenty of evidence from the Christian spiritual tradition that all forms of prayer are basically a matter of attention. In vocal prayer one has to pay attention at least to the words, to pronouncing them well, etc. On this point, the most striking account I know is that of the eminent French mystic, Marie de l'Incarnation who, during choral prayer used to fix her attention on the psalm-verse each time it was her side's turn to psalmodize. For Marie's own description, see Henri Bremond, *Histoire littéraire du sentiment religieux en France*, VI: *La conquête mystique*: *Marie de l'Incarnation*; *Turba magna* (Paris: Bloud et Gay, 1922) 172. In the prayer of petition one must actually "think of what one is asking." But it is especially in mental prayer that attention is absolutely necessary: "Mental prayer is thought itself, affection itself. Through these we elevate ourselves towards God, and without attention they do not exist anymore. Manifestly, this prayer stops when the spirit ceases to pay attention." Thus mental prayer is seen as "a loving, simple and permanent attention of the mind to the divine things." As for the psychological description of attention, it is "a modality of the conscious life common to all the functions." Consequently, attention is a compound as well as a dynamic phenomenon. And this is of particular interest, for it is here that imagination appears as part and parcel of attention, so much so that one can distinguish sensory attention, which implies complementary images, imaginative attention, intellectual and volitional attention. Also and quite interesting again, expectative attention, tending to an object that is absent, or to a fuller possession of it when present, for instance "at moments of aridity in prayer." In addition one should keep in mind that attention is the core point of Simone Weil's anthropological and religious view. "God," this mystic

God by being attentive to the things that represent him: words, images, feelings, etc. At this point one may wonder whether the distinction between both forms of mental tending is not a useless subtlety. However, the proper sense of intending should not be lost: that one directs one's attention toward something while being ready to go beyond this object, and indeed every object. Thus the attention mystics advocate is an open-ended concentration. The "object" of their awareness being the Other, the definitely different, they are even more concerned than the phenomemologist about doing justice to human consciousness as intending what is beyond.

Sartre, we have seen, also presents reflective consciousness as a secondary phenomenon. In order to be aware of what is going on within me — for instance, "I have an image" — I need to call my attention back from the object it intends spontaneously. As a follower of Husserl — "consciousness is about something" — he is keen to show that what affects consciousness, the "Erlebnisse," the "vécu," does not primarily concern my consciousness but certain objects beyond. The mystics are in their own way as touchy as the phenomenologists about what they perceive as a danger: that reflection might play a prominent role in their awareness of God. Some of them even use the same word as Sartre: "reflection."[39] So John of the Cross in *The Ascent of the Mount Carmel*

and philosopher affirms, "is only present in as far as there is attention ... Attention is linked to desire." See her *Cahiers* III (Paris: Plon, 1974) 158; see also how she prays, for instance concentrating on the Our Father, in *Waiting for God* (New York: Harper and Row, 1973) 68-69 and passim. More recently this same appreciation of attention has been demonstrated by Iris Murdoch. See *The Sovereignty of Good* (London: Routledge and Kegan Paul, 1970).

[39] "Reflection" is a graphic word: instead of looking at what is not-me although represented in me, I am mirrored, like Narcissus, in experiencing my *vécus*, as the French put it.

devotes an entire chapter to "the harm caused from reflection upon this supernatural knowledge." And when Maria Petyt becomes mystically aware of God — "my unimaged Beloved and All" — she characterizes her consciousness as "without reflection" (*sonder reflexie*). She observes that as soon as she tries to capture the divine light by reflecting upon it, it disappears: "The slightest thought or reflection of the human mind upon that light is too much, for it serves no useful purpose but only darkens the path to the light that appears."[40]

So far we have seen the mystics agreeing on the main issues of *L'Imaginaire*: intention is highlighted and reflection is put in its proper place. In addition, Sartre has pointed out that the image needs to go together with some knowledge of the object intended. It is worth noting that on this point too there appears to be a correspondence, at least in the following sense. Contrary to what often seems to be the accepted truth, mystics do not say that in order to become aware of God, the always Other who is always beyond, the mind's intending should be a tabula rasa, reaching out into the blue with no foreknowledge whatsoever — "launch out naked into the Unknown," as is commonly said, with "no-thought" towards the "no-thing", etc. The fact is that even those

[40] See book III, chapter 8. For Maria Petyt, see Albert Deblaere, *De mystieke schrijfster Maria Petyt 1623-1677* (Ghent: Secretarie der Academie, 1962) 46. And there is an acute description by Francis of Sales of how contemplative attention that lacks the dynamic of intending turns into self-attention. The mentality of some contemplatives is such that "if God gives them the sacred rest of his presence, they leave it voluntarily in order to see how they behave in it and to examine whether they feel really satisfied, concerned about knowing if their quietness is quite quiet and their calm quite calm." Quoted by Vernay, "Attention," 1070. Obviously, this sense of the importance of attention and reflection is not a monopoly of Christian mysticism. Plotinus for one has much to say about this topic. See Pierre Hadot, "Les niveaux de conscience dans les états mystiques selon Plotin," *Journal de psychologie* 23 (1980) 249, 250 and 253-254.

mystics who most drastically underline that God is forever unknowable, point out at the same time that what we do know of him — mainly from religious tradition — is useful and indeed needed. "Scripture *does* lead us to God," as Claesinne van Nieuwlant, an extremely apophatic Flemish mystic, asserts. And when Ruusbroec comes to describe, in the *Spiritual Espousals*, the transition from the non-mystical to the mystical life, he indicates that one needs to climb the tree of faith that has twelve branches, namely the twelve articles of faith.

To close this section, a possible misunderstanding needs to be removed. There is no question here of cross-pollinating modern phenomenology and traditional mysticism by interweaving psychological analysis and descriptions of God-experience. Evidently, Sartre and Ruusbroec are not to be put in the same box, if only for the following reasons. Sartre's view of imagining consciousness only takes into account the *absence* of a visible object: the "Pierre" intended by the image of "Pierre" is a distant human thing. In the perspective of Ruusbroec the image is being used with an eye to the *presence* of an invisible object, or rather of the primordial Subject. For Sartre, then, the image is self-made, produced by the person who imagines. It does not come to that person as given by or emanating from the intended object. For the contemplative the image has been received as the self-expression of the Person looked for. Here the person who imagines accepts the image from tradition as a common divine present, or as a personal gift "shown" to him in the visionary experience, or "impressed" upon him in mystical union. In brief, mysticism has been exposed here to phenomenology in order to indicate that the contemplative who makes use of images is basically following a natural procedure of the human mind. As usual, the mystic proves to be an exceptionally normal person.

Image and Idol

According to Iris Murdoch, "there is good and bad 'imagination'."[41] Referring to Plato, Kant and Simone Weil, she points to the ambivalence of imagination with regard to our knowing reality. Consequently, she comes to distinguish "between egoistic *fantasy* and liberated truth-seeking *imagination*." She even wants to "see the contrast… in terms of two active faculties, one somewhat mechanically generating narrowly banal false pictures (the ego as all-powerful), and the other freely and creatively exploring the world." In her view, then, the familiar word "imagination" has a positive sense. It designates "something (good by definition) to which the contrast with fantasy (bad by definition) gives substance. The human mind is naturally and largely given to fantasy." For this deep-seated power of fantasy, Murdoch could also have called upon the Bible: while Adam has nothing more to show to Eve than what he actually is, namely God's creature, Satan conjures up a vision — "you'll be like God himself."

Undoubtedly Murdoch has a point here: our imaginative activity may either open consciousness or close it. And one must not blame the moralist for moralizing this dual movement: fantasy is characterized as "egoistic and bad," imagination as "good." However, we may perhaps let our imagination wander beyond this dichotomy, and wonder whether there is not some grasping ego in that definitely "good" imagination. If it is not egoistic, is it possibly egocentric? If, unlike fantasy, imagination does not delude us with visions of the "ego as all-powerful", is it not the case that even in our reality-minded and noble imagining the ego is alive

---

[41] Murdoch, *Metaphysics as a Guide to Morals*, 315. The entire chapter 11 is devoted to "imagination." Further quotations from pp. 321-322.

and kicking?[42] So much so that this unique spiritual force, "good by definition," appears as so very precious that one cannot imagine there being any reason why it might ever be surrendered.

Mystical authors are aware of fantasy and its mirages. Simone Weil mercilessly keeps bursting any dream-bubble. And Ruusbroec tells us, for instance, that "within" we need to "flee from impure fantasies and images (*fantasye ende beelden*) ... lest we become filled with images" (*verbeelt*, literally 'imaged').[43] However, in the mystic's perspective this attack on fantasy is only an initial diagnosis. It appears specifically in the description of the first stages of the contemplative life. From the moment the mystic speaks in his capacity as mystic, that is, as the person touched by Presence, he does not confine himself to probing fantasy. Then it is not fantasy but imagination which appears as his main target. A well-known passage from Ruusbroec's *Sparkling Stone* may illustrate this point.[44] Here is first how he characterizes the "faithful servant," who personifies the exterior kind of person: "He is more filled with the images of the works he does than with God he works for." If fantasy is the source of these hampering images, it cannot be called bad for, obviously, the faithful servant is doing good. If, on the other hand, imagination is the origin, it cannot simply be called good. Apparently, the mystic is looking beyond the level of morality, searching for the root cause that makes itself felt in good imagination as well as in bad fantasy. Ruusbroec's

---

[42] Ibid., 331.The person who is "liberated from selfish fantasy, can see himself as others see him, imagine the needs of other people."

[43] Ruusbroec, *The Seven Rungs, Werken* III, 228.

[44] See *Opera Omnia* X, 223-400. (The two quotations that follow are 291-292 and 328-329). Ruusbroec here makes a distinction between hired servants, faithful servants, secret friends and hidden sons. This is a graphic way of describing the different stages or aspects of a person's spiritual life.

description of the "secret friends", who stand for the interior person, indicates where that original sin is to be found. Undoubtedly, these secret friends represent an advanced stage in the contemplative life, which implies a high degree of morality. And yet, "they are caught up with themselves and their works in the manner of images and intermediaries." At this point our imagining as a whole, including the creations of imagination as well as the concoctions of fantasy, is shown in its true colours. When all is said and done, when moral reflection and action have reached a high standard, it appears that all our images are egocentric, even when they are not egoistic. And the reason for this manifold self-centeredness is that they spring from the radical reflectiveness of our self-image. There, in that being "imaged with oneself", as Ruusbroec puts it literally, lies the fundamental intermediary that unduly turns reality into "my" world. And in the mystic's view it is not by living a morally perfect, altruistic life that the ego's hiding-place is discovered but by the felt presence of an Other. No wonder then, as will soon be shown, that the vital principle of all idols is auto-idolatry.

As for the scriptural view of idols and idol worship, the starting point must be the prohibition of images. While God's self-revelation is the positive reason for this commandment, the negative one lies in the essential relation between image and idol. Every image is indeed a potential idol: instead of referring to the Unimaginable, it always carries the risk of captivating the spectator's attention. That is why for Jews and Christians alike the temptation is always lurking to fall before idols. Even at the end of the Bible, there is the ominous appearance of the beast that survives, and allures humans to "erect an image in honour of the beast which had been wounded by the sword and yet lived. It was allowed to give breath to the image of the beast, so that it could even speak and cause all who would not worship the image to be put to death." Throughout the Bible, idolatry is taken very seriously. If the idols as such, as images "shaped by human craftmanship and design", are seen as "mute and deaf", or as just "nothing", the act of worshipping them is considered a surrendering of the human person to demonic powers.[45]

Triggered by Nietzsche's striking statement that religion is just idol worship, modern philosophical reflection too has taken seriously the idolatrizing tendency of the human mind. Recently a thorough discussion of this topic has been presented by J.-L. Marion, who draws attention to several points worth taking into account here.[46] One must not try to dispose of idolatry just by labeling it as fake religion. To get the right perspective on it, one has to pay attention to the idol's function. The idol does not personify the divine in the sense of presenting itself to the worshipper as the god in person. In that case, idolatry would be sheer imposture indeed.[47] In fact the idol represents the way in which humans — the artist and his milieu — experience the unseen divine. From a religious point of view, therefore, this experience is not per se unauthentic, nor is the idol necessarily false for being what it actually is: the visible form given by the artist to a genuine human awareness of the invisible.[48]

[45] The last two quotations are from *Revelation* 13,14-15 and *Acts* 17,29. In the Bible, idolatry is often connected with magic. See John P. Meier, *A Marginal Jew: Rethinking the Historical Jesus*, 2: *Mentor, Message and Miracles*, Anchor Bible Reference Library (New York: Doubleday, 1994) 535-575. In *Penser la Bible*, André LaCocque points out that in Moses' asking the name of God there is a trace of (Egyptian) magic. It is not an innocent question.

[46] See Jean-Luc Marion, *L'idole et la distance* (Paris: Grasset, 1977); *Dieu sans l'être* (Paris: Fayard, 1982); *Prolégomènes à la charité* (Paris: Editions La Différence, 1986).

[47] For confirmation of this point, see Pierre Miquel, "Images (culte des)," c.1504-1505. Not all idolaters feel that the idol captivates their attention.

[48] Marion, *L'idole et la distance*, 23: "L'idole nous renvoie, dans le visage d'un dieu, notre expérience du divin."

However, it is precisely by being the perceptible expression of the experience of the divine, as it appears in the consciousness of a human group, that the idol becomes dubious. By giving a form to the divine it curbs the original religious awareness. The idol abolishes the distance between the human and the divine. It blunts the intending consciousness. The idol disposes of the hiddenness that initially characterizes the divine. The visible image comes to screen off the Invisible, the light so close by outshines the darkness beyond. The touchable and touching figure eliminates the divine reservedness. Eventually, the idolater indulges in familiarity with the god, who turns into an entity one can get a hold on.[49]

The second point to be retained from Marion's discussion of idolatry regards the appreciation of our concepts with a view to our knowledge of God. In fact, the main purpose of this philosopher's reflection is to come to grips with the question of "ontotheology."[50] Is all speculative theology just a way of confining the divine within the concept of "Being"? Marion takes the affirmative view, and he goes on to show that our concepts are the most refined and, therefore, very effective and tenacious idols we bow before: "The concept, like the idol, provides a presence without the divine distance, in a god who reflects our own experience or thought in a way that is familiar enough to enable us to hold the reins."[51]

Here again, it is interesting to see how the philosopher, following his own path, arrives at a conclusion that is similar to the discernment reached by the mystics. With regard to our knowledge

---

[49] At this point the idol is likely to become an amulet, and magic enters the picture.

[50] For a critical appreciation of Marion's view on "ontotheology," see Paul Ricoeur in *Penser la Bible*, 364-369.

[51] Marion, *L'idole et la distance*, 27.

of God, the mystics keep pointing out that the sense of image must not be limited to representations that figure the divine.[52] In their perspective, image includes, to put it in the terms of Ruusbroec, every "means" (*middel*) of which we make use. All of them, the conceptual as well as the imaginative ones, belong to the realm of the "intermediaries" (*middel*). Our soundest and most sophisticated intellectual tools as well as the holy words-and-thoughts warranted by Christian tradition, are all images that may, instead of directing our "intending" (*meynen*) to God, hamper it. That is why the mystic keeps repeating that, for the Other to become present to us, all our mental categories, all our "modes and manners" (*wise ende maniere*) must give way.

In this same line, Marion highlights an insight that demystifies a certain "apophatic" mysticism often welcomed nowadays with a feeling of liberation, liberation, that is, of all superfluous thinking. The paradox here is, that when negation constitutes the last and only word of our God-talk, it turns into an inverted affirmation. "If negation remains categorical, it remains idolatrous." Such a never-ending negation "destroys precisely what the negations aimed at in the first place, namely the Absolute."[53] By a remarkable coincidence, a learned and sympathetic student of Buddhism, Hans Waldenfeld, makes the following reflection: "The East… runs the risk of destroying the mystery in a negative way. Eastern speculation often overlooks the fact that negations can also limit and thereby undo the possibilities of the mystery…, that negations

---

[52] In *The Spiritual Tabernacle* Ruusbroec states that, "if we want to feel God's indwelling in us," we need to "strip our memory of sensual images and our understanding of spiritual images" (*Werken*, II, 359-360). However, Geert Grote (see above note 17) claims that, unlike the images linked to the senses, Aristotelian concepts do not hamper our knowing of God.

[53] Marion, *L'idole et la distance*, 192.

can also be expressions of human arbitrary construction (*Eigen-mächtigkeit*)."[54]

Finally, in Marion's view, idols originate with human self-idolatry.[55] This appears all the more conspicuously in the case of persons who feel they have reached a purely intellectual insight or a purely spiritual experience. They may be left with the impression that their true self is an otherworldly entity than which there is nothing "higher", so much so that they come to see — to imagine — themselves as a god. Instead of "making a god of their belly" they "make an idol of their spirit."[56]

Ruusbroec has considered very carefully what he calls "natural contemplation" or "going inward without grace."[57] He appreciates the experience of these contemplatives who reach the "highest a person can by nature reach." Yet they come finally to self-idolatry:

> And because they are without practice and do not cling to God in love, they do not go beyond themselves but rest and idle in their own essence. And so their essence is their idol (*afgod*) for they think they have and are one essence with God, and that is impossible.[58]

The Icon

This introductory chapter has been merely a way of mapping out the vast territory of the image. The aim has been to clarify the

---

[54] Quoted by Jan Van Bragt in *Mysticism Buddhist and Christian*, 73.

[55] Marion, *Dieu sans l'être*, 192 and, in the context of love and its object, *Prolégomènes à la charité*, 96-97.

[56] *Philippians* 3,19. In this context Marion quotes from Paul Valéry's *Monsieur Teste*: "Je confesse que j'ai fait une idole de mon esprit." (See Marion, *L'idole et la distance*, 43 n. 3).

[57] See Mommaers, *Mysticism Buddhist and Christian*, part 3.

[58] Ruusbroec, *Four Temptations*, Opera Omnia X, 177-80.

issue of the image and, particularly, of the Image of images — the humanity of Christ — in "imageless" mystical experience. Naturally there are no tangible results as yet regarding this "Riddle of Christian Mystical Experience." In the meantime, however, it will help to bring into focus the figure of the Godman by asking to what extent this Image too may turn out to be an idol for the ordinary, non-mystical beholder. Two widely acknowledged data deserve to be taken in consideration here. The first concerns the way in which Jesus appears in the gospel narrative, the second the manner of representing him in the icon.

Apparently, the prime fallacy of religious imagery lies in its tendency to imagine God as an extension of man's self-image. Two main elements come together here: my imagined "real I" poses as essentially spiritual as well as all-powerful. Consequently, the God that corresponds, of course in the grand divine style, to this human self-portrait appears as the Absolute, reflecting humanity's supposedly spiritual nature, and as the Almighty mirroring their powerfulness. But is not our inclination to idolize to be found in this religiously-colored projection, whose root cause can be diagnosed as auto-idolatry?

Now, the way in which the Humanity appears in the gospel narrative is bound to curb this high-flying projection. And it is precisely by his being so thoroughly corporeal that Jesus has this demystifying effect. As to our bent for spiritualizing both ourselves and our God, throughout Jesus' public life the "Image of the invisible God" comes to the fore as a shockingly physical person. Words like "incarnated" or "embodied" fail to do justice to this aspect of the evangelist's picture of the "son of man." What John says about having "felt him with our own hands" (1 John 1), is simply characteristic of Jesus' way of living. He is again and again touching people bodily and himself being touched by them. And as this tangible life comes to an end, he takes leave of his friends with the words "this is my body." To say the least, this Humanity is not an easy object for spiritual projection and this Image does not represent God as the utterly detached Absolute. The ordinary beholder's attention is not captivated here by any spiritualizing charm.

As for the question whether the Humanity lends itself to be regarded as the image of human as well as divine omnipotence, the impotence of the man who suffers and dies in the way he actually does, provides the answer. What is there to be seen which gives material for idolizing imagery? Significantly, those who witness the crucifixion are looking at something quite visible — it is a "spectacle" — even as they appear to respond to an invisible event. As it comes into contact with this Image, the human gaze at once sees, falters and opens onto what cannot be seen. Luke's description of Jesus' last moments deserves to be quoted here:

> Then Jesus gave a loud cry and said: 'Father, into thy hands I commit my spirit'; and with these words he died. The centurion saw it all, and gave praise to God. 'Beyond all doubt', he said, 'this man was innocent.' The crowd who had assembled for the spectacle, when they saw what had happened, went home beating their breasts. His friends had all been standing at a distance; the women who had accompanied him from Galilee stood with them and watched it all.[59]

The other factor that merits particular attention here, is the way in which the icon represents the Godman.[60] In this case the Face

---

[59] Luke 23,46-49. For this insight into Luke's text, see Claude Flipo, "Regarder autrement: Images du ciel, images de la terre," *Christus* 181 (1999) 23.

[60] "Icon" refers in the first instance to the Byzantine-style paintings of Christ or the saints. However, not only icons in the strict sense exhibit the characteristics we are occupied with here. So, I have been touched, in the oratory of Campion Hall, by the iconic force of the painting of Christ's face by Quinten Metsys. The context to this way of representing the Humanity is most aptly expressed in Paul's letter to the Colossians: "He is the image (*eikôn*) of the

appears as the focus of the Humanity, which is no surprise. For there is, on the one hand, the deep-seated biblical view of Yahweh's Face, which is seen as God himself being effectively present, regarding his creatures and thus evoking their regard. So much so that the privilege granted to Moses, as well as the hope of every believer, is to see God face to face. And there is, on the other hand, the specific human fact that we know each other by looking into each other's faces. So much so that people with totally expressionless faces "would have nothing human about them."[61] However, this expressiveness of the human face is precisely what makes figuring it so difficult. According to legend, even the most skillful painter was not able to represent Jesus' features. Only images "not made by human hands", such as the one impressed upon the veil of Veronica, could reproduce the Face. And there is, I surmise, a connection here with something we learn from personal experience: we can imagine the features of the beloved only with great difficulty, which is not the case with other people.[62] Mutatis mutandis one may say, perhaps, that in both cases the person's life, showing in the face, outshines the features.

It may suffice here to draw attention to a distinguishing mark of the icon that is most apt to show how this kind of image of the Image checks any inclination to idolize it. The principle underlying the attitude of both the artist and the spectator is an inverted perspective. This implies quite a "conversion." For, obviously,

---

invisible God" (1,15). It goes without saying that we are not following here in C.S. Peirce's wake, whose perspective is anthropocentric and whose "icon" is constituted by an intrinsic duality that leads one to think of something while considering something else.

[61] Wittgenstein's words. See chapter 5, note 36.

[62] So, I am again and again astonished to see that, even as I try to call up the face(s) that have been most expressive for me, it is in fact the features as fixed in some snapshot that appear.

the perspective is usually anthropocentric, in the sense that the spectator is supposed to play the leading part: the perceptual current originates from him, only to return to him, and to result in his seeing the image in his way. The Byzantine iconolatry breaks through this circle. As one commentator puts it, the main question for these people was "how to paint God... how to paint him as he is in himself, and not as he is in our view." And the solution they invented was "as simple as it is surprising: by inversing the relation between the one who regards and the one who is being regarded; by imposing God not as an object anymore to be contemplated but indeed as a subject that contemplates us... The whole secret lies in their having discovered that the image is able to assume the quality of a person."[63]

---

[63] See Pierre Miquel, "Icône, II: Théologie de l'icône," c. 1234.

CHAPTER II

MYSTICAL REPORTS: FEELINGS INTO IMAGES

Given the scope of this study one is obliged to pay special attention to visionary mystical texts. For this is where one meets a phenomenon that seems to be particularly problematic. Are not many visions so overwhelmingly imaginative as to appear to be the clearest evidence of the obstacles that images constitute on the path to the "image-less" experience of God? And is not the focus of the visionary experience mainly Jesus in his outward appearance, for instance as the Suffering Man, so much so that his Humanity seems to screen off the Divinity?

Here we will concentrate on those visions that the visionaries themselves consider to be an effect of God's influence, distinguishing them from self-induced imaginations or illusions. And we will focus on the account of their visions written by three women mystics. In all three cases the figure of Jesus appears to be central. However, in each particular case the reception of this picture imposing itself on their consciousness is different. For the first, Julian of Norwich, the impressive presence of Jesus, the image of God, is no problem. Her visionary experience is unceasingly concentrated upon Jesus but this does not hamper her mystical experience of God. Here, Christocentrism and theocentrism go together as a matter of course, or rather the one lives in the other.

For the second, Teresa of Avila, things are not that simple. She has difficulty with a Jesus who is supposed to take the first place in her contemplation, while she is being taught to approach God not only without images but also without thoughts. In her account,

Teresa raises the problem quite clearly, and she shows how she is favoured with visions of the Humanity that do not hamper the imageless contemplation of the Divinity. However, in the end she fails to make sufficiently explicit how Jesus can be at the centre of even her most advanced mystical contemplation.

The third visionary, Maria Petyt, is gifted with abundant visionary experiences although she has a dislike of visions. She is the one who raises the problem in all its clarity, relates how she finds her way towards a contemplative solution and, finally, describes in detail how even the Suffering Man can be at the heart of imageless contemplation.

The *Showings* of Julian of Norwich

A short reminder of a few facts concerning the author and her book are appropriate.[1] The sixteen visions occurred 8-9 May, 1373. At that date Julian was 30 years old, and she then wrote the first version of her *Revelations,* known now as the "short text". We do not know how soon after the visionary experience she drafted her book.[2] Some twenty years later she writes the long

---

[1] There is no need here to dwell on the problem of dating exactly Julian's life and literary work, questions that have been recently revived by Nicholas Watson. See, for a succinct presentation of the question, Julian of Norwich, *The Revelations of Divine Love*, trans. Elizabeth Spearing (Harmondsworth: Penguin Books, 1998) XII-XIII. I will be quoting from this translation. As for the original text, citations are from *A Book of Showings to the Anchoress Julian of Norwich*, eds. Edmund Colledge O.S.A. and James Walsh S.J., Pontifical Institute of Medieval Studies: Studies and Texts 35 (Toronto: Pontifical Institute of Mediaeval Studies, 1978).

[2] That this first text was written soon after the visionary event does not imply that it is the 'original' version, in the romantic sense of reporting immediately an unadulterated experience. The short text should not be considered to be free of

version of the *Revelations*. At that moment she integrated into the 'showings' (viz. into what years ago had been shown to her and happened in her) the growing insight that she had acquired in the meantime.

Julian presents the 'showings' she had as unexpected gifts, both in their visual and in their spiritual aspects: "Then I suddenly saw the red blood trickling down"; "the Trinity suddenly filled my heart with the greatest joy" (ch. 4, p. 45-46). Students of mystical texts recognize this "suddenly" as the word used again and again throughout the ages to evoke the passivity that characterizes the mystic's experience. Does this "suddenly" imply that there was no preparation at all? Of course not. Initially, one has to bear in mind a general, well-established fact of culture: a mystic never appears out of thin air, no matter how divine or original her or his experience may be. In addition, Julian is a mystical *writer*, which implies even more the presence of a strong cultural background. She may call herself a "simple uneducated creature" or "a woman, ignorant, weak and frail,"[3] but one is well advised to take this "unlettered" *(that cowde no letter)* with a pinch of salt. More probably, Julian should be seen as one of those educated medieval women, each officially regarded as a *femina rudis et idiota,* who created an "Illiteraten-Literatur".[4] This is not the place to dwell on

interpretation in contrast with the long text. On the relation between experience and interpretation, and our modern tendency to oppose these two (always inter-twined) strands of descriptive writing, see Alois Haas, "La mystique comme théologie," Revue des sciences religieuses 72 (1998) 261-288. In the notes which follow, we shall refer to the so-called "short text" as ST, and the so-called "long text" as LT.

[3] LT ch. 2, p. 42 and ST ch. 6, p. 10-11.

[4] This expression has been coined by Herbert Grundmann. See, among other works, his "Litteratus-Illiteratus: Der Wandel einer Bildungsnorm vom Altertum zum Mittelalter," *Ausgewählte Aufsätze*, III: *Bildung und Sprache,* Schriften der Monumenta Germaniae Historica 25/3 (Stuttgart: Hiersemann, 1978). Not all

the educational influences. But one needs to face the fact that Julian appears as immediately prepared to receive exactly the visions she does have. On the one hand, the mystical "suddenly" does not alter the fact that the imagination of the visionary-to-be is disposed towards the coming 'showings'. Just before they take place, she feels she is dying. The curate comes to visit her, doing exactly what was prescribed by the *Ordo Visitandi*. He sets a crucifix before Julian's face so that she can look at it. And, lowering her eyes that "were looking fixedly upwards," she fixes her eyes on it instead.[5] And there must have been, of course, a lot more

medieval women writers presented themselves in this way. Hadewijch, for example, who was "lettered" enough to read and translate Latin texts, said about the Brabantine Middle Dutch she used to evoke her mystical experience: "Words enough and Dutch enough can be found for all things on earth, but I do not know any Dutch or any words to answer my purpose. Although I can express everything insofar as this is possible for a human being, no Dutch can be found for all I have said to you, since none exists to express these things, so far as I know". See Hadewijch, *The Complete Works,* trans. Mother Columba Hart, The Classics of Western Spirituality (New York: Paulist Press, 1980) Letter 17, 112, p. 84. For more about Hadewijch, see chapter 4.

[5] See Eamon Duffy, *The Stripping of the Altars: Traditional Religion in England 1400-1580* (New Haven and London: Yale University Press, 1992) 314: "It was this gesture which provided the trigger for the most remarkable theological achievement of the English late Middle Ages, the 'Showings' of Julian of Norwich." It would be interesting to know exactly which kind of crucifix Julian had before her at that moment. Was Christ mainly, if not exclusively, presented as a human being who has suffered cruelly in the body, a body which then looks like the "'empty envelop' from which the life-giving spirit has departed," as M. Meany puts it in *The Image of Christ in the Revelations of Divine Love by Julian of Norwich* (London: University Microfilms International, 1975) 147. Meany's survey (pp.132-150) of the different ways in which Christ is presented on the cross through history deserves attention. In this context the description of Francis of Assisi's vision of Christ on Mount Alverna is most interesting in relation to Julian's 'showings': "[Francis] beheld ... a man as a seraph with six wings, who stood over him, with arms outstretched and feet together, nailed to a cross ... He rejoiced exceedingly, and was filled with intense delight at the kindly and

imaginative material feeding the visionary's mind. Take that most vivid and dread passage, in LT chapter 16, where Jesus' body hanging on the cross is shown as slowly drying out. It was prefigured in the "Fifteen Odes of St Bridget," "quite certainly the most distinctive and probably the most popular, of all prayers in medieval England."[6]

Julian seems, on the other hand, also affectively ready for the visions that are about to occur. She had longed to be actually there, when Jesus was suffering:

> And therefore I longed to be shown him in the flesh (*I desyred a bodely sight*) so that I might have more knowledge of our Saviour's bodily suffering and of our Lady's fellow-suffering ... I never wished for any other sight or showing of God (*other sight nor shewing of god desyred I never none*) until my soul left my body.[7]

One may wonder, of course, whether this desire to see the Man's body in agony points to a strange impulse surfacing here. Is Julian obsessed with the painful bodily presence of Jesus, to the point that she is about to induce it? The *Revelations* themselves answer these questions. Just before the account of the 'showings' begins,

gracious look with which he saw the Seraph regarded him, for his beauty surpassed all conception. But the way the Seraph was nailed to the cross and the bitterness of his suffering greatly frightened the Saint" (quoted by Meany on p. 148, from Celano's *Vita Prima*).

[6] Duffy, *The Stripping of the Altars*, 249. It is interesting to learn from Duffy that these popular prayers had in fact a solid theological content. They were even "learned" prayers: "The Odes never lose sight of the dialectic between the human and the divine in the Incarnation, and though their systematic progress through the details of the Passion signals their indebtedness to the affective tradition, they never slip into mere emotionalism by slackening the theological tension which gives them their distinctive power" (250-251). This sounds almost like a comment on the way Julian's *Showings* present Christ and the way she responds to him.

[7] LT ch. 2, p. 43. See Colledge and Walsh (eds.), *A Book of Showings to the Anchoress Julian of Norwich*, 286:12-17.

there is a passage that recapitulates in a masterly way all that has been indicated before, and all that we need to know about this point. Some time before, Julian had "conceived a great longing to receive three wounds in my life." Now, she wishes for the second wound:

> That my whole body should be filled with remembrance and feeling (*that my bodie might be fulfilled with mynd and feeling*) of his blessed Passion; for I wanted his pains to be my pains, with compassion, and then longing for God. Yet in this I never asked for a bodily sight or showing of God (*in this I desyred never no bodily sight ne no maner shewing of god*), but for fellow-suffering, such as a naturally kind soul might feel for our Lord Jesus ... so I wanted to suffer with him.[8]

The personal quality of this self-description — a woman, "a naturally kind soul," expressing at once the bodily depth and spiritual height of her intimate love for this Man — makes one hesitate to analyse it. Two marginal comments may suffice: first, that, when the moment of the 'showings' has come, Julian's initial passion for sight of the body has already been relativized; second, that she has a full appreciation of the body as the seat of real love, a love that unites with the human person and at once leads to the divine: "his pains to be my pains, with compassion, and then longing for God (*and afterward longing to god*)."

It is time now to have a look at the text of the *Revelations*. On a cursory reading, Julian's visions appear striking, not to say showy. Here is the beginning of the first revelation:

> Then I suddenly saw the red blood trickling down (*sodenly I saw the reed bloud runnyng downe*) from under the crown of thorns, hot and fresh and very plentiful (*hote and freyshely, plentuously and liuely*),

---

[8] LT ch. 2, p. 43 and ch. 3, p. 45. See Colledge and Walsh (eds.), *A Book of Showings to the Anchoress Julian of Norwich*, 292: 44-293: 51.

as though it were the moment of his Passion when the crown of thorns was thrust on his blessed head.[9]

This is what Julian calls a "bodily sight". Does she mean to say that she had a "corporeal vision" (to use the set expression), which would imply that she had the perception of somebody there, actually present in front of her, just as a thing which is present impinges upon the external senses? Do mystics have this sort of materialistic "real" visions? In this case there is a definite answer, which eliminates a pseudo-problem that might have hampered our approach to Julian's account. There simply are no corporeal visions; in fact they are all imaginative. It is from within that the visionary's internal senses are being stirred without any external thing being there to affect them. Julian seems to support this current general understanding of so-called corporeal visions.[10] The fourth *Revelation* starts in much the same way as the first, with a very striking "bodily" sight indeed and, in addition, the visionary's own level-headed remark:

> I saw, as I watched, the body of Christ bleeding abundantly (*I saw beholdyng the body plentuous bledyng*), in weals from the scourging ... the hot blood ran out so abundantly that no skin or wound could be seen, it seemed to be all blood ... nevertheless, the bleeding continued for a while so that it could be observed attentively (*tyll it myght be seen with avysement*). And it looked so abundant to me (*to my syght*) that I thought if at that moment it had been real, natural

---

[9] LT ch. 4, p. 45. See Colledge and Walsh (eds.), *A Book of Showings to the Anchoress Julian of Norwich*, 294: 3-6.

[10] See the excellent survey of Pierre Adnès, "Visions," *Dictionnaire de spiritualité* XVI (1994) 949-1002, c. 999-1000. For an in-depth discussion, see Karl Rahner, "Ueber Visionen und verwandte Erscheinungen" *Geist und Leben* 21 (1948) 179-213. For Julian's questioning the authenticity of her own visionary experience as a whole, see LT ch 66-70, p. 157: "And I said openly that I had been delirious (*and I seyde I had ravyd to day*)." See Colledge and Walsh (eds.), *A Book of Showings to the Anchoress Julian of Norwich*, 632: 16-633: 17.

blood (*if it had ben so in kynde and in substance*), the whole bed would have been blood-soaked and even the floor around (*and haue passyde over all about*).

That bodily sights are in reality imaginative ones, does not alter the fact that the vividness of these visions is most impressive. If this kind of showing does not occur 'out there', it certainly looks like a gripping interior film-show: a motion picture indeed, and in technicolour at that. Is this almost photographic representation of Jesus' bodily suffering what the *Showings* are about? Does this establish that the Christian contemplative is, as it were, captivated by the Image and consequently disinterested in the Imageless?

In order to clarify this issue, a second reading of Julian's text is necessary. And, in order to focus the reading, three questions need to be answered: what does Julian say she is really seeing? what kind of seeing is this? and, is anything else happening to her while she is seeing?

As for the object of the visionary's seeing, one notices in the first place that Julian did feel the normal, deep-rooted drive to search for God-in-the-highest, and she has, so to say, been tempted to go beyond the Man. As she seemed to be dying, the priest set the cross before her face, and she "consented" to look at it, be it at that moment for rather physical reasons:

> It seemed to me that I was well as I was, for my eyes were looking fixedly upwards into heaven, where I trusted that I was going with God's mercy. But nevertheless I consented to fix my eyes (*I ascentyd to sett my eyen*) on the face of the crucifix if I could, and so I did, because I thought that I might be able to bear looking straight ahead for longer than I could manage to look upwards.[11]

After the eighth revelation, however, this initial change of focus shows its mystical meaning. Julian's heaven is to be Jesus:

---

[11] LT ch. 3, p. 44. See Colledge and Walsh (eds.), *A Book of Showings to the Anchoress Julian of Norwich*, 291: 24-28.

At this point I wanted to look up from the cross (*I wolde have lokyde fro the crosse*), but I dared not ... Then a suggestion came from my reason (*had I a profyr in my reason*), as though a friendly voice had spoken, 'Look up to his Father in heaven.' And then I saw clearly with the faith that I felt (*sawe I wele with the feyth that I felt*) that there was nothing between the cross and heaven which could have distressed me. Either I must look up, or I must answer. I answered with all the strength of my soul (*I answeryd inwardly with alle the myght of my soule*) and said, 'No, I cannot, for you are my heaven' .... Thus I was taught to choose Jesus as my heaven, though at that moment I saw him only in pain.[12]

It is, then, all the more striking that the experience of this visionary, who concentrates all her attention on the Humanity, proves to be primarily a perception of the Divinity. Returning to the first *Revelation*, we see that the colourful description of the suffering Jesus continues as follows:

And as part of the same showing the Trinity suddenly filled my heart with the greatest joy (*fulfilled my hart most of joy*). And I understood that in heaven it will be like that for ever ... For the Trinity is God, God is the Trinity ... And this was shown in the first revelation, and in all of them (*in the first syght and in all*); for it seems to me that where Jesus is spoken of (*for wher Jhesu appireth*), the holy Trinity is to be understood ... With this sight of the blessed Passion, along with the Godhead that I saw in my mind (*in my understanding*) ...[13]

Obviously, the grace bestowed here upon the visionary is not that she is enabled to stare at Jesus' bleeding flesh as such. The gracious revelation consists properly in that she is conscious of the Divinity being present in — not beyond — this particular Humanity, which

---

[12] LT ch. 19, p. 69. See Colledge and Walsh (eds.), *A Book of Showings to the Anchoress Julian of Norwich*, 370: 2-371: 16. See also ST ch. 10, p. 17.

[13] LT ch. 4, p. 45-46. See Colledge and Walsh (eds.), *A Book of Showings to the Anchoress Julian of Norwich*, 294: 9-296: 24.

is suffering in precisely this painful way. Here Julian is not so much confessing her faith in the Trinity and the Godman, nor is she following a line of thought — e.g., "from incomprehensible human suffering to divine bliss" — and there is no apparition of the Trinity. In brief this is a passive, mystical experience of God in Jesus.

Undoubtedly, this awareness of the Trinity is the core of all Julian's *Showings:* "And this was shown in the first revelation (*syght*), and in all of them." Or, as she puts it a little later, "the strength and the foundation of everything was shown in the first vision (*the strenght and the grounde of alle was schewed in the furst syght*)."[14] And finally she affirms:

> I was able to touch, see and feel (*I had in perty touchyng, syght and feelyng*) some of the three properties of God on which the strength and meaning of the whole revelation is based (*the strenght and the effecte of alle the revelacion stondyth*); and they were seen in every showing and most characteristically in the twelfth, where it often says, 'It is I' (*I it am*).[15]

Concerning the way in which Julian "sees," it is clear that it corresponds to the compound object of her seeing. In the initial description of the first 'showing', that was taken as a starting-point, it appears already that along with the sight of the Passion goes a seeing "in my mind" (*in my understanding*). And later in the first *Revelation* this combination of two manners of seeing is explicitly confirmed:

---

[14] LT ch. 4, p. 46 and ch. 6, p. 50. See Colledge and Walsh (eds.), *A Book of Showings to the Anchoress Julian of Norwich*, 309: 63-64. Moreover the conclusion of Julian's book reads as follows: "Thus ends the revelation of love of the Holy Trinity shown by our Saviour Christ Jesu ..."

[15] LT ch. 83, p. 176. See Colledge and Walsh (eds.), *A Book of Showings to the Anchoress Julian of Norwich*, 722: 2-5.

> And all the time that God was showing in spiritual sight (*in gostely syght*) what I have just described, the bodily sight of the plentiful bleeding from Christ's head remained (*I saw the bodely syght lastyng*). The great drops fell down from under the crown of thorns like pills (*pelottes*) ... The beauty and the vividness of the blood are like nothing but itself.[16]

As for the third question — is anything else happening to Julian while she is seeing the compound divine object? — the same initial passage of the first *Revelation* already indicates the answer. While the 'bodily' sight unrolls before the visionary's eyes, causing her cruel pain, something very different happens to her. Unexpectedly she feels herself being changed; her heart's grief is converted into joy, and at once she "understands" this transformation as the Trinity being actually present — "the Trinity suddenly filled my heart with the greatest joy." This is where the mystical character of Julian's experience is clearly seen. For in the first instance the mystic's perception is not a matter of seeing something somewhere, but of being affected, "touched," in an unforeseen and incomparable way, so much so that it is precisely through the quality of the effects produced in this person's consciousness that he or she comes to perceive an Other. The mystic's own manner of "seeing" God arises from undergoing such a personal transformation: the divine Object makes itself known through the human subject's own emotion.[17]

---

[16] LT ch. 7, p. 50-51. See Colledge and Walsh (eds.), *A Book of Showings to the Anchoress Julian of Norwich*, 311: 12-312: 21.

[17] "Emotion," from the Latin *e-movere,* is taken here in the strong, non-sentimental sense of a person's consciousness being "moved out" of its usual, self-poised state by something undeniably present and yet incomprehensible. That is why mystics often refer to their "admiration". Cf. Paul Mommaers, "Is Hadewijch emotioneel?," *Emoties in de Middeleeuwen*, eds. R.E.V. Stuip and C. Vellekoop, Utrechtse Bijdragen tot de Mediëvistiek 15 (Hilversum: Verloren, 1998) 135-156.

Thus, from the beginning of the first *Revelation*, Julian describes in no uncertain terms what may be considered the distinguishing feature of her experience. Two different and yet interconnected ways of seeing — the bodily and the spiritual in unison — accompany a twofold feeling — pain changing into joy — and so manifest the presence of the Divinity in the Humanity. For present purposes it will be helpful to have a look at a few more passages where the founding experience of the first *Revelation* reappears. These are texts where, thanks to Julian's talent for expression, the reader is enabled to see together with her (so to speak) how, in the dying Jesus, indestructible Joy and Life appear, how, in the Humanity, withering to death on the cross, the glorious Divinity appears, and finally how this utterly poor man manifests himself as the Glad Giver.

The eighth *Revelation* starts with the hopeless vision of the dying of Jesus, which is seen here as a slow drying out:

> Loss of blood and pain drying him from within (*blodlessehed and payne dryed with in*), and blasts of wind and cold coming from without, met together in the dear body (*swete body*) of Christ ... So I saw Christ's dear flesh dying (*thus I saw the swete flessch dry in my syght*), seemingly bit by bit drying up with amazing agony (*with mervelous payne*) ... This long agony (*peyne*) made it seem to me that he had been dead for a full week (*as if he had be sennyght deede*) ... yet dying continually (*contynually dyeng*).[18]

The reader has to wait until the ninth *Revelation* to see joy emerge from the suffering, and the divine from the human — the most miserably human. At this point the paradox is carried to the extreme. Whereas in the first *Revelation* the joy in Julian's heart appeared as developing from the pain of the man who is still alive

---

[18] LT ch. 16, p. 65. See Colledge and Walsh (eds.), *A Book of Showings to the Anchoress Julian of Norwich*, 358: 17-359: 29.

— "the red blood trickling down from under the crown of thorns" — it now springs from the man whose life "to all appearances could last no longer". And again we notice how the seeing of the visionary goes along with her own transformation: "the changing of his blessed expression changed mine":

> And I watched for the last breath with all my might (*and I lokyd after the departyng with alle my myghtes*) and expected to see the body completely dead. And just at the very moment when it seemed to me that to all appearances his life could last no longer and the end must be revealed, suddenly I saw while looking at the same cross, that his blessed expression changed (*sodenly I beholdyng in the same crosse he channgyd in blessydfulle chere*). The changing of his blessed expression changed mine (*the channgyng of hys blessyd chere channgyd myne*), and I was as glad and happy as it was possible to be. Then our Lord made me think happily (*brought oure lorde meryly to my mynd*), 'Where is there now one jot of your pain (*any poynt of thy payne*) or your sorrow?'[19]

And this same man, whose end seems so irremediably final, reveals himself as the living lover, the "glad giver"[20], whose suffering for love is "a joy, a delight and an endless happiness," and in whose Manhood, then, the triune Godhead appears as "three heavens":

> Then our good Lord Jesus Christ spoke, asking, 'Are you well pleased (*apayd*) that I suffered for you?' I said, 'Yes, my good Lord, thank you ...' Then Jesus, our kind Lord, said, 'If you are

---

[19] LT ch. 21, p. 71. See Colledge and Walsh (eds.), *A Book of Showings to the Anchoress Julian of Norwich*, 379: 3-10.

[20] "And with these words: 'It is a joy, a delight and an endless happiness to me' (*It is a joy, a blysse and endlesse lykyng to me*) he brought to my mind the nature of a glad giver (*propyrte of a gladde geaver*): a glad giver pays little attention to the thing he is giving, but his whole desire and intention is to please and comfort the one to whom he gives it."(LT ch. 23, p. 75. See Colledge and Walsh (eds.), *A Book of Showings to the Anchoress Julian of Norwich*, 392: 37-40.

pleased (*apayde*), I am pleased (*apayde*). It is a joy, a delight and an endless happiness (*it is a joy, a blysse, an endlesse lykyng*) to me that I ever endured suffering (*sufferd passion*) for you, and if I could suffer more, I would suffer more.' And as I became conscious of these words my understanding was lifted up to heaven (*in thys felyng my understandyng was leftyd vppe*) to heaven, and there I saw three heavens ... And though I saw three heavens, and all of them in the blessed Manhood of Christ, none is greater, none is lesser, none is higher, none is lower, but they are all equally full of supreme joy (*evyn lyke in blysse*) ... For the first heaven Christ showed me his Father ... I saw in Christ what the Father is (*I saw in Crist that the father is*).[21]

And then follows the passage of the *Revelations* that shows most aptly how Julian's Christocentric experience is inextricably theocentric. The words Jesus had spoken to Julian ("it is a joy, a delight and an endless happiness to me") now suddenly open. What at first had appeared as referring only to Christ — "to me" — is understood now as the expression of the Trinity's love:

By the joy I understood the pleasure of the Father; and by the delight, the glory of the Son (*and for the blysse the wurshyppe of the sonne*); and by the endless happiness, the Holy Ghost.[22]

Finally, there is in the sixteenth *Revelation* — "conclusion and confirmation of all the other ones" — the following graphic presentation of the core of Julian's experience:

And then our Lord opened my spiritual eyes (*gostely eye*) and showed me my soul in the middle of my heart. I saw the soul as large as if it were an endless world and as if it were a holy (*blessyd*) kingdom ... In the centre of that city sits our Lord Jesus, God and

---

man (*very god and very man*), a handsome person and of great stature ... He sits in the soul, in the very centre, in peace and rest. And the Godhead rules and protects heaven and earth and all that is: supreme power, supreme wisdom and supreme goodness. It seems to me (*as to my syght*) that in all eternity Jesus will never leave (*he shall nevyr remoue withouten ende*) the position which he takes in our soul; for in us is his most familiar (*homelyest*) home and his everlasting (*endlesse*) dwelling.[23]

This attempt to investigate the text of the *Revelations* is based on the conviction that the author wishes to say lucidly what she is actually saying. In fact this reading of the Lady Julian's "book" ("begun by God's gift and grace but ... not yet completed"[24]) has brought out a number of points that may well help to clarify the "riddle of Christian mystical experience".

Primarily, Julian's *Revelations* are meant to testify to a passive (mystical) experience of the "Godhead," and are not intended to reproduce self-induced visions of the "Manhood". Thus the purpose of Julian's focusing on the Passion can, perhaps, best be rendered as follows: this imaginative and affective concentration of the senses upon a senselessly suffering and destroyed human figure — the disconcerting image — is for this woman the only possible way to be personally touched in the spirit — that "soul in the middle of my heart" — by indestructible joy, life, love, and the imageless Reality. The *Revelations* are in the very first place a *felt* revelation of Love:

---

[23] LT ch. 68, p. 163. See Colledge and Walsh (eds.), *A Book of Showings to the Anchoress Julian of Norwich*, 639: 2-641: 17. The original text is more explicit: *He syttyth in the soule evyn rygthe in peas and rest, and he rulyth and zemyth hevyn and erth and all that is. The manhode with the godhed syttyth in rest, the godhede rulyth and zemeth withoutyn ony instrument or besynesse. And the soule is alle occupyed with the blessyd godhed, that is soueryne myghte, souereyne wysdom and souereyn goodnesse.*

[24] LT ch. 86, p. 179.

And from the time that this was shown, I often longed to know what our Lord meant. And fifteen years and more later my spiritual understanding received an answer, which was this: 'Do you want to know what our Lord meant? Know well that love was what he meant. Who showed you this? Love. What did he show? Love. Why did he show it to you? For Love.

> *And fro the tyme that it was shewde, I desyerde oftyn tymes to wytt in what was oure lords menyng. And xv yere after and mor, I was answeryd in gostly understondyng thus: What, woldest thou wytt thy lordes menyng in this thyng? Wytt it wele, loue was his menyng. Who shewyth it the? Love. What shewid he the? Love. Wherfor shewyth he it the? For love.*[25]

The *Revelations* attest to a psychic phenomenon mentioned by other mystics, for instance, as they try to clarify how action and contemplation can go together in the single experience of being one with God. Two different levels of consciousness may be activated simultaneously without the person's psyche falling apart. This power of the human soul allows, in Julian's case, for a double "showing". So, through the parable of the Lord and the Servant, she comes to see the "double expression" of the Lord:

> The first was shown outwardly, very gentle and kind (*outward, full mekely and myldely*) ... The second expression was shown inwardly (*that other chere was shewde inwarde*); it was more elevated but it was all one with the first (*and that was more hyly and all one*) ... Nothing comes between the first and the second, for all is one love, and this one blessed love now works doubly in us (*for it is all one love, whych one blessyd loue hath now in us doubyll werkyng*).[26]

---

[25] LT ch. 86, p. 179. See Colledge and Walsh (eds.), *A Book of Showings to the Anchoress Julian of Norwich*, 732: 13-733: 18.

[26] LT ch. 52, p. 127. See Colledge and Walsh (eds.), *A Book of Showings to the Anchoress Julian of Norwich*, 552: 74-553: 90.

Teresa of Avila's Visions of Christ

Undoubtedly Teresa of Avila (1515-1582) is one of the most striking personalities in the history of Christian spirituality. Graced with an overwhelming and multi-faceted mystical experience, she also had great talent for expression. She was able to put into writing even the most delicate phenomena of contemplation with the vivacity of the spoken language. In addition to being very influential as a mystical author, Teresa left her mark on modern spirituality by founding the reformed Carmelite nuns who effectively spread her contemplative teachings. But it is not without significance that Teresa de Ahumada assumed a different name, Teresa of Jesus, in 1562, precisely at the moment that she set to work on this daring religious reform. In fact, the figure of Jesus Christ was to be pivotal throughout Teresa's religious life, as well as in her mystical career.[27]

Before looking more closely at those passages in Teresa's writings where she comes to grips with the exact issue under discussion here, it will be as well to make a few observations, as in the case of Julian of Norwich, if only to avoid some false problems. First of all, Teresa shares Julian's conviction as to the nature of her visions. She knows that none of them is actually corporeal, in the sense of something tangible that impinges upon the senses from outside.[28] Secondly, Teresa was almost obsessed from the

[27] See, for the milestones in the development of Teresa's Christ-centered life, Thomas Alvarez, "Thérèse de Jésus (sainte)," *Dictionnaire de spiritualité* XV (1991) c. 616-618.

[28] All quotations here and hereafter are from the English translation by E. Allison Peers, *The Complete Works of Saint Teresa of Jesus* (London: Sheed and Ward, 1946). Hereafter cited as CW. References to *The Complete Works* will include the title of the specific work from which the quotation is drawn. For the Spanish text and the numbering of paragraphs, cf. Santa Teresa de Jesús, *Obras Completas,* eds. Efrén de la Madre de Dios O.C.D. and Otger Steggink O.Carm

outset of her contemplative career with distinguishing authentic from illusory mystical experiences. If it had not been for her learned counsellors demanding written evidence, we would not now have at our disposal the *Life* and the *Spiritual Relations*. No wonder, then, that this visionary was particularly aware of the possibility of visions being self-induced and fully 'imaginary'.[29] Next, this seer is anything but endowed with a talent for visual imagination: she says she had "so little ability for picturing things in my mind that if I did not actually see a thing I could not use my imagination, as other people do, who can make pictures to themselves and so become recollected." So much so that "of Christ as Man I could only think: however much I read about his beauty

(Madrid: La Editorial Catolica, 1972). Hereafter referred to as OC. References to the *Obras Completas* will also include a reference to the specific work from which a quotation is taken. "When it is a question of exterior sight, I can say nothing about it, for the person I have mentioned, and of whom I can best speak, had not experienced this." See CW (*Interior Castle*), 315. See also CW (*Life*), 179 where Teresa asserts: "Although this vision is imaginary, I never saw it, or any other vision, with the eyes of the body, but only with the eyes of the soul". And she goes on then to distance herself from the *theory* of there being corporeal vision, "seen with the eyes of the body."

[29] Peers correctly translates *visión imaginaria* as "imaginary vision" instead of "imaginative vision". On this point Teresa questions her own visions. See CW (*Life*), 179-180: "And no sooner had the vision faded — the very moment, indeed, after it had gone — than I began to think ... that I had imagined it". And she is well aware of the capacity of contemplation-minded people to "create" their visions: "When the soul is able to remain for a long time looking upon the Lord, I do not think it can be a vision at all. It must rather be that some striking idea creates a picture in the imagination (*fabricada en la imaginación alguna figura*): but this will be a dead image by comparison with the other." Some come to "think they can actually see everything that is in their mind." See CW (*Interior Castle*), 316. In fact, this tendency to make oneself imagine the sight of Christ is no more than a specific case of wishful thinking: "When a person has a great desire for something, he persuades himself that he is seeing or hearing what he desires, just as those who go about desiring something all day think so much about it that after a time they begin to dream of it." See CW (*Interior Castle*), 319.

and however often I looked at pictures of him, I could never form any picture of him myself."[30]

And finally, one finds that, for Teresa, the meaning of the ordinary image lies in its use. On this point she falls into line with the general view indicated in chapter 1. The image in its capacity to represent something else compensates for the absence of the real thing, it substitutes for its tangible presence. In particular, Teresa agrees to some extent with Marguerite Porete as to the role of the image. It can be said to bridge the distance from the Beloved; it is a substitute for his felt presence: "Especially when communicating, I would wish I had His portrait and image always before my eyes, since I could not have it as deeply engraven on my soul as I should like."[31]

Teresa's first awareness of the riddle of the Humanity in contemplation

It first dawned on Teresa that the Humanity of Christ may cause a problem for the contemplative when she came into contact with *The Third Alphabet* (*Tercer Abecedario*) of Francisco de Osuna, the exponent of the Franciscan spiritual movement of "recollection" (*recogimiento*).[32] Osuna offered her a method of prayer

---

[30] CW (*Life*),55 and see below the text corresponding to note 39. See also CW (*Life*), 24: "My imagination is so poor that, even when I thought about the Lord's Humanity, or tried to imagine it to myself, as I was in the habit of doing, I never succeeded."

[31] For Porete, see chapter I, the text that corresponds to note 27: "To have his image does not alter the fact that I am in a strange land and far from the palace where the very noble friends of this Lord dwell." For the text from Teresa, cf. CW (*Life*), 138.

[32] Cf. chapter 4, § 6-8, of CW (*Life*). See also CW (*Interior Castle, Mansions* IV, chapter 3). Francisco de Osuna (1492-1540), a Friar Minor, is nowadays

which she followed "with all my might". Soon she was successful: "The Lord began to be so gracious to me on this way of prayer that He granted me the favour of leading me to the Prayer of Quiet, and occasionally even to Union, though I did not understand what either of these was." At this moment, there is no question yet of Teresa seeing the Humanity as a hampering image, which should be left behind in order to enter recollection. But there appears already the tension between having before the mind's eye the image of a particular figure and turning inward beyond all images. Teresa tries as hard as she can to "think of Jesus Christ ... as present within me, and it was in this way that I prayed. If I thought about any incident in His life, I would imagine it inwardly."[33] Obviously, by so internalizing the Humanity,

considered the "first and greatest master of Teresa of Jesus, the principal master and codifier of the mysticism of *Recogimiento*, the dominating and fundamental mysticism of the 16th, 17th and 18th centuries in Spain." See Melquiades Andrés Martin, "Osuna (François de)," *Dictionnaire de spiritualité* XI (1982) c. 1050. It may suffice here to note that Osuna himself received his contemplative formation in the religious houses where "recollection" (*recolección*) was being practised. That is also where the mystical *recogimiento* flourished, which Osuna systematized in his *Third Alphabet*, the third book in a series of six, while in the *Fourth Alphabet* he tackles the pseudo-mystical imitation of *recogimiento*, namely *alumbradismo* (contemplatives who feel directly "illuminated") which implies a *dejamento* (the "abandonment" of all interior and exterior activity, such as meditating on the Passion, *no meditan la pasión*). Briefly, the *recogimiento* (bringing together; concentrating) is a method that leads to interior rest by quieting the affective and spiritual faculties. Then one does not meditate on a particular subject by using the will and the imagination/understanding, but one tries to *no pensar nada*, "not to think of anything" (as the well-known expression had it). Thus *recogimiento* implies that one looks for God within oneself, where he may be reached without the intermediary of images and thoughts, beyond the ordinary, active levels of consciousness.

[33] "Procurava lo más que podía traer a Jesucristo ... dentro de mi presente ... si pensava en algun paso (de la Pasión), le representava en lo interior." See OC (*Vida*), ch. 4, §8.

Teresa expects to meet the Man actually and personally, but this endeavour to perceive him within her seems to have been of little avail.[34] She is not able to keep thinking about Jesus nor to imagine him, which leads her to take refuge in reading "good books". For, indeed, this mystic-to-be is wary of growing dull in prayer:

> For if the will has nothing to employ it and love has no present object with which to busy itself the soul finds itself without either support or occupation, its solitude and aridity cause it great distress and its thoughts involve it in the severest conflict.

Thus Teresa is aware of an interior void looming up, if the Humanity is bound to just disappear.

It will be useful to examine in detail the *Prologue* of *The Third Alphabet* for that is where Osuna, as an adept of *recogimiento*, presents his view on the Humanity.[35] To start with, he states that the Humanity "in itself neither impedes nor hampers recollection, regardless of how refined and lofty it is." The same applies even to all creation, for "no created thing in itself can impede

---

[34] It will take Christ-centered visionary experiences to lead her to actually perceive the Humanity as present in her. In chapter 40 she describes a vision which "seems to me a very beneficial one for recollected persons *(personas de recogimiento)*, for it teaches them to think of the Lord as being in the very innermost part of their soul." At the risk of running ahead of things, I quote this impressive account by Teresa here: "On one occasion, when I was reciting the Hours with the community, my soul suddenly became recollected and seemed to me to become bright all over like a mirror: no part of it — back, sides, top or bottom — but was completely bright, and in the centre of it was a picture of Christ Our Lord *(se me representó Cristo nuestro Señor)* as I generally see Him. I seemed to see Him in every part of my soul as clearly as in a mirror, and this mirror — I cannot explain how — was wholly sculptured in the same Lord by a most loving communication which I shall never be able to describe" *(este espejo se esculpía todo en el mesmo Señor por una comunicación que yo no sabré decir, muy amorosa)*. See CW *(Life)*, 292; OC *(Vida)*, ch. 40, § 5.

[35] Quotations are from Francisco de Osuna, *The Third Spiritual Alphabet*, trans. Mary E. Giles (New York: Paulist Press, 1981) 38-44.

contemplation, however lofty." Any hindrance, then, is caused by our imperfection. And Osuna goes on to specify this deficiency. In contrast with the condition of the saints in whom "all parts harmonize with one another and one does not disturb the other or weaken its force," we lack this psychic integration. Consequently, "we are unable in our smallness to deal with everything at once." Because of this impotence to perceive and enjoy the visible and the invisible together, we resemble the apostles: Christ had to deprive them of his bodily presence, for it was "necessary for them as people who were not yet capable of delighting in everything at once." Thus Osuna's solution to the contemplative's difficulty with the Humanity is tinged with paradox. He asserts that the height of contemplation does not require constant abstracting from the Humanity to reach the Divinity. Such an abstraction should be only a passing phase in anticipation of the moment when one would be enabled to "rise to a higher state":

> Since it was beneficial to the apostles, therefore, that they cease contemplating the Humanity of Our Lord for a while so as to be more freely occupied solely in the contemplation of the Divinity, it also seems appropriate for all who desire to rise to a higher state.

The most sigificant passage of Osuna's *Prologue,* however, reads as follows:

> If all creation constitutes a ladder for the feet of wise people to climb to God, how much more so is the Humanity of Christ, the way, the truth, and the life, who came to give us life more abundantly so that going in by his Divinity and out by his Sacred Humanity we might be nourished.

The crucial phrase here is "going in ... going out". In *The Third Alphabet,* Osuna has been essentially influenced by Flemish mystical literature. Through the works of Hendrik Herp *(Harphius,* † 1477), also a Friar Minor, he had come into contact with the teachings of Jan van Ruusbroec († 1381).[36] Now, as will be clear further on, the expression "going in ... going out" is not only a key phrase in Ruusbroec's general description of mystical union but also, in particular, in his phenomenological elucidation of the role of the Humanity in the experience of the most advanced contemplatives. Given Osuna's familiarity with Flemish writings and his awareness of the contemplative problem caused by the Humanity, it is all the more striking that he does not make use of this notion of "going in ... going out" to clarify that it is possible for the highest contemplative experience to be, and to always remain, centered upon Christ. In Osuna's treatment this inherited and helpful expression loses its *contemplative* significance. It is reduced to a statement of principle: Christ is the "objective" cause of the Christian's life, and only the "going in," in the sense of "climbing to God," is emphasized. Surely this is true of all the other passages quoted from the *Prologue*.[37]

[36] Herp is deservedly called the "herald of Ruusbroec": it is mainly through his works, written for the most part in Latin and published by the Carthusians of Cologne, that his master's mystical teaching spread throughout Europe. As for Osuna, it appears that the third part of the *Abecedario* "se rattache, pour l'essentiel, à la doctrine de Ruusbroec et de Herp, sans pourtant jamais les mentionner." (Etta Gullik and Optat de Veghel, "Herp (Henri de, Harpius)," *Dictionnaire de spiritualité* VII/1 (1969) c. 363.

[37] Geert Grote (see ch. 1, note 17) is worth mentioning once more: in his *De Quattuor Generibus Meditabilium* he uses the same expression (*ingredi ... egredi*), but unlike Osuna he is more faithful to Ruusbroec's teaching. He argues that finally the images — *sensibilium phantasmata* — have simply to disappear: "*licet non praecipitanter, licet non ex propria praesumptione nec propriis viribus, non subito sed paulatim eliminanda et evacuanda recedunt, vel potius transformantur in spiritualem quandam armoniam, ut tam homo interior quam exterior, tam ingrediens quam egrediens, ut ait Christus, pascua inveniat*" (line 838-843). — The gospel reference is John 10,9: "I am the gate. Whoever enters by me will be saved, and will come in and go out and find pasture." See also Guido de Baere, "Het 'ghemeine leven' bij Ruusbroec en Geert Grote,"*Ons Geestelijk Erf* 59 (1985) 172-183.

In chapter 9 of the *Life*, Teresa returns to her practice of the prayer method she learnt about from Osuna's *Abecedario*. Again she points out how she "would try to make pictures of Christ inwardly,"[38] but her "representing" him does not yield his felt presence. Unable to imagine the Man, she can only think of him, and not perceive him. Teresa's description of this contemplative limitation deserves particular attention:

> Of Christ as Man I could only think: however much I read about His beauty and however often I looked at pictures of Him, I could never form any picture of Him myself. I was like a person who is blind, or in the dark: he may be talking to someone, and know that he is with him, because he is quite sure he is there — I mean, he understands and believes he is there — but he cannot see him. Thus it was with me when I thought of Our Lord. It was for this reason that I was so fond of pictures.[39]

Up to this point the author of the *Life* has only hinted at the problem for a Christian contemplative that arises from the prayer method of *recogimiento*. In chapter 12 of the *Life,* the dubiousness of methodically leaving the Humanity behind in contemplation becomes more apparent. After drawing attention once more to the inner desert awaiting the soul that ceases in prayer to use its understanding,[40] Teresa now focuses on what she considers to be a temptation that creeps up on the future mystic. Her concern is that one may be lured into suspending, on one's own initiative, the activity of the understanding. She warns the person who wants to "pass beyond ... and lift up his spirit" of the lethargy to which he or she will fall prey: "we shall remain stupid and cold". And she explains the contradiction in terms (the "foolishness") that such a

---

[38] CW (*Life*), 54. "Procurava representar a Cristo dentro de mí."

[39] CW (*Life*), 55-56.

[40] "When the understanding ceases to act, the soul remains barren *(desierta)* and suffers great aridity" CW (*Life*),71.

self-induced suspension implies. Far from denying that in prayer a passive suspension may take place, she is all the more opposed to the fruitless attempts of those who "try to rise unless they are raised by God." For in such cases there is no Presence to fascinate one: the soul lacks the "something which both amazes it and keeps it busy":

> What I say we must not do is to presume or think that we can suspend it ourselves; nor must we allow it to cease working ... When the Lord suspends the understanding and makes it cease from its activity, He gives it something which both amazes it *(de que se espante)* and keeps it busy ... To keep the faculties of the soul busy and to think that, at the same time, you can keep them quiet, is foolishness ... It is lost labour, and the soul feels slightly frustrated, like a man who is just about to take a leap and is then pulled back.[41]

Teresa's own abandoning of the Humanity

It is time now to have a good look at Teresa's description of how she came to disavow, in contemplation that is, the "image of the invisible God".[42] The occasion for this devotee of Christ to become so thoroughly disturbed about Jesus is the impact on her of the method of *no pensar nada* as it was being practised in the contemplative circles of the *Recogimiento*. She first came across this way of praying in Osuna's *Third Alphabet*, apparently without being then upset by it.[43] Years later, when she was about forty

---

[41] CW (*Life*),71-72.

[42] The key passages are CW (*Life*), ch. 22 and *Mansions* VI, ch. 7, §10-15. It may suffice here to concentrate on the first.

[43] Teresa had been an assiduous reader of the *Tercer Abecedario* ever since she was twenty-two. Osuna treats of *no pensar nada* in chapter 5 of *Treatise* XXI. A few passages that show his sharp wit and make us understand why Teresa enjoyed reading him deserve to be quoted here. Osuna begins his chapter 5 by saying that *no pensar nada* appears questionable indeed to those who are "not

years of age, Teresa came into contact with another contemplative authority promoting *no pensar nada*: Francisco de Laredo (1482-1540). She read his *Ascent of Mount Sion*,[44] and again she was not shocked. On the contrary, she affirms that he helped her to see clearly into her own experience, for in Laredo's description of the prayer of union she found "all the symptoms I had when I was

practised in spiritual matters". These people "reduce it to a matter of thinking nothing at all. But if we have to put our understanding to rest and intimately quiet it, clearly this requires us to think of something. If you really were to think of nothing, then we could apply to this devotion the words of the satirist: 'Nothingness can come from nothing and nothingness can return to nothing'." "The recollected do not consider that perfection is tantamount to thinking nothing at all; if that were the case, those who sleep, unless they dream, and the stunned would be perfect" (563). "The memory and understanding of those experienced in this devotion are so quiet and still when they are with God ... that they do not consider anything at all, not even what engages them at the moment, for they are totally absorbed and inebriated by what they feel in the soul. This state results from profound attention like that we experience when speaking so reverently with some lord that we do not think about the person in whose presence we find ourselves" (565). "You must not consider this exercise any less good because a philosopher or a Jew availed himself from it ... Nor should you think that because something is common to both good and evil people, it is less good, for it works in each according to his disposition without its intrinsic worth being affected" (566-567). "In these forms of recollection the understanding is not so quieted as to be totally deprived, for there always remains a tiny spark, sufficient for the soul to know it is enjoying something and that it is from God ... Raptures or degrees of recollection may also occur, causing the understanding to cease functioning altogether, as if the soul had no intelligence, but then it discovers again the living spark of simple knowledge" (574).

[44] Teresa read the second edition (Sevilla 1533) of the *Subida del Monte Sion*. See Robert Ricard, "Laredo (Bernardin de)," *Dictionnaire de spiritualité* IX (1976) c. 277-281. For a thorough study, with plenty of quotations from the *Subida,* see Fidèle de Ros, *Le Frère Bernardino de Laredo: Un inspirateur de Sainte Thérèse* (Paris: Vrin, 1948). See especially pp. 244-254: "La Sainte humanité est-elle parfois un obstacle à la pure contemplation?"; pp. 325-326: "no pensar nada".

unable to think of anything. It was exactly this that I was always saying — that when I was experiencing that type of prayer I could think of nothing" *(no podia pensar nada).*

One may ask who, among the authors advising the method of *no pensar nada,* was the one who put Teresa's Christ-centered prayer life at such risk, so much so that after some time she came to realize that by following his teaching she had been "committing an act of high treason"?[45] The Franciscan lay brother, Barnabé de Palma († 1523), has been identified as the guide who mainly mis-led Teresa, for it is possible to find in his *Via Spiritus* sentences that correspond to those with which Teresa describes this critical development.[46] Thus we need to have a close look at chapter 22 of the *Life,* where the first version of this account appears.[47]

To start with, Teresa outlines the method launched by de Palma and kindred spirits. It certainly has a harsh ring to it, for in order to make progress the contemplative is told to "rise aloft in humility". This means in real terms that one is supposed to empty one's consciousness of everyhing corporeal and to maintain untiringly this interior state. Obviously, there is no place for the Humanity in this lofty contemplation:

> And these books advise us earnestly to put aside all corporeal ima-
> gination and to approach the contemplation of the Divinity. For they

---

[45] CW (*Life*), p. 137.

[46] Published in Flanders in 1541, the full title was *Via spiritus o de la perfec-ción espiritual del ánima.* For the correspondence between Teresa's text and the *Via spiritus,* see Tomás de la Cruz, Introduction to the facsimile edition of Teresa's *Camino de Perfección* (Vatican City: 1965) 58 n. 2. For this last refer-ence, see Tomas de la Cruz, "Humanité du Christ, IV: L'école carmélitaine," *Dictionnare de spiritualité* VII/1 (1969) c. 1099.

[47] In *Mansions* VI, ch. 7, §5-15, Teresa returns to this disturbing matter. There her critique seems to be less radical: "I may be wrong and we may all be meaning the same thing" (CW, 304).

say that anything else, even Christ's Humanity, will hinder or impede those who have arrived so far from attaining the most perfect contemplation.[48]

In addition to this objective statement of the method in question and of its Christological implications, Teresa offers a description of what happened to herself as she followed it. This is where the Carmelite mystic's account goes to the very heart of the problem being studied here. She recognizes the authenticity of her experience of God through this procedure and thus accounts in passing for her "contriving" to maintain this "recollection". So far so good, and yet there is a catch in this endeavour to remain so concentrated. Three almost synonymous terms suddenly appear: "delight," "joy," and "pleasure".[49] This kind of contemplation bestows on Teresa a spiritual satisfaction which, fusing together with the genuine "advantage" of her experiencing God, makes her commit her "act of high treason": "no one could have made me return to meditation on the Humanity":

> When I began to gain some experience of supernatural prayer — I mean the Prayer of Quiet — I tried to put aside everything corporeal,

---

[48] See CW (*Life*), 136. A little later Teresa indicates the basic contemplative principle of these spiritualizing authors. They "think that, as this work is entirely spiritual, anything corporeal may disturb or impede it, and that what contemplatives must contrive to do is to think of themselves as circumscribed, but of God as being everywhere, so that they may become absorbed in Him."

[49] *(Oración) sabrosa, deleite, gusto. Gusto* is in Teresa's writing an appreciative term, as can be seen from her treatment of the difference between *contentos* ("sweetness or tenderness in prayer") and *gustos* ("consolations") in *Mansions IV*, ch. 1 and 2. "What I call consolations from God *(gustos de Dios),* and elsewhere have termed the Prayer of Quiet ... "(CW, 236). However, there is something tricky even about these gifts from God, for they can turn into an ordinary satisfaction: "The devil might mislead (the soul) with regard to the consolations *(gustos)* which God gives ... and (let it) be living in a state of permanent absorption *(y dejarla en un embevimiento ordinario)"* (CW, 231).

> though I dared not lift up my soul, for, being always so wicked, I saw that to do this would be presumption. But I thought I was experiencing the presence of God, as proved to be true, and I contrived to remain with Him in a state of recollection. This type of prayer, if God has a part in it, is full of delight, and brings great joy. And in view of the advantage I was deriving from it and the pleasure it was bringing me, no one could have made me return to meditation on the Humanity — on the contrary, this really seemed to me a hindrance.[50]

What strikes one first here is that Teresa, at this stage, sees the contemplative's real — "supernatural" — union with God as happening only in the Prayer of Quiet. This kind of prayer, then, appears as the "perfect contemplation," a peak experience.[51] By the same token, the state of recollection is considered to be the sole form of consciousness that allows this real union to take place. Obviously, the contemplative who strives for perfection is supposed to apply herself to a variety of virtues and spiritual exercises — one will not reach the top unless one climbs the mountain paths of, say, charity and meditation — but with that quiet recollection being seen as the summit, all outer and inner activity appear necessarily as simply a preparation. Moreover, this peak view of mystical union is reinforced by feelings of "delight," "joy," and "pleasure" that accompany the presence of God experienced in recollection. These *gustos* are so enjoyable that the contemplative gets "absorbed" in them and wants this state to go on always. Teresa knows a number of people who have been granted "perfect contemplation and who would like to remain in possession of it for ever." They come to "think it would be a very great

---

[50] CW (*Life*), 137.

[51] "Perfect contemplation" appears again and again, and Teresa likes to use such expressions as "the most sublime kind of prayer," "the summit of contemplation". See CW (*Interior Castle*), 307; CW (*Life*) 139.

thing to be enjoying these gifts all the time." Teresa then advises those who enjoy these gifts to "become less absorbed in them" and even to "make every effort to avoid this absorption". She knows by experience how attractive the *gustos* are, for she herself had been "going about in that state of absorption". And when she was first granted the "Prayer of Quiet, and often, too, the Prayer of Union," she "began to be afraid, for the delight and the sweetness which I felt were so great and often I could not help feeling them".[52] On the negative side, all inner and outer activity appears to be not only a hindrance to quiet contemplation but also a deprivation of the spiritual "delight".

Consequently in the experience of the perfect contemplative, Jesus suffers the same fate as "everything corporeal," because in order to keep this human figure in mind, one needs to cultivate the inner activity of meditation,[53] which does not yield the *gusto* that goes with quiet recollection. As a result, for this contemplative to "think of Jesus" turns into a tasteless occupation. Although Teresa had not gone so far as to "think that meditation on the most sacred Humanity can actually harm you," she confesses to her own lack of taste for the Humanity:

> It was only that I would take less pleasure than previously in thinking of Our Lord Jesus Christ and would go about in that state of absorption, expecting to receive spiritual consolation.[54]

Letting herself be led by the champions of *no pensar nada,* Teresa comes to see real, "perfect" contemplation as only taking place in a most enjoyable and almost ecstatic state of consciousness. Thus she faces a dilemma: either one reaches the summit of prayer life

---

[52] CW (*Interior Castle*) 305, 308, 309; CW (*Life*), 145.

[53] For a description of meditation, see CW (*Interior Castle*), 307.

[54] CW (*Interior Castle*), 308, 309.

and finds no contemplative reason to return to the Humanity, or one keeps attending to Jesus and gets stuck in an inferior form of prayer. In general terms, all images and intermediaries, the Humanity included, appear to Teresa, looking down on them from the blissful height of "perfect contemplation," as a kind of necessary evil.

Does the author of the *Life* and the *Interior Castle* break out of this Christological impasse in the passages she devotes in these works to reaffirming the role of the Humanity in contemplation? Not really. To put it bluntly, Teresa tries to by-pass the unacceptable view of the Humanity as a necessary evil by emphasizing that it is a necessary condition. However, as she argues for the permanence of Jesus in contemplation, all the reasons mentioned refer to the conditions for the Prayer of Quiet or to the inevitable moments of its absence. Not a single one has reference to "perfect contemplation" as such. To start with, Teresa asserts that Jesus is the "door that we must enter if we wish his Sovereign Majesty to show us great secrets," and "even if you reach the summit of contemplation (you) must seek no other way: that way alone is safe."[55] Obviously the Humanity is, according to the Christian faith, the "objective cause" of the salvation and union with God of every human being. Consequently, just like all ordinary persons, contemplatives are bound to base their whole lives on this Man. But this is to say that Teresa is not giving here a *contemplative* argument in favour of the role of Jesus through all the stages of prayer life.

Next, there is Teresa's diagnosis of the motives for wanting to leave the Humanity behind. In chapter 22 of the *Life*, she points to "a certain lack of humility" and the desire to "become angels

---

[55] CW (*Life*), 139. The "door" and the "way" refer to John 10,9 and 14,6. See also, for the same argument based on John, CW (*Interior Castle*), 305.

while still on earth."[56] These are solid points indeed, and they carry weight as far as the general attitude of the person at prayer is concerned, but they do not show the *contemplative* need for those who enjoy "perfect contemplation" to "meditate on something so precious" as the Humanity.

And why should one not leave the Humanity behind? The answer is because, in actual practice, it is not possible for humans to remain permanently in the state of quiet.[57] Even those who have attained the height of prayer and its consolation need Jesus, but this is, apparently, in order to live through the periods of desolation. This is when they will engage in what, for perfect contemplatives, can only be a contemplative imperfection, that is, the activity of looking at him and thinking of him:

> When we are busy, or suffering persecutions or trials, when we cannot get as much quiet as we should like, and at seasons of aridity, we have a very good Friend in Christ. We look at him as a Man; we think of his moments of weakness and times of trial; and He becomes our Companion. Once we have made a habit of thinking of Him in this way, it becomes very easy to find Him at our side, though there will come times when it is impossible to do either the one thing or the other.[58]

[56] CW (*Life*), 140. We already came across the temptation of the contemplative soul to "rise before the Lord raises it," as Teresa specifies this lack of humility in CW (*Life*), 72. As for the angelic tendency, see CW (*Interior Castle*), 304, where she admits (ironically) that "angelic spirits ... may remain permanently enkindled in love."

[57] Teresa describes her own experience on this point as follows: "All the joys it (her soul) had experienced had come in little sips, and, once these were over, it never experienced any companionship, as it did later, at times of trial and temptation." See CW (*Life*), 138.

[58] CW (*Life*), p. 140-141. In the same chapter 22 of the *Life*, Teresa had also indicated that "our temperament, or some indisposition, will not always allow us to think of the Passion because of its painfulness." There too she refers to the possiblity of considering Jesus glorified as "our Companion," "so good a Friend, so good a Captain at our side." See CW (*Life*), 138-139.

The final phrase of this passage shows in its very poignancy how difficult it is for the perfect contemplative to contemplate the Humanity. There are times when neither the one thing, the prayer of quiet, nor the other, the prayer of meditation, is possible. These are the moments, or indeed periods, when even the lowly substitute for lofty contemplation is unavailable, when one finds it impossible to "look at" Jesus or to "think of" him. These are the seasons of utter aridity that bring the experience of no experience. And it is then that the pressing questions arise. Is the person whose life's fulfilment lies in the consolation of God's felt presence in a position to make sense (as a contemplative) of this desolation? Has the contemplative who feels at home in recollection the capacity to integrate in the experience of union with the divine this inevitable distraction that so evidently belongs to the human condition? Is it possible to have one's perception fixed upon the Humanity while all meditation upon Jesus has become blocked?

When reading Teresa's apology for the Humanity, as playing a permanent role throughout prayer life, even in "perfect contemplation," one is left with the impression that it falls short on two crucial points. First, the author does not really explain how contemplation as such is able to interconnect with meditation and desolation, that is, with the Humanity and the sheer human condition. She only shows that the Humanity is necessarv before and after the peak experience of perfect contemplation. Next, Teresa does not offer any description of the transition from actively meditating upon the Humanity to passively experiencing the Divinity, from approaching God through the intermediary of the Image to enjoying him in immediate mystic union. Briefly, in Teresa's writing no genuine to-and-fro appears between perfect contemplation and the rest of prayer life, no intimate interaction between consolation and desolation.

However, there is more to Teresa's treatment of the contemplative's difficulty with the Humanity. What she fails to do in the direct defence presented in chapter 22 of the *Life* and chapter 7 of the sixth of the *Mansions* — to advance strictly contemplative arguments — she makes up for to a large extent through the description of her own further mystical experience. For, after the critical period she first related in chapter 22 of the *Life,* her prayer life developed beyond the prayer of quiet and of union. And it is only then, "in the last two Mansions," that she felt how the contemplative issue of the Humanity was being clarified.

In fact, Teresa repeatedly emphasizes that the insight into the Humanity's abiding, even in the most advanced contemplation, is essentially connected with the gift of going beyond the prayer of quiet and entering the last two *Mansions:*

> I can well believe that anyone who attains to union and goes no far-
> ther — I mean, to raptures and visions and other favours granted by
> God — will think that view (of the Humanity being a hindrance) to
> be the best, as I did myself.[59]

And, putting it the other way round, Teresa assures those people who "on set purpose withdraw from" the Humanity that "they will not enter these last two Mansions; for if they lose their Guide, the good Jesus, they will be unable to find their way".[60] Thus we reach the decisive moment in Teresa's answer to the riddle of the Humanity. What happens to her in the last two *Mansions* that allows for the Man to be permanently present in her mystical experience of God? When specifying the contemplative progress that brought her beyond the prayer of quiet, Teresa mentions again and again "appearances and visions":

> In order, sisters, that you may ... see that the farther a soul pro-
> gresses the closer becomes the companionship with this good Jesus,
> it will be well for us to consider how, when His Majesty so wills, we

---

[59] CW (*Life*), p. 137
[60] CW (*Interior Castle*), 305.

cannot do otherwise than walk with Him all the time, as is clear from the ways and methods whereby His Majesty communicates Himself to us, and reveals His love for us by means of such wonderful appearances and visions.[61]

Obviously, visions are integral to the most advanced stages of Teresa's prayer life, and by the same token we are faced with an intriguing paradox. It is by way of visions that the Image is shown to be part and parcel of the experience of the Unimaginable. How can it be possible that in the seventh *Mansion* the "soul never ceases to walk with Christ Our Lord but is ever in the company of both His Divine and His Human nature"?[62]

---

[61] CW (*Interior Castle*), 309. Looking back on her own abandoning of the Humanity in contemplation, she says: "All my life I had been greatly devoted to Christ (for this happened recently: by 'recently' I mean before the Lord granted me these favours — these raptures and visions)." See CW (*Life*), 137.

[62] CW (*Interior Castle*), 306. As for the meditation upon the Humanity, Teresa distinguishes two manners of "meditating". One can, for instance, "reason about the Passion" *(discurrir en la Pasión)* or "think about the Passion" *(pensar en la Pasión)*. The first, discursive way of meditating implies quite some mental activity, which easily results in the soul's "labouring hard at meditation" *(si mucho trabajase en el discurrir)*. So much so that meditation in this active sense may turn into a hindrance to God's own acting on the soul. And this intense inner "working" is also the reason why those who are granted the passive experience of God in "perfect contemplation" feel impotent to practice this kind of meditation. The second way of meditating consists in a different form of attention. The mind is not on the move now. It is still active but in a much quieter, simplified way. Instead of making the understanding "run through" *(dis-currir)* a number of ideas or images that represent facts so as to make sense of them by connecting them, the soul lets the understanding be impressed by "truths" *(verdades)* or "mysteries" *(misterios)* that appear in the object of meditation. These truths and mysteries are "signs of His love" which are "understood in a more perfect way": "First, the understanding will picture them to itself and then they will be impressed upon the memory, so that the mere sight of the Lord on his knees, in the Garden, covered with that terrible sweat, will suffice us, not merely for an hour, but for many days. We consider, with a simple regard, Who He is and how ungrateful we have been ..." See CW (*Interior Castle*), 304-303; *Mansions* VI, ch. 7, §6-12.

Teresa's finding the Humanity anew

It is then beyond the prayer of quiet — in the "last two Mansions" — that the Humanity appears as being central to Teresa's contemplative experience. And this resurgence of the Man in the "recollected" consciousness of this "perfect contemplative" occurs mainly by way of visions. The first question to be raised now is, what does Teresa mean, in this context, by "vision"? In chapter 27 of the *Life* she describes how she was introduced to an original way of perceiving Christ. She is granted an invisible vision: "I had not seen Him at all." There is nothing "imaginary" here, no "form," and no hampering of her soul's recollection:

> I was at prayer on a festival of the glorious Saint Peter when I saw Christ at my side — or, to put it better, I was conscious of him, for neither with the eyes of the body nor with those of the soul did I see anything. I thought He was quite close to me and I saw that it was He Who, as I thought, was speaking to me. Being completely ignorant that visions of this kind could occur ... All the time Jesus Christ seemed to be beside me, but, as this was not an imaginary vision, I could not discern in what form: what I felt very clearly was that all the time he was at my right hand, and a witness of everything I was doing, and that, whenever I became slightly recollected or was not greatly distracted, I could not but be aware of His nearness to me ... my confessor asked me in what form I had seen Him. I told him that I had not seen Him at all ... that when in the Prayer of Quiet my soul was now much more deeply and continuously recollected.[63]

[63] CW (*Life*), 107. See, for the other version of the same experience, CW (*Interior Castle*), 310-311. Before this crucial contemplative event, Teresa had already been favoured, although fleetingly, with mystical experience. From chapter 4 of the *Life* it appears that she had been elevated several times to the "Prayer of Quiet, and occasionally even to Union, though I did not understand what either of these was" (CW (*Life*), 23). And, resuming this matter in chapter 10, Teresa points out that these instantaneous perceptions of God's presence were "in no sense a vision," and that there was, so to say, some vagueness about the God she

Is there any plausible reason for Teresa to describe as a "vision" that which she sees "neither with the eyes of the body nor with those of the soul"? This question can be answered satisfactorily by remembering a linguistic feature that all mystical authors have in common. The distinctive characteristic of the mystic as such is that he or she knows by perception what otherwise is an object of faith. Teresa puts it this way:

> So that what we hold by faith the soul may be said here to grasp by sight *(lo entiende por vista),* although nothing is seen by the eyes, either of the body or the soul, for it is no imaginary vision.[64]

The mystical writer, then, wants her text in the very first place to convey the perceptual nature of her subject matter. She is intent on making her readers sense that she is describing an experience, and not at all treating of conceptual or imaginative things. She puts into words a personal event, that is, the phenomenon of something making itself present to her: *presencia,* as Teresa pointedly says.[65] But the problem with this "something" is that, while being strikingly perceptible, it does not make itself felt by sense perception.

came to know then (p.58). However, she considers these moments to be forebodings of the visionary event that is about to leave an indelible stamp on her further contemplative life with the figure of the Godman.

[64] CW *(Interior Castle),* 332; *Mansions* VII, ch. 1, §7.

[65] Or *estar allí.* See how aptly Virginia Woolf expresses the same point: "That is one of the experiences I have had here in some Augusts; and got then to a consciousness of what I call 'reality': a thing I see before me: something abstract; but residing in the downs or sky" (thus connecting "a thing I see" with "abstract" and "in the downs"): See *A Writer's Diary* (London: Triad Grafton Books, 1978)163-169. And another extremely lucid woman, Simone Weil, has this to say about her experience of "a real contact, person to person, here below, between a human being and God": "Moreover, in this sudden possession of me by Christ, neither my senses nor my imagination had any part; I only felt in the midst of my suffering the presence of a love, like that which one can read on a beloved face." See *Waiting for God* (New York: Harper and Row, 1973) 68-69.

So much so that mystics often feel that they are equipped with senses of another kind, "interior" or "spiritual" senses. Thus, Teresa says that the first degree of "supernatural" prayer is "an interior recollection felt in the soul, which seems to have acquired new senses, corresponding to its exterior senses."[66] What can the mystic do when wanting to evoke in common language — the only one that makes sense — this uncommon perception by the "interior" senses, especially when, at the same time, she needs to prevent her readers from interpreting her "spiritual" vision as somehow abstract? There is nothing left but to resort to the idiom of sense perception;[67] one is bound to make use of such ordinary words as "fragrance," smoke," "heat": "I only put it in that way so that you may understand it":

> The fragrance (the soul) experiences, we might say, is as if in those interior depths there were a brazier on which were cast sweet perfumes; the light cannot be seen, nor the place where it dwells, but the fragrant smoke and the heat penetrate the entire soul, and very often ... the effects extend even to the body. Observe ... that no heat is felt, nor is any fragrance perceived: it is a more delicate thing than that; I only put it in that way so that you may understand it. People who have not experienced it must realize that it does in very truth happen; its occurrence is capable of being perceived, and the soul becomes aware of it more clearly than these words of mine can express it.[68]

Far from being just an interior spectacle yielding some divine information, the vision Teresa has in mind here is *presencia*. This leads us to pay attention to its most striking feature: this invisible

---

[66] CW (*Spiritual Relations*), 327; *Cuenta de conciencia*, 54a, §3.

[67] As appears from the passage that will be quoted next, a positive reason for the mystical writer to use the language of the senses is that "the effects (of the 'spiritual' perception) often extend to the body."

[68] CW (*Interior Castle*), 238.

vision, or rather the Something that is being perceived, "impresses itself" on the soul. So much so that it is precisely through this "impression" that the visionary's awareness is brought about: "Though He remains unseen, so clear a knowledge is impressed upon the soul".[69] Thus the object of the vision proves to be an acting subject. It represents itself to the visionary's soul by impressing itself upon it, and "to impress" is to be taken here strictly, i.e. in the sense of an impressed stamp rather than of an impressive performance. After reporting, in chapter 27 of the *Life*, her first imageless vision of the Humanity,[70] Teresa goes on to comment on it. She quotes her inquisitive confessor asking who told her it was Jesus Christ, and gives her answer: " 'He often tells me so Himself', I replied; but before ever He told me so, the fact was impressed upon my understanding."[71] It is by being "impressed" or "engraven" that the soul can understand what, or rather Who, is present to her, prior to any image or word:

> The Lord is pleased that this knowledge should be so deeply engraven upon the understanding that one can no more doubt it than one can doubt the evidence of one's eyes.[72]

To be granted a vision means, then, to undergo an "in-formation". The visionary suffers a change within: far from being the awareness of shown images or spoken words, the seeing and hearing are the consciousness of an effect produced from within. But even more is involved in the causing of this impression. It dawns on Teresa that the change produced in the understanding is the

---

[69] See the significant passage in CW (*Life*), 171-173; OC (*Vida*), ch. 27, §5-7: "*sin verse se imprime*". Apart from *imprimir* Teresa likes to use in this context *esculpir*, "engrave".

[70] See above, the quotation that corresponds to note 63.

[71] CW (*Life*), 171-172; OC (*Vida*), ch. 27, §5: "se emprimió en mi entendimiento que era El".

[72] CW (*Life*), 172.

repercussion of something that is happening in the soul beyond the realm of the spiritual faculties, at a deeper level. It is the "inmost part of the soul," which later she will call the "centre," that undergoes the divine influence in the first place:

> The Lord introduces into the inmost part of the soul what he wishes that soul to understand, and presents it not by means of images or forms of words, but after the manner of this vision aforementioned.[73]

Rather surprisingly, Teresa's explanations of the way in which the Image appears to her do lead the reader to grasp that something invisible is being done to her in the centre of the soul. In order to express this divine action upon the core of the human being, she shows a preference for two literary devices. On the one hand, she evokes the image of the "little butterfly" and, on the other hand, she takes over two corresponding phrases from Saint Paul: "It is no longer I who live, but it is Christ who lives in me," and "For to me, living is Christ and dying is gain."[74] The escape of the "little butterfly"[75] represents the thorough change of the deeper ego, of which the mystic becomes conscious on attaining

---

[73] CW (*Life*), 172; OC (*Vida*), ch. 27, §6: "en lo muy interior del alma, y *allí* lo representa sin imagen ni forma de palabras." And Teresa goes on to make the following comparison: "It is as if food has been introduced into the stomach without our having eaten it or knowing how it got there ... In this experience, I do know Who put it there, but not how He did so, for my soul saw nothing and cannot understand how the operation took place."

[74] Galatians 2, 20 and Philippians 1, 21.

[75] This key image used by Teresa refers to the metamorphosis of the silkworm. The "little butterfly" (*mariposilla, mariposica*) is the silkworm moth at the exact moment of its coming into being — into a new, free existence — through the transformation of its caterpillar form. Teresa makes this delicate comparison in chapter 2 of the fifth of the *Mansions*: "Then, finally, the worm, which was large and ugly, comes right out of the cocoon a beautiful white butterfly." See CW (*Interior Castle*), 253.

full contemplative development, on reaching the seventh *Mansion.* That is when the process of "undoing" the self reaches completion and new life emerges.[76]

In the context of clarifying the riddle of the Humanity a significant element appears here. At the high point of Teresa's mystical writing the image of the butterfly is closely linked to the words of Saint Paul. This means that the Carmelite mystic's experience of union with God in the imageless depth of the soul coincides with being identified with the Image at that same depth. Thus, the butterfly-like experience, which can be understood in a general way — "this is what all mystics however different go through" — has as its core the particular Pauline experience of Christ. Or, conversely, Teresa's 'sight' of the invisible Image is tantamount to her perceiving that she is one with the Unimagined. In chapter 2 of the seventh *Mansion,* she describes the difference between "spiritual betrothal" and "spiritual marriage". This is how she finally characterizes the latter:[77]

> And (Saint Paul) also says: *Mihi vivere Christus est, mori lucrum.* This, I think, the soul may say here, for it is here that the little butterfly… dies, and with the greatest joy, because Christ is now its life.[78]

[76] Describing a previous stage in her contemplative career — the prayer of union — Teresa reports how she wondered "what the soul is doing then?" She was told: "It dies to itself wholly *(deshácese toda),* daughter, in order to fix itself more and more upon Me; it is no longer itself that lives, but I". See CW (*Life*), 110; OC (*Vida*), ch. 18, §14.

[77] It is interesting to notice how Teresa, just before the key passage about to be quoted, tries out a few general comparisons in order to evoke the definite union of "spiritual marriage": "But here it is like rain falling from the heavens into a river or a spring; there is nothing but water there ... Or it is as if a tiny streamlet enters the sea ... or as if in a room there were two large windows through which the light streamed in: it enters in different places but all becomes one." See CW (*Interior Castle*), 335.

[78] CW (*Interior Castle*), 335-336. For Paul's text, from Philippians 1,21, see above, note 74.

Teresa then goes on to describe the effects of this being "endowed with life by God"; at times, this in-depth transformation drives her to say: "*Oh, vida de mi vida*", "0 life of my life", and at the beginning of chapter 3, she returns to the same Christocentric theme:

> As we were saying, then, this little butterfly has now died, full of joy at having found rest, and within her lives Christ. Let us see what her new life is like ...[79]

This is where the decisive question concerning the role of the Humanity in Teresa's fully developed mystical experience arises. One wonders how, at this stage, the perception of Christ *living* in her includes an awareness of Jesus, of that particular Man who lived and died in a particular way. For in the seventh *Mansion* the soul is "called to enter into its own centre," and the "secret union" of spiritual marriage "takes place in the deepest centre of the soul".[80] Consequently, this experience occurs beyond the grasp of the soul's faculties: here all imagining and understanding fails. How, then, can the person who, in this inconceivable depth,[81] feels "endowed with life by God," be conscious not just of the divine Christ, but of the very human Jesus being alive in her?

Teresa gives a preliminary answer in the form of a vision she describes at the beginning of chapter 2 of the seventh *Mansion*. Strikingly enough, it is an imaginative vision, and it is meant to assure the passage from spiritual betrothal to spiritual marriage:

> When granting this favour (of spiritual marriage) for the first time, His Majesty is pleased to reveal Himself to the soul through an

---

[79] CW (*Interior Castle*), 338-339. Obviously, the combination of finding "rest" and discovering "life" is all the more significant as one remembers Teresa's earlier quietist temptations due to her following the method of *no pensar nada*.

[80] CW (*Interior Castle*), 331 and 334.

[81] "This 'centre' of our soul ... is something so difficult to describe, and indeed to believe." See CW (*Interior Castle*), 338.

imaginary vision of His most sacred Humanity, so that it may clearly understand what is taking place and not be ignorant of the fact that it is receiving so sovereign a gift ... To the person of whom we have been speaking (=Teresa) the Lord revealed Himself one day, when she had just received Communion, in great splendour and beauty and majesty, as He did after His resurrection, and He told her it was time she took upon herself His affairs as if they were her own and that He would take her affairs upon Himself ... This ... left her quite confused ... also because, in the interior of her soul, where He revealed himself to her, she had never seen any visions but this. For you must understand that there is the greatest difference between all the other visions we have mentioned and those belonging to this Mansion ... All that has so far been described seems to have come through the medium of the senses and faculties and this appearance of the Humanity of the Lord must do so too. But what passes in the union of the Spiritual Marriage is very different. The Lord appears in the centre of the soul, not through an imaginary, but through an intellectual vision.[82]

This imaginative vision of exceptional "force" and depth — it is seen in the "interior of her soul" — has a pedagogical ring. Its purpose is to enable Teresa, who has now been admitted to the most profound mystical union, to "clearly understand what is taking place and not be ignorant." Apparently, this impressive appearance comes to prevent her from ever forgetting that it is through the Humanity that "so sovereign a gift" as this divine marriage has been granted. However, the figure that appears here

[82] CW (*Interior Castle*), 334. See also the description of the same visionary experience in *Spiritual Relations* XXXV (=*Cuenta* 25a), where Teresa mentions John of the Cross wanting to "mortify" her by giving her only half a host at communion. There is a representation here of the wedding: "He gave me His right hand, saying to me 'Behold this nail. It is a sign that from to-day onward thou shalt be My bride'." See CW, 351-352. For an example of the imaginative visions of the Humanity, which had been granted Teresa earlier on, see CW (*Life*), 179.

is the glorified Humanity: "in great splendour and beauty and majesty," and there is no visionary impression of the downtrodden Man. Far from looking like the cruel instrument used on Calvary, the "nail" Teresa receives is a blissful "sign".[83] In any case, this vision is only a preparatory experience, as the last lines of the passage quoted make quite clear. The definite answer to the question of the Humanity is not to be found in any imaginative vision perceived through the "medium of the faculties," but in intellectual visions that directly act upon the "deepest centre of the soul, which must be where God Himself dwells".[84]

It is time now to have a look at this last kind of visions in order to see whether and in what way they represent the Humanity by impressing it upon the soul's core. Here is the account of the key vision that made Teresa experience the height of mystical union. As a matter of fact it is a Trinitarian one:

> (The soul) is brought into this Mansion by means of an intellectual vision, in which, by a representation of the truth in a particular way, the Most Holy Trinity reveals Itself in all Three Persons. First of all the spirit becomes enkindled and is illumined, as it were, by a cloud of the greatest brightness. It sees the three Persons, individually, and yet, by a wonderful kind of knowledge which is given to it, the soul realizes that most certainly and truly all these three Persons are one Substance and one Power and one Knowledge and one God alone; so that what we hold by faith the soul may be said here to grasp by sight, although nothing is seen by the eyes, either of the body or of the soul, for it is no imaginary vision. Here all Three Persons communicate Themselves to the soul and speak to the soul and explain to it those words which the Gospel attributes to the Lord — namely, that He and the Father and the Holy Spirit will come to dwell with the soul which loves Him and keeps His commandments.[85]

---

[83] See the version from the *Spiritual Relations* quoted in note 82.
[84] CW (*Interior Castle*), 334.
[85] CW (*Interior Castle*), 331-332.

So far Teresa's account of the seventh Mansion has yielded two significant passages concerning the role of the Humanity in her most advanced mystical experience. The first describes the imaginative vision of Christ that led Teresa from spiritual betrothal to spiritual marriage; the second evokes the intellectual vision of the Trinity that brought her into the seventh Mansion.[86] These texts establish two points: as the glorified Humanity — "in great splendour and beauty and majesty" — Christ is the key figure in Teresa's final contemplative progress, and as the divine Person, he is central to her ultimate experience of the "one Substance ... one God alone."

However, the reader who expected to discover at last whether and how the concrete humanity of Jesus is integral to Teresa's highest mystical awareness may not feel satisfied. These Christ-centred visions fail to answer the precise question that Teresa herself raised after having been taken in tow by the spiritualizing masters of *recogimiento* and *no pensar nada*. The "recollected" Carmelite nun, favoured with "perfect contemplation," had "put everything corporeal aside" so well, and enjoyed such "delight," that "no one could have made me return to meditation on the Humanity".[87] Teresa passed this critical stage. Through visions and reflection she came to focus her contemplative attention once again upon the Humanity. So much so that her experience of the presence of the Godman has developed into the central theme of her mystical writing. Moreover, the issue of the Humanity has become of such crucial importance for Teresa that she tells her reader it can only be clarified definitively in the "last two Mansions". And yet all this does not alter the fact that the reader, even

---

[86] CW (*Interior Castle*), 334 and 331-332.

[87] CW (*Life*), 137. See above, the subdivision: *Teresa's own abandoning of the Humanity*.

after being introduced to the two great visions of the seventh Mansion, cannot see how Jesus is part and parcel of the bride's "secret union" with Christ and the Trinity. By now one is so accustomed to the abundance and significance of Teresa's visions, that one tends to look for yet another vision to provide an answer. But no more visions appear in the seventh *Mansion*.[88] Teresa wrote this final part of the *Interior Castle* in 1577. In 1581 she sent her confessor *Relation* VI which confirms what can be seen in the seventh *Mansion:* "The imaginary visions have ceased, but I always seem to be having this intellectual vision of the three Persons and of Christ's Humanity."[89]

Is this, then, Teresa's final, and rather frustrating, clarification of the riddle of the Humanity in contemplation? When all is said and done, does Christ in his majesty outshine Jesus in his very human form?

---

[88] Here it is worth having a look at chapter 38 of the *Life,* where Teresa describes the "sublimest vision the Lord had granted me grace to see". She had been favoured with this same vision "on three other occasions": "I saw the most sacred Humanity in far greater glory than I had ever seen before. I saw a most clear and wonderful representation of it in the bosom of the Father *(representóseme por una noticia admirable y clara estar metido en los pechos de el Padre)* ... without seeing anything, I seemed to see myself in the presence of the Godhead. I was amazed, so much so that I believe several days must have gone by before I was completely myself again. I seemed all the time to have present with me that Majesty of the Son of God ..." See CW *(Life),* 273-274; OC *(Vida),* ch. 38, §17. See also above, note 34, for the description of another important vision of Christ in CW *(Life),* chapter 40.

[89] CW *(Spiritual Relations),* 335. OC *(Cuentas de conciencia),* 66a, §3. *"Lo de las visiones imaginarias ha cesado."* For Teresa it is now "so impossible to doubt the presence of the three Persons that I seem clearly to be experiencing the truth of those words of Saint John, that He will make His abode with the soul (John 14,23). And this not only through grace, but because He is pleased to make the soul conscious of that presence" *(quiere dar a sentir esta presencia).* See CW *(Spiritual Relations),* 336-337; OC *(Cuentas),* 66a, § 10).

"The Spiritual Marriage, of which are always born works, works" [90]

Before going on to examine the seventh *Mansion* for some more samples of 'embodied' Teresian experiences of the Humanity, one should be reminded that the main factor in this mystic's experience is her being affected by the Presence so as to feel transformed. So much so is this the case that Teresa's visions are not, in the first instance, a matter of seeing an image or understanding a truth, but of undergoing the "impress" of Reality. This truth will be a great help as no visionary illustrations are available to those trying to find in the seventh *Mansion* the height of Teresa's mystical life along with her solution to the riddle of the Humanity.

In Teresa's description of the seventh Mansion, attention has already been drawn to the "centre" of the soul. As has been seen, the secret union of spiritual marriage "takes place in the deepest centre of the soul," and the three Persons, who "communicate themselves" to Teresa, do so "in the interior of her heart — in the most interior place of all and in its greatest depths."[91] The distinguishing mark of this core of the human being is its hiddenness, for such is its profundity that even the soul's own spiritual powers are unable to grasp it. The centre lies somewhere beyond the reach of the peripheral faculties, so much so that

> when Our Lord brings the soul into this Mansion of His, which is
> the centre of the soul itself (for they say that the empyrean heaven,

---

[90] "Oh, my sisters, how little one should think about resting ... For if the soul is much with Him ... its whole thought will be concentrated upon finding ways to please Him and upon showing Him how it loves Him. This, my daughters, is the aim of prayer: this is the purpose of the Spiritual Marriage, of which are always born works, works" *(de que nazcan siempre obras, obras)*. See CW *(Interior Castle)*, 346; *Mansions* VII, ch. 4, §6.

[91] CW *(Interior Castle)*, 334, and *332: "en lo muy muy interior, en una cosa muy honda"* *(Mansions* VII, ch. 1, §8).

> where Our Lord is, does not move like the other heavens), it seems,
> on entering, to be subject to none of the usual movements of the fac-
> ulties and the imagination, which injure it and take away its peace.[92]

Peacefulness and steadiness are the characteristics of the unitive experience that takes place there, in the person's depth: now the soul "remains all the time in that centre with its God"; it "neither moves from that centre nor loses its peace"; it is "almost always in tranquillity".[93] In order for her sisters to form some idea of this unimaginable centre of the soul and of the undisturbed peace she keeps experiencing there, Teresa offers them a comparison that "makes me smile":

> A king is living in his palace: many wars are waged in his kingdom
> and many other distressing things happen there, but he remains
> where he is despite them all. So it is here: although in the other
> Mansions there are many disturbances and poisonous creatures, and
> the noise of all this can be heard, nobody enters this Mansion and
> forces the soul to leave it.[94]

It is time now to have a closer look at the nature of the peace Teresa enjoys in her soul's centre. What strikes one immediately

---

[92] CW (*Interior Castle*), 337.

[93] CW (*Interior Castle*), 335, 336 and 341.

[94] CW (*Interior Castle*), 338. This representation of the soul at the height of mystical union as a sovereign is obviously not exclusively Teresian. A passage from Hadewijch, who will be studied in detail in chapter 4, is in place here: "(God's) perfection gives the peers of the kingdom the lordship over their land, like the sovereign dominion of the sovereign soul I am speaking of who, with a sovereign and perfect will and perfect works, has obtained her noble mode of liv-ing by all the will of Love ... In this way the emperor himself remains free and in peace, because he commands the officials to administer the law and invests the kings, dukes, counts, and chief peers with the high feudal tenure of his domain and the true legal rights of Love. This same Love is the crown of the blessed soul, who can help all according to their needs while, at the same time, seeking after nothing of its own except in the love of its Beloved." See Hadewijch, *The Complete Works*, 85.

is that there is no possibility here of "peace" as a kind of terminal rest. On the contrary, however steady and tranquil it is, this repose manifests itself at once as dynamic: motionless it sets in motion; inactive it activates; having a centre it radiates. While experiencing the quietness of this peace, the mystic is also aware of its centrifugal force. There appears in the soul an "impulse" which is

> now felt very gently, but it proceeds neither from the thought nor from the memory, nor can it be supposed that the soul has had any part in it. This is so usual and occurs so frequently that it has been observed with special care: just as the flames of a fire, however great, never travel downwards, but always upwards, so here it is evident that this interior movement proceeds from the center of the soul and awakens the faculties.[95]

Again and again, Teresa points to the vivifying capacity of the peace bestowed on her in the seventh Mansion. Now the time of those extraordinary inner states — ecstatic raptures,[96] self-involved recollection, mesmerizing absorption in God — that previously happened to make her unfit for ordinary human activities, has passed. Do not think, she tells the reader, who tends perhaps to conceive of this in-depth quietude as some sort of abstracted inwardness,

> that such a person will not remain in possession of her senses but will be so completely absorbed that she will be able to fix her mind upon nothing. But no: in all that belongs to the service of God she is more alert than before; and, when not otherwise occupied, she rests in that happy companionship.[97]

The foundress gives her sisters fair warning against misrepresenting the inner peace she refers to as resulting in idleness:

---

[95] CW (*Interior Castle*), 340-341.

[96] CW (*Interior Castle*), 342: "On reaching this state, the soul has no more raptures."

[97] CW (*Interior Castle*), 332.

> You may think that I am speaking about beginners, and that later on one may rest: but ... the only repose that these souls enjoy is of an interior kind; of outward repose they get less and less, and they have no wish to get more. What is the purpose ... of these messages which are sent by the soul from its innermost centre to the folk outside the Castle and to the Mansions which are outside that in which it is itself dwelling? Is it to send them to sleep? No, no, no.[98]

Instead of turning the accomplished mystic into a disembodied weakling, this God-given peace has humanizing effects. It strengthens the body, while inwardly urging the soul to "attempt much more":

> It is quite certain that, with the strength it has gained, the soul comes to the help of all who are in the Castle, and, indeed, succors the body itself. Often the body appears to feel nothing, but the strength ... overflows into the weak body ... In this life, then, the soul has a very bad time, for, however much it accomplishes, it is strong enough inwardly to attempt much more.[99]

Only now has Teresa reached the summit of her contemplative career. In the seventh Mansion the bride finally discovers mystical union in its fullness, that is, as an essentially compound experience. "Peace" goes together with "works, works," and being "deeply recollected" goes with being "more alert than before". "Martha and Maria walk together in each other's company."[100] Now the "service of the Lord" ceaselessly draws the contemplative's

---

[98] CW (*Interior Castle*), 347.

[99] CW (*Interior Castle*), 347. In order to clarify somehow the paradox of this deep-seated peace being combined with the soul's inner and outer motion, Teresa makes use of the theory of a "division of the soul": "The essential part of her soul seemed never to move from that dwelling-place. So in a sense she felt that her soul was divided ... we know that there is some kind of difference, and a very definite one, between the soul and the spirit, although they are both one." See CW (*Interior Castle*), 333.

[100] CW (*Interior Castle*), 344 and 348.

attention, so much so that the desire to "die and thus enjoy Our Lord" is matched by "an equally strong desire to serve Him."[101] In chapter 7 of the sixth Mansion, Teresa describes in advance what awaits the contemplative in the seventh Mansion:

> In a wonderful way the soul never ceases to walk with Christ Our Lord but is ever in the company of both His Divine and His Human nature.[102]

In the original text this passage ends in a simpler way, omitting the speculative term "nature": *"divino y humano junto es siempre su compañía,"* "the divine and the human joined together is always accompanying her". And here again, the exact point at issue remains unanswered: where is this *humano* — the sheer human of the Humanity — to be found in Teresa's culminating experience? Is the mystic, even at this stage, (still) aware of the Man? And if such is the case, what kind of perception is this supposed to be? Here it is essential to remember that mystical consciousness is in the first instance one of being "impressed," of undergoing the influence of a Presence. Thus one can understand that Teresa's "walking with" and "being in the company of" are not to be interpreted as if she were somehow looking at Christ and seeing his twofold "nature". Similarly it would appear that if the bride of the seventh Mansion contemplates the Godman, she does so by suffering his "impression," a twofold impression that involves both the divine and the human.

Thus we come to what may perhaps be labelled Teresa's 'inexplicit' contemplative Christocentrism: almost without mentioning

---

[101] CW (*Interior Castle*), 339-340. See also *Relation* VI, p. 334: "All I want is to serve."

[102] CW (*Interior Castle*), 306; *Mansions* VI, ch. 7, §9: *"es muy contino no se apartar de andar con Cristo nuestro Señor por una manera admirable adonde divino y humano junto es siempre su compañía."*

Jesus, she has shown how his Humanity is perceptibly present at the height of her prayer life. It is precisely through discovering that mystical union is a compound experience that she clarifies the issue of the Humanity of Jesus. To reformulate what has been seen extensively above: Teresa comes to realize that the *divine* impression is such that it causes its *human* expression. There is for her no inmost, peaceful enjoying of *Christ,* the Lord, without also feeling his "impulse," an "interior movement that proceeds from the centre of the soul and awakens the faculties". And what are the human powers so strongly urged on to do? To serve and to suffer in the way that *Jesus* did.

This is where the reader would like Teresa to have expressed more clearly this imageless experience of the Humanity in "perfect contemplation". However, at least a few passages from the seventh Mansion make the inexplicit a little more explicit: she explains there that those who have attained to the last Mansion

> have with them the Lord Himself and it is His Majesty who now lives in them. His life, of course, was nothing but a continual torment and so He is making our life the same, at least as far as our desires go.[103]

> For His Majesty can do nothing greater for us than grant us a life which is an imitation of that lived by his Beloved Son. I feel certain, therefore, that these favors are given us to strengthen our weakness ... so that we may be able to imitate Him in his great sufferings.[104]

> Do you know when people really become spiritual? It is when they become the slaves of God and are branded with his sign, which is the sign of the Cross, in token that they have given Him their freedom. Then He can sell them as slaves to the whole world, as He Himself was sold ...[105]

---

[103] CW (*Interior Castle*), 340.

[104] CW (*Interior Castle*), 345.

[105] CW (*Interior Castle*), 346.

A Reluctant Visionary: Maria Petyt

Unlike Julian of Norwich or Teresa of Avila, Maria Petyt (1623-1677) enjoys no international prestige, nor is she recognized within the Flemish mystical tradition as a leading figure. Yet, there is a fascinating freshness about the reports of her contemplative experience in which visions and the figure of the God-man hold a prominent place.

By way of introduction, one should note that the historical period to which she belongs is not an age of decline in the mysticism of the Low Countries.[106] If the medieval flowering, marked by authors of such genius as Hadewijch and Ruusbroec (13th and 14th century) has passed, the early modern period shows continued growth. Moreover, it is precisely during the 16th-17th centuries that Middle Dutch mystical literature spread throughout Europe. First translated into Latin, the works of Ruusbroec and his followers soon appeared in all the Romance languages.[107]

For the present study, one salient characteristic of contemplative life in this period is particularly interesting. The role of the

---

[106] See Paul Mommaers, "Pays-Bas, IV. Les XVIe et XVIIe siècles," *Dictionnaire de spiritualité* XII/1 (1984) c. 730-750. I shall borrow from it here without giving detailed references.

[107] In the 15th-16th centuries the Carthusians of Cologne undertook an enormous translation project — exceptional in quantity as well as in quality — rendering into Latin all the major mystical works from Brabant and the Rhineland. Thus they published the complete works of Ruusbroec and the *Mirror of Perfection* (*Spieghel der volcomenheit*) of Herp (see above, note 36), which appeared as the *Directorium aureum contemplativorum*. And a priest who collaborated with the Carthusian monks translated the anonymous *Evangelical Pearl* (*Evangelische Peerle*), henceforth widely known as *Margarita Evangelica*. As a matter of fact, these followers paved the way for Ruusbroec himself to enter the European literary scene. See Paul Mommaers, "Internationale uitstraling van de Nederlandse mystieke literatuur," *Nederlands in culturele context* (Antwerpen: IVM, 1994) 133-151.

Humanity of Christ was not only brought into prominence in some remarkable mystical works; it also became the focus of repeated, and at times ferocious, public debate. The major literary achievement was the *Evangelical Pearl* (short text, 1535; long one, 1537-38), whose leading theme is the "birth of Christ in the soul". The female author is keen to show how the contemplative becomes conscious of this birth taking place at the different levels of the personality. The Godman "is born in him, lives, walks, works, suffers, resuscitates, is joyful, and he is pleased to have found a person after his heart. Thus this person abandons all his own activity or desolation, his words and works, and he has lost certainly not the essence but the appearance, for he himself does not live anymore but Jesus Christ lives in him."

Another outstanding mystical text is the *Dialogue* (*Tsamensprekinge*) of Claesinne van Nieuwlant (1587). Here the leitmotiv is the soul's "annihilation". Therefore, the way in which this beguine from Ghent evokes her experience of the presence of Christ is all the more striking. Mystical union with the Godman appears as both ascent and descent combined in one single feeling: "The higher the spirit goes upwards into God ... the deeper also the exterior man goes downwards into the Humanity of Christ. Christ is God and Man, and the one is not separated from the other. In the same way these two movements cannot be separated."

As for the controversy caused by the issue of the Humanity, it came mainly in two waves. First, toward the end of the 16th century (roughly 1585 — 1598), there was relentless opposition among the Flemish Capuchins between those who stood for union with God in "abstract," imageless contemplation, which is reached by way of "introversion," and those who advocated union with God through meditation upon the life and passion of Christ.[108]

[108] For details, see Paul Mommaers, "Union mystique et imitation de Jésus-Christ: Une controverse cruciale chez les capucins Flamands vers la fin

Later, between 1607 and 1611, the Spanish Carmelites appear on this troubled Flemish scene. They feel it is the duty of the followers of Teresa of Avila to convert the Northern contemplatives to the Humanity. This is how Anna of Jesus, the foundress of the first reformed Carmel in the Low Countries (Brussels 1607), reacted to the kind of prayer she discovered at that moment:

> For me it is necessary that (the novices) consider and imitate Our Lord Jesus Christ, for here they do not remember him much: it all takes place in a simple view of God. I do not know how this can be. Since the days of Saint Denys, who wrote the Mystical Theology, all have continued to apply themselves to God by suspension rather than by imitation. That is a strange way of proceeding; really, I do not understand it.

Thus public debate flared up again. This time two renowned Spanish Carmelites, Jerónimo Gracián and Tomás de Jesús, attacked the Flemish Capuchins who supposedly failed to do justice to Jesus. Perhaps the best outcome of this hawkish encounter was that it brought into existence some excellent explanatory texts from the Capuchin side.

A Carmelite tertiary going in for imageless contemplation[109]

At eighteen Maria Petyt joined the reformed Carmelite nuns in Ghent but her sight proved to be so poor that she was unable to read the office. She left the convent and moved to the "Small Beguinage" of Ghent where she lived together with a few companions. Now a member of the Carmelite Third Order, she followed

---

du XVIe siècle," *I Francescani in Europa tra Riforma e Contrariforma* (Perugia: Edizioni Scientifiche Italiane, 1987) 27-49.

[109] I shall make use here of the fundamental and brilliant study by A. Deblaere, *De mystieke schrijfster Maria Petyt 1623-1677* (Ghent: Secretarie der Academie, 1962).

the rule of the Carmel. In 1657 she moved to Mechelen (Malines) following Michael of Saint Augustine, her Carmelite spiritual director.

To start with, Maria succeeded in praying in an imageless way. This meant that she succeeded in calming down and emptying all the faculties of the soul so as to reach a state of "idleness": the traditional Flemish term to indicate this psychic condition is *ledicheit,* a word which evokes at once "emptiness" and "idleness". In such a state, images and concepts are "annihilated," and thus the "ground" of the soul, where God can be reached in an imageless way, is laid bare:

> At times all I have is an interior, essential turning towards the imageless divine Object, which turning towards is being practised solely through a simple looking at this Object and by way of excluding all other activities of the faculties and the senses.[110]

So far so good: Maria is on her way to perfect contemplation. However, a problem arises. She begins to get visions, or rather visions are forced upon her, for she does not want these at all. She considers the visionary path "full of dangers," so much so that she hides these unwelcome favours from everyone, even from her spiritual director for fear he might approve of them. However, after some time she cannot but give in to the visionary influx, and the "imageless" contemplative now has to come to grips with the paradox of seeing the Unseen.

Like her predecessors, Maria proves to be quite lucid about this way of seeing. She is aware that there are no exterior objects impinging upon the senses. Her reports are full of such cautious expressions as "it seems" and "as if": "All these different manifestations occur through the inner sight of the soul, when Jesus

---

[110] Deblaere, *De mystieke schrijfster Maria Petyt,* 43: "the imageless divine Object," *"den onverbeelden goddelijcken Voorworp".*

shows himself as if from the outside, then I see him as I would see someone with my bodily eyes."[111] Maria also distinguishes visions from illusions. Thus, when the devil appears to her while she is ill, she brushes this aside as "*imaginatie*," "imagination". And she goes on to characterize as "illuminations" those insights that are impressed upon her understanding in an imaginative way. So, when she "sees" the needs of other people, she calls this beholding "*beeldelijcke indruckinghe*," "imaginative impression". Finally, the decisive criterion for her to winnow the chaff from the grain in her visions is the down-to-earth evangelical one: observe the verifiable effects.

In any case, Maria's visions of Christ are the core of her entire visionary experience, and are those she describes most accurately. For example, she reports how on one occasion her prayer passed through three different phases. First, there is her contemplative activity: she makes use of the most representative of Christian images, the crucifix, and by meditating upon it — with "reflection" and affectionate "speaking" — she tries to approach Christ:

> I went again to prayer. Taking a crucifix in my hand, I started ... to speak to him in that crucifix, my mouth against the holy wound in his side.

Then a crucial change occurs, from activity to passivity and from image to vision. Instead of tending towards Christ through the crucifix, the contemplative now perceives the presence of his Humanity "in the spirit" and feels she is being united with it:

> Next, while the reflection upon that material crucifix was disappearing, I had Jesus present in the spirit, in a very lively and explicit manner, and I joined myself quietly to his holy wound. And see,

---

[111] Ibid., 117. For the context, see below, the extended quotation that corresponds to note 113.

> suddenly I felt myself being placed therein, and at once I came nearer to his divine heart and rested therein ...

Finally, Maria reaches what for the time being she considers perfect contemplation, namely an imageless awareness of the Divinity:

> and gradually the image of his holy Humanity disappeared, more and more, and I seemed to be taken up in the spirit to contemplate the Divinity.[112]

This is not the place to dwell further on Maria's visionary experiences, but one more description deserves to be quoted here as it gives a significant account of the difference between an "exterior" and an "interior" vision of the Humanity:

> How do I see Jesus glorified in my interior? This happens in a very different way from when I see him next to me, before me, above me as somehow elevated as between heaven and earth. Although all these different manifestations occur through the inner sight of the soul, when Jesus shows himself as if from the outside, I see him as I would see somebody with my bodily eyes, while being aware of myself and the things around me ... For instance, when Jesus of late manifested himself on my right side and seemed to embrace me ... then I felt that I was different from him and not one with him, receiving that embrace as if from someone outside me, although not in as sensuous and rough a manner as it may sound ... It seems to take place on the outside, but it penetrates the interior, and thus it is spiritually sensuous and sensuously spiritual.
>
> But it is something quite different when Jesus shows himself in my interior. I do see him with the same glorified body, but in such a way that I am more united with him. My interior is then so broadened and expanded in him, and he in me, that my interior seems to be swallowed up and one with him. And yet, I do not sense myself nor my body, in such a way as to imagine that I am enclosing that huge Christ in my narrow body. But my spiritual interior appears to be so broadened and expanded that the whole world and all that is

---

[112] Ibid., 111.

contained in it, even the whole of the sky, could appear therein and be seen.[113]

It is little wonder that Maria's Carmelite director felt uneasy about her imageless contemplation. He told her to give a central place to Christ in her prayer. The "spiritual daughter" did not fail to react in writing to her master's request, presenting a clear definition of the problem of the Humanity in contemplation:

> I thought I had no other aim (in prayer) than to adhere nakedly to the unimaged Divinity, to rest therein, and to be satisfied with that only, and to forget myself therein ... This exercise, then, is wholly inward and spiritual, and it has nothing to do with any imagination, conception or other thoughts. How should I then be occupied with the unimaged Divinity, where all imagination has to be left behind, and at the same time imagine the bodily Humanity? This comes to the same thing as having to see while being blind.[114]

Torn between her inclination for dangerous "abstraction" and the director's desire for secure "meditation," Maria was at an impasse, and from the way she describes her problem it seems that, if she had remained within this perspective, there would have been no chance of it ever being resolved. Plainly, her view of contemplation was determined by a twofold assumption. On the one hand, Maria was making an absolute of the imageless perception of the Divinity: one should have "no other aim" in prayer and be "satisfied with that only." Thus, the advanced contemplative's consciousness must be empty and by all means remain so. On the other hand, Maria could not help conceiving of the "bodily Humanity" as simply an object for the contemplative to look at: Jesus is to be "seen". Evidently, this last premise entailed that the Humanity should occupy that same consciousness which otherwise was supposed to be empty. Was there a way out of this impasse?

[113] Ibid., 117-118.
[114] Ibid., 183.

Jesus as the active "subject" of Maria's contemplation

In fact, Maria succeeded in overcoming, step by step, the contemplative difficulty raised by trying to do justice to the Humanity. To start with, she had a vision of Christ as "united with his glorified Humanity," with the result that

> I do not find it difficult anymore nor do I feel a hindrance but rather a great lightness and pleasure in contemplating Jesus, the Godman. This is particularly so since, on Easter Sunday evening, Jesus manifested himself to me all glorious ... Little by little I feel this so much as a habit and lightness that it seems impossible to me to have the Beloved in mind in any other way than thus united with his blessed and glorious Humanity.[115]

But however genuine and helpful this experience was, as a contemplative Maria was not yet sure of herself. The Carmelite tertiary felt the need to justify this awareness of the Humanity by referring to the proper authority and by engaging apologetically in the current controversy with the adepts of "naked" and "annihilating" contemplation. In fact her analysis of this particular form of consciousness and her elaboration of it are not very satisfactory:

> I am saying with Saint Teresa that one must not leave aside the Humanity of Christ under the pretext of more purity and elevation of the spirit. And one is not allowed to reckon this Holy Humanity among the corporeal things which should be rejected by spiritual souls and annihilated in God in order for them not to be hindered in their inner turning towards God. As if that Holy Body would carry a hindrance regarding the contemplation of the Godhead ... for, although it is the case that this Holy Body causes an imagination as a Man, this Man is also truly God ... [116]

---

[115] Ibid., 188.

[116] Ibid., 188. Apparently, Maria is familiar with chapter XXII of Teresa's *Life*: "Christ's most sacred Humanity must not be reckoned among these corporeal objects." "For they say that ... even Christ's Humanity will hinder or impede

There is a certain dryness about this Christological arguing, but from her description of the way in which Maria now perceives Christ's presence it appears that she has come to a decisive experiential discovery. On the one hand, for the first time, "contemplation" is seen to be the awareness of becoming one with Christ. The Godman is no longer the object of Maria's spiritual seeing, but is now the One who makes her exist in him: "and in this way I live in him, I converse with him in prayer as well as out of prayer, and it seems I cannot do otherwise." On the other hand, this union is something the contemplative undergoes; it is a matter of mystical passivity: "for this is not my doing but ... a certain impression or showing which the Beloved by himself does to my soul."[117]

Fully aware now of her being impotent to attain by herself the experience of the Godman, Maria prays to the Beloved to teach her how to be occupied "with your Divinity and at the same time with the Humanity." Thereupon she feels "a light and clarity being poured into my inner self. This took possession of my soul and formed therein something divine which I cannot by any words give to understand." Obviously, there is no vision here nor any representation, but this does not prevent Maria from doing what mystical writers are bound to do: she gives a comparison. This "something divine" resembles a throne. Then she goes on to evoke her imageless perception of Christ as follows:

those who have arrived so far from attaining to the most perfect contemplation." See CW (*Life*), 140, 136.

[117] Ibid., 188. See also p. 189 where the passive nature of Maria's experience of Christ is very evident in the following observation: "I resolved to follow the counsel ... of your Reverence and to practise contemplating the Godman, and to live in Christ, etc. And when I turned to do so, I felt a headache and my brains getting strained because, in order to impress upon the mind the Image of the Holy Humanity, I did this in too active and rough a way."

> On that throne I see my Beloved resting, reigning over my soul, therein working, bringing it to life, as if he were the life and the soul of my soul. As I see it, he thinks, he prays, and he does everything through me, and I am only holding myself passively in all he wants to do. This governing comes out of the most inner ground, out of that clarity and rest of the mind without there being anything else mingled with it.[118]

With this the crucial step to discovering imageless contemplation of the Image has been taken. "Contemplation" has definitely developed from looking at the Godman into perceiving him as the Other who lives within oneself. "Imitation" of Jesus as the outer model one imagines with affection has been changed into identification with his Humanity as being one's own vital principle. The accomplished contemplative now appears as the person who feels the "in-formation with (*overvorminge met*) Christ, the Godman," which

> comes about through ... a simple turning towards and adhering to Christ, who in my prayer appears to be praying himself. When I speak, or do something, it is the Spirit of Christ who does it through me. This is to be understood in the sense that union with Christ proves so strong that the soul does not remember herself anymore, nor does she feel herself as something different from Christ ... now she does not perceive her doings, her limbs as hers, as she did before, but as the limbs and doings of Christ ... In this kind of union I seldom lose the full use of my senses and limbs, nor does it carry me along into rapture, but the soul remains free and able to do everything.[119]

It must be obvious that the role of the Passion is the most questionable point in the riddle of the Humanity. Is it not simply out of the question that the contemplative can have the suffering figure

---

[118] Ibid., 190

[119] Ibid., 191-192.

of the Godman present while praying in a "perfect," imageless way? Is there any religious event more likely to fill and fix a person's imagination and affection than what happened on the Via Dolorosa and on the hill of Calvary? The following text shows how the problem was solved for Maria, no longer by means of arguments, nor by trying to imagine Jesus' one-time suffering in Jerusalem, but by realizing his actual suffering in herself, here and now:

> This union with the abandoned and suffering Jesus begins with a simple, quiet turning (to the Father) ... simply remembering that this movement was also that of Christ. This remembering comes spontaneously and is given from above. Next follows a quiet, inner joining of the soul to Christ, and an impressing of the soul into Christ, like a seal is impressed into the wax and adheres to it. This happens while there is great simplicity and quietness in the faculties. And after that there follows the union of the soul with the abandoned and suffering Jesus, so much so that the soul seems to be solely one with him. And what thereby comes about is that the soul does not perceive or feel her abandonment and pains as being in her, but she regards, loves and embraces them as the pains of Christ with whom she is united, and at that moment she is also forgetting herself.[120]

---

[120] Ibid., 193-194.

CHAPTER III

THE FALLACY OF ECSTASY[1]

The great debt that Christian mysticism owes to a pagan mystic, namely to the *nobilissimus Plotinus*, as Saint Bonaventure calls him, should never be overlooked. Essential themes and terms, that run like golden threads through successive Christian descriptions of mystical union till at least the seventeenth century, have been taken over from Plotinus. One of these is the spatial metaphor that presents the contemplative path as an "ascent": the mystic-to-be approaches the presence of the Other by psychological concentration and moral purification which are seen as an upward climb.

---

[1] On the meaning of "ecstasy," one should note with the *Oxford English Dictionary* that this is initially a Greek term derived from the verb *ek-istanai*, "to put out of place." Thus "ecstasy" was (and still is?) in the first instance a pejorative term that refers to "insanity," "bewilderment," the typical Greek expression being *ek-istanai phrenoon*, "to drive a person out of his wits." By this evocation of the dehumanizing phenomenon of alienation, "ecstasy" points significantly to the subhuman, and it is this pointing beyond the human that has led mystical literature to adopt the same word, but in order to refer to the superhuman. In any case, it is clear from the outset that ecstasy is at odds with the human as such. The development of attitudes to ecstasy can be seen from a comparison between the frenzy of the Bacchae, the poetic flight of the Romantic artists and the fact that today "ecstasy" is a pill taken at parties. For the way in which Christian authorities — *Doctores Mystici* — defined ecstasy up to the seventeenth century, a useful work is Maximilianus Sandaeus, *Pro Mystica Theologia Clavis* (Cologne: Gualteriana, 1640; facsimile Heverlee: Éditions de la Bibliothèque S.J, 1963) 190-193. I am making use here of the richly documented article of Charles Baumgartner, "Extase," *Dictionnaire de spiritualité* IV/2 (1961) c. 2045-2189. This is rather a series of essays describing the phenomenon of ecstasy as it appears in different spiritual traditions (starting from shamanism), expanding on ecstasy in Christianity, and presenting the chief findings of a psychological approach.

And this ascent is intimately connected with another spatial image that contrasts the "external" with the "internal," to the point that the going *inward* is at once a going *upward*. By penetrating into oneself, a person ascends into God.

These are the two most influential themes of Plotinus. As for key words borrowed from him by Christian mystics, "vision" and "contemplation" are the most conspicuous. However, and this point is too often overlooked, Plotinus also makes use of words evoking "presence" and "contact," terms which reappear in Christian descriptions of mystical union with God. As Paul Henry points out, it "is noteworthy that a Greek philosopher should prefer, in describing the mystical union, expressions which are more appropriate to the sense of touch than to the sense of vision." And he refers to the following passage: "There, indeed, it was scarcely vision, unless of a mode unknown; it was a going forth from the self ... a reach towards contact ..."[2] Seen from the perspective of Christian mysticism, Plotinus' preference for the sense of touch is remarkable indeed.[3] The word *gherinen*, "to touch," is Ruusbroec's fixed term for the specificity of mystical experience, and the same is true of John of the Cross who makes use of *tocar* and *toque*.

In Plotinus' last Tractate (according to Porphyry's account), "On The Good, or The One" (*Enneads* VI, 9), there appears the well-known description of the highest stage of mystical union. A reading of this text (from §9) is appropriate here as it brings out the Plotinian theme of ecstasy, and illustrates the points made so

---

[2] See Paul Henry, "Introduction," in Plotinus, *The Enneads*, 2nd rev. ed., ed. B. S. Page, trans. Stephen MacKenna (London: Faber and Faber, 1956) xlv-xlix. The quotation is from *Enneads* VI. 9, 11, 24.

[3] Pierre Hadot observes that the importance for Plotinus of the "mysticism of light" must not be exaggerated. He refers to a passage where the "loving Spirit" is said to "experience the Good by a kind of touch." See Plotinus, *Traité 38* (VI, 7), ed. Pierre Hadot (Paris: Cerf, 1988) 60.

far. First, one notices how "touch" appears at the moment when Plotinus evokes mystical union: "So that with our being entire we may cling about This, no part in us but through it we have touch with God." And, in the second place, we see how "vision" is actually union, "we ... become that very light":

> Thus we have all the vision that may be of Him and of ourselves; but it is of a self wrought with splendour, brimmed with the Intellectual light, become that very light, pure, buoyant, unburdened, raised to Godhood or, better, knowing its Godhood.

And §10 continues to describe the same unifying experience: "In this seeing, we neither hold an object nor trace distinction; there is no two. The man is changed, no longer himself nor self-belonging ..."

There is an enthusiastic, liberated ring about both paragraphs 9 and 10, enhanced by the use made by Plotinus of the vivid language of the mystery religions. Yet one cannot fail to be struck by the sad note that is heard in the transition between the two paragraphs. The spiritual delight of the person who has become "unburdened" seems to be under the threat of a relapse. The self that is "all aflame," may be "crushed out once more if it should take up the discarded burden," as paragraph 9 concludes. And the reason why the highest union is so precarious is given: "the soul has not yet escaped wholly: but there will be the time of vision unbroken, the self hindered no longer by any hindrance of the body." The joyful, absolute union Plotinus is evoking appears to be only a momentary experience. It is far from being an "unbroken vision."

In paragraph 11, Plotinus goes on to describe the experience of the contemplative when "this ascent is achieved." He makes use of very strong expressions to indicate the contact with the One, such as "this mingling with the Supreme." And this is where the terms "rapture" and "enthusiasm" are prominent: "Reasoning is in abeyance ... and even, to dare the word, the very self: caught away (*harpasteis*), filled with God (*enthusiasas*)."[4] To this rapturous "filled with God" corresponds the "it was a going out from the self" (*ekstasis*). But the painful consciousness that this highest vision-union cannot be a lasting state appears once again. For the person who "has penetrated the inner sanctuary," the temple images will necessarily "become once more first objects of regard when he leaves the holies." And although the "self thus lifted ..., we have won the Term of all our journeying," this rest seems to be of short duration: "Fallen back again, we waken the virtue within until we know ourselves all order once more; once more we are lightened of the burden ...".

Taking into account the legacy of Plotinus to Christian mysticism, and the particular question we are trying to clarify (what is the role of the Humanity of Christ in mystical union?), this "ecstasy" deserves particular attention. Paul Henry remarks that it "is doubtful whether we ought to apply to this 'rapture' the term *ekstasis*, which is very rarely found in Plotinus and does not necessarily bear the sense which it bore for Philo and which it will later receive from the Christian mystics, the sense of 'ecstasy'." Thus the word "ecstasy" does not appear in MacKenna's translation: he renders the Greek word *ekstasis* by "a going forth from self." In this way, "the voluntary tension is emphasized at the expense of the passivity." But the passivity of Plotinus is a "relative passivity," which does not "imply any corresponding initiative or activity on the part of the object of contemplation."[5]

Whatever the degree of passivity Plotinus may have experienced, there is no doubt that the mystical union he knew was ecstatic. So much so that Pierre Hadot gives the first place to

---

4 Pierre Hadot translates: "arraché à lui-même et ravi par l'enthousiasme."
5 Henry, "Introduction," xlix.

ecstasy among the six main characteristics of the Plotinian mystical experience, which he describes as follows:

> This union is a momentary 'ecstasy' and not a state ... It is a kind of grace one can neither provoke voluntarily nor retain indefinitely. Consequently, the Plotinian spiritual life consists in the alternance of lengthy states, during which the philosopher studies theology and lives 'according to the Spirit', in order to prepare himself for union, and rare and short moments of ecstasy during which the soul unites itself to the good. On the one hand, the long-lasting desire of the soul in pursuit of the good, on the other hand, the sudden illumination. In Plotinus' school the mystical experience was considered a rare and exceptional phenomenon: Porphyry reports that during the seven years he lived with him, Plotinus reached the 'goal' only four times.[6]

However, an interesting problem arises: Paul Henry has warned us not to give Plotinian ecstasy the "sense which it ... will later receive from the Christian mystics," while Pierre Hadot seems to assert the opposite: "most of the Christian mystics allude to the alternation of the presences and absences of the Bridegroom," "Plotinian philosophy corresponds with" the mystical experience described by Bernard of Clairvaux, i.e., "a lengthy preparation to short but fulgurant moments of ecstasy."[7] So, is Christian mystical experience ecstatic in the Plotinian sense?

To start with, an evident fact has to be taken into account. Plotinian ecstasy was not the only kind of ecstasy to enter the

---

[6] Hadot in Plotinus, *Traité 38* (VI, 7), 58-59.

[7] Hadot in Plotinus, *Traité 38* (VI, 7) 59. Surprisingly enough, in footnote 67, Hadot refers to the experience of John of the Cross, who is supposed to have experienced the Plotinian "alternation," in the following way: "More precisely, in the permanent state of union of the soul with God, there is an alternance of 'rest' (periods of a continuous experience of union) and 'awakenings' (periods of more intense activity)." As will be shown further on, this "permanent state" is particularly important.

Christian tradition, nor was it accepted like some sort of cut diamond. This appears clearly from the work of Gregory of Nyssa (c. 335 — c. 395), the first Christian theologian and mystic to bring ecstasy into prominence.[8] Gregory, who had a deep influence upon subsequent Christian spiritual tradition, was imbued with (Neo)platonism.[9] Yet in his presentation of ecstasy he is dependent on Philo of Alexandria (c. 2O BC — 50AD), a Jewish eclectic thinker and, possibly, a mystic. In addition, Gregory draws on the Bible to illustrate his views, evoking such 'ecstatic' figures as Abraham and Saint Paul. The pertinence of Paul Henry's warning can be seen here: there is in Gregory's account of ecstasy a sense of mystical passivity which does not appear in the descriptions of Plotinus. According to Gregory, it is God who acts in mystical union, making himself present to the human person in an overwhelmingly abundant way. And when this effective presence of the other reaches a certain degree of intensity, it may 'put out of place', that is, draw the contemplative out of his or her self. Ecstasy is thus a kind of "e-motion," from the Latin *e-movere*, the phenomenon of being "moved out of" one's usual state, on God's initiative and through his attractive influence.[10]

---

[8] Cf. Jean Daniélou, "Mystique de la ténèbre chez Grégoire de Nysse," *Dictionnaire de spiritualité* II (1953) 1876-1885; Baumgartner, "Extase," c. 2099.

[9] He proved himself a master in adjusting its themes to his own theology and spirituality. On Gregory's coining of the label "achieved philosopher" to describe the Christian, and on his interpretation of "seeing God in one's own soul," see Paul Mommaers, "Gregorius van Nyssa (c. 335 — c. 395): De mens is nooit voltooid," in *Denk-wijzen, 4: Een inleiding in het denken van Plato, Aristoteles, Plotinus, Gregorius van Nyssa*, ed. Harry Berghs (Leuven: Acco, 1989) 93-120.

[10] Emotion in this basic, non-sentimental sense, plays an important role in mystical experience. This is why "admiration" appears often in mystical texts. See Paul Mommaers, "Is Hadewijch emotioneel?, *Emoties in de Middeleeuwen*, ed. R.E.V. Stuip, C. Vellekoop, Utrechtse Bijdragen tot de Mediëvistiek 5 (Hilversum: Verloren, 1998)135-156.

In some cases the impact of the divine presence on the human psyche is such that the mystic is no longer aware of anything else, all the soul's functions being put out of action. This occasional aspect of ecstasy — "the psychological fact of a suspension of the senses" — is not prominent in Gregory. He treats it as a side effect, and focuses on the "mystical fact of the intensity of the divine presence which seizes and absorbs the soul so as to capture all its attention." By distinguishing the spiritual motion in ecstasy from its psychosomatic repercussions, Gregory establishes a decisive religious criterion, but as we shall see, subsequent mystical authors did not always take it into account.

Thus the mystic's passivity, provoked by God's gracious and "suddenly" experienced presence, is the core of Greogory's ecstasy, and shows sufficiently the difference between it and Plotinian ecstasy. However, the variety and emotional strength of the ways in which Gregory expresses this experience make that difference still more abundantly clear.[11] Among the expressions he uses to characterize ecstasy are "inebriation," "sleep," "vertigo," "madness" and "wound." These last two images belong to the vocabulary of passionate love. And it is indeed the lovableness of the divine presence — manifesting itself as the absolutely lovable Person — that drives the human person out of himself. Ecstasy is essentially ecstatic love, a loving extroversion effected by eros and agape together, a remarkable combination, some people might say, in a mystical author inspired by Christian charity:

> As it sees the inexpressible beauty of the Bridegroom, the soul is wounded by the incorporeal and burning arrow of love (*eros*). This is indeed how the intensity of charity is called.[12]

---

[11] And, as we shall see further on in the texts of Bernard of Clairvaux and others, these striking expressions of the Greek Church Father have left their stamp on later mystical language.

[12] See *Homily 13 on the Song of Songs*, in *Patrologia, Series Graeca* 44, c. 1048c: "Epitetamenè gar agape eros legetai."

But Gregory goes further in his view of mystical union with God. He does not see it as consisting in some separated peak experiences of being taken out of oneself and momentarily lost in the Other. For Gregory, mystical union with God, instead of being at best an infrequent repetition of ecstasies, which appear as identical in so far as they are unrelated to the usual state of consciousness, is a constantly growing experience. It is a steady possessing of God by being possessed, but this steadiness has nothing static or terminal about it. It has the permanence of life developing and intensifying. The God presenting himself in the mystical experience described by Gregory is the Inexhaustible, who really gives himself, as the forever overflowing Reality. Consequently, for the human being to possess this Abundance is a most lively state. Here satisfaction goes together with desire. One keeps longing for more, while being "filled to capacity." That is why Moses made such a paradoxical demand:

> And although lifted up through such lofty experiences, he is still unsatisfied in his desire for more. He still thirsts for that with which he constantly filled himself to capacity, and he asks to attain as if he had never partaken.[13]

To help us clarify the role of the Humanity of Christ in mystical experience, this Gregorian yearning for more, while being one with God,[14] will prove a most valuable feature of the mystic's union with God. For in this case the overwhelming presence of the divine does not obliterate the human, nor does it serve as a sporadic escape from our normal state. While being steadily one with God, the mystic, for Gregory, keeps feeling the difference, desiring

---

[13] Gregory of Nyssa, *The Life of Moses*, trans. Abraham J. Malherbe, Everett Ferguson (NewYork, Ramsey, Toronto: Paulist Press, 1978) 114.

[14] Gregory's term is *epectasis*, which refers to Paul's "straining towards what lies ahead" (Philippians 3,13).

more and more: in God, the person is never "achieved." So it is
not just by chance that Ruusbroec — the master, as we shall see,
of Christ-centred mysticism — was particularly impressed by this
insight of Gregory. As leitmotif for his *Spiritual Tabernacle* he
selected a passage of identical import from Paul's Letters, namely,
"Run in such a way that you may comprehend."[15] And the mystic
from Brabant develops this expression into a paradoxical sentence
reminiscent of Gregory's *epectasis*:

> ... One falls into Resting, and then one will possess and compre-
> hend; and comprehending one will run and running one will com-
> prehend, and this is eternal life.[16]

Pseudo-Denys the Areopagite (c. 590) is the second important
author to have introduced the notion of ecstasy into the Christian
tradition, again adjusting it in accordance with his own experience. For his terminology on ecstasy he borrows not only from
Plotinus but also from Philo and Gregory. Indeed, ecstasy can be
seen to be at the centre of the Areopagite's writings, so much so
that the "whole Dionysian Corpus prepares for ecstasy and deter-
mines its conditions."[17] Here it may suffice to pay attention to two
points. In the first place, for Denys, too, ecstasy is caused by love
when it reaches a climax of ardour, and again no distinction is
made in this love between eros and agape: "In my opinion, the
sacred writers regard yearning (*eros*) and love (*agape*) as having
one and the same meaning." In the second place, it appears that
Denys, who is often described as a Christian mystic without Christ,

---

[15] See 1 Corinthians 9, 24 ("comprehend" means here "to grasp"): Ruusbroec made use of the Vulgate: "sic currite ut comprehendatis."

[16] Jan van Ruusbroec, *Werken* II, 2-3. This sentence construction is used elsewhere. Compare the end of *The Spiritual Tabernacle*: "See, thus we will run and
comprehend. And comprehending we will run; and running we will comprehend."

[17] Daniélou, "Mystique de la ténèbre," c. 1896.

puts Jesus Christ at the center of the mystic's ecstatic transition into God:

> This divine yearning brings ecstasy so that the lover belongs not to self but to the beloved ... This is why the great Paul, swept along by his yearning for God and seized by its ecstatic power, had this inspired word to say: 'It is no longer I who live, but Christ who lives in me.' Paul was truly a lover and, as he says, beside himself for God, possessing not his own life but the life of the One for whom he yearned, as exceptionally beloved.[18]

There can be no doubt, then, that the Plotinian view of contemplation was thoroughly christianized from early on. This does not alter the fact, however, that his concept of mystical union as a momentary peak experience has made itself felt throughout the Christian tradition. Moreover the predominant role given to ecstasy was bound to call into question, or at least to complicate, the position of the Humanity in advanced contemplation. Hence there is a need to investigate how a number of leading Christian mystics were able, more or less successfully, to integrate ecstasy and Christ-centered contemplation.

Initially two eminent mystical authors from the twelfth century deserve attention: on the one hand, the Cistercian monk recognized as the father of medieval mysticism and, in particular, as the initiator of contemplative devotion to the Humanity, Bernard of Clairvaux (1090-1153); on the other, one of the leading figures of the Augustinian abbey of Saint-Victor, a writer famous for the prominence he gives to ecstasy, Richard of Saint-Victor († 1173).

---

[18] Pseudo-Dionysius, *The Complete Works,* trans. Colm Luibheid (New York: Paulist Press, 1987) 82: *Divine Names* 709b and 712 a.

Bernard of Clairvaux: "Oh little while, little while! How long a little while!"

There is no need to expatiate here on the key position that Bernard of Clairvaux occupies in the history of the Christian spiritual tradition: it is no exaggeration to say that all mystical experience from the twelfth century onwards originates with the *doctor mellifluus*. He was the teacher who made religious love-experience flow from Scripture. Obviously Bernard's ideas on contemplation were not completely his own invention: he had assimilated remarkably well such distant predecessors as Augustine and Gregory the Great, also learning from his friend William of Saint-Thierry (1085-1149). And, more noteworthy still, he came to be the catalyst of the new cultural-religious tendencies that mark his century as the first Renaissance. For, after about 1050, a genuine humanism had come into existence.

There appears in the Christian West a change of mentality that "took the form of a greater concentration on man and on human experience as a means of knowing God. This was a significant step towards the restoration of the dignity of man, for it made the study of man an integral part of religious life. The search for God within the soul became one of the chief preoccupations of the monastic leaders of the late eleventh and twelfth centuries and this search expanded into a general demand for self-knowledge."[19] It was Bernard's contribution to put self-knowledge and the inner life at the centre of spirituality. He "popularized the method of introspection and made it the property of a school of monastic writers." And Richard William Southern goes on to show how, in Bernard's time, and especially in the monastic milieu, the experience of friendship

[19] Richard William Southern, *Medieval Humanism and Other Studies* (Oxford: Basil Blackwell, 1970) 33, 34-36.

came to the fore, for "without the cultivation of friendship there can be no true humanism." This sense of wonder at the exquisiteness of human friendship kindles a new feeling for the divine: "the experience of friendship lay along the road to God." So much so that the twelfth century also rediscovered friendship between God and man. And here we meet again with the subject that occupies us in this study: "There were many forces working in this direction. One of them was just a new way of thinking about God. Prayers, poems, devotions of all kinds, poured forth from the twelfth century onwards, which had one predominant theme — the humanity of God." Once more, Bernard was the writer who placed this devotion in the forefront, focusing it upon the sufferings of the Man.[20] So, in Sermon 43 on the Song of Songs, he comments on "My beloved is to me a bundle of myrrh that lies between my breasts" (1,21).[21] He interprets this "bundle" as representing the sufferings of Jesus, and he urges his audience: "Never permit even for an hour that this precious bunch of myrrh should be removed from

[20] Southern, *Medieval Humanism*, 36, observes that already "since the days of St. Anselm the God of human sufferings and emotions had become an object of tender contemplation. The whole creation had become filled with humanity." Even the theme of sin and misery "has been sweetened by the common humanity of God and man." It is worth noting here that another formidable thinker, similar in stature to Anselm (1033-1109), namely, Peter Abelard (1079-1142), also displayed a genuine devotion towards the Humanity. In his *Hymnarius Paracletensis*, he expresses his compassion — or "sympathy," in the strong, original sense of the word — with the suffering and struggling Jesus. However, for Abelard, the Godman is the human example that appeals to him from without, and not the divine life that feeds him from within. This is one of the reasons why Abelard came to be a privileged target for the polemical arrows of Bernard of Clairvaux. Bernard criticized him for reducing Christ to a person who gave doctrine, but not life.

[21] I shall be quoting from *The Works of Bernard of Clairvaux*, 4 vols. (Kalamazoo: Cistercian Publications, 1976-1981). For Sermon 43, see *On the Song of Songs II*, 220-224.

your bosom. Preserve without fail the memory of all those bitter things he endured for you, persevere in meditating on him." Bernard then goes on to express his own feelings and — something to be noted — he emphasizes the fact that he himself never leaves these "sentiments" behind:

> As for me, dear brothers, from the early days of my conversion ... I made sure to gather for myself this little bunch of myrrh and place it between my breasts. It was culled from all the anxious hours and bitter experiences of my Lord; first from the privations of his infancy, then from the hardships he endured in preaching, the fatigues of his journeys, the long watches in prayer ... the insults, the spitting, the blows, the mockery, the scorn, the nails and similar torments ... Among the teeming little branches of this perfumed myrrh I feel we must not forget the myrrh he drank upon the cross and used for his anointing at his burial. Hence as you well know, these sentiments are often on my lips, and God knows they are always in my heart. They are the familiar theme in my writings, as is evident. This is my philosophy, one more refined and interior, to know Jesus and him crucified.

As for Bernard's notion of contemplation, his basic terms are *experientia* ("experience") and *affici* ("to be affected"). The "experience" he has in mind consists in the kind of knowledge a person can be favoured with only in loving, and this love-experience is in the first instance a matter of feeling. Thus, the contemplative comes to know God by the way in which his heart is being "affected." As Bernard puts it in Sermon 74, after having described his personal mystical experience of Christ the Word: "Only by the movement of my heart *(ex motu cordis),* as I have told you, did I perceive his presence."[22]

---

[22] *On the Song of Songs IV*, 91; §6. Here is part of Bernard's description of this personal experience, one of the very great texts from the Christian mystical tradition: "I want to tell you of my own experience ... I admit that the Word has also come to me — I speak as a fool — and has come many times. But although

Obviously, it would be an anachronism to narrow down (as is current today) the sense of "heart" to refer to the (symbolic) organ of a person's sentimental feelings. Bernard still draws on the biblical tradition that sees the heart primarily as the core of the human person, which integrates both spiritual and affective power. And the "movement" he has in mind should not be reduced to a simple psychological reaction. It comprises also, as he puts it (a little further on in Sermon 74), the "renewal and remaking of the spirit of my mind, that is of my inmost being."[23] However, this broader sense of "heart" and the efficacity of the "movement" need not entail that human sensitivity is excluded. Certainly not in the case of Bernard, who contributed decisively to the development of affection in contemplation, and who, to be more specific, made heartfelt love for the Humanity the hub of spirituality and mysticism.

On this point, it will be useful to examine in detail Sermon 20 *On the Song of Songs*. Bernard starts, so to speak, "from above," expressing a love — that one can assume to be spiritual — for the "Lord Jesus," that is, for "the one through whom I have my

he has come to me, I have never been conscious of the moment of his coming. I perceived his presence, I remembered afterwards that he had been with me; sometimes I had a presentiment the he would come, but I was never conscious of his coming or his going ... The coming of the Word was not perceptible to my eyes, for he has no color; nor to my ears, for there was no sound; nor yet to my nostrils, for he mingles with the mind, not with the air; he has not acted upon the air, but created it. His coming was not tasted by the mouth, for there was no eating or drinking, nor could he be known by the sense of touch, for he is not tangible. How then did he enter? ... I have ascended to the highest in me, and look! The word is towering above that. In my curiosity I have descended to explore my lowest depths, yet I found him even deeper. If I looked outside myself, I saw him stretching beyond the furthest I could see, and if I looked within, he was yet further within" (89-90).

[23] *On the Song of Songs IV*, 91; §6.

being, my life, my understanding." But soon he descends to express a different reason for loving the Godman:

> But there is something else that moves me, arouses and enflames me even more. Good Jesus, the chalice you drank, the price for our redemption, makes me love you more than all the rest. This alone would be enough to claim our love. This, I say, is what wins our love so sweetly, justly demands it, firmly binds it, deeply affects it.[24]

Such is what Bernard goes on to call the "love of the heart," which "relates to a certain warmth of affection." And this is how the abbot tries to arouse his monks to the pleasurable quality of this affectionate love and its curing effect:

> Your affection for your Lord Jesus should be both tender and intimate, to oppose the sweet enticements of sensual life. Sweetness conquers sweetness as one nail drives out another.[25]

However, this "love of the heart," though essential, should not stand on its own. It needs to be accompanied by two more spiritual kinds of love: the "love of the soul" and the "love of strength." Thus Bernard relativizes the status of affectionate love but, interestingly enough, he does not want the advancing contemplative simply to renounce it or leave it behind. To make this clear, he refers first to a passage from the New Testament that has been seized upon again and again by those contemplatives who champion a purely spiritual love. When Jesus was about to ascend into heaven, he said to his disciples whose affectionate love for him was now to be frustrated: "It is good for you that I am going."

---

[24] *On the Song of Songs I*, 148; §2.

[25] *On the Song of Songs I*, 150; §4. Bernard refers again and again to this purifying aspect of affectionate love for the Humanity; e.g. in the case of Jesus' disciples "it was only by his physical presence that their hearts were detached from carnal loves." — "But that carnal love is worthwhile since through it sensual love is excluded ..." (pp.152 and 154).

For a moment Bernard seems to accept the spiritualizing interpretation: "Their love was more tender than prudent, it was sensual but not reasonable; they loved with the whole heart but not with the whole soul." But soon he marks his distance from the "spirituals" by making a sharp distinction. By telling his disciples that this separation was good for them, Jesus did not intend to "correct their feelings but their foresight." The same is true, Bernard goes on to assert, of Peter, "who loved him so dearly" that he "tried to stand in the way" (of Jesus' Passion). When Jesus rebuked Peter, "what was it but his imprudence he was correcting?" He meant to say: "you do not love wisely, you are following your human feeling in opposition to the divine plan."[26]

Evidently, Bernard is putting the love of the heart into its proper perspective. He will admit that the gift of being "nourished by the sweetness of (Christ's) humanity" is most suitable for "beginners" because they lack as yet the capacity to "perceive the things which are of the Spirit of God." But he also hastens to emphasize that "there is no love of Christ at all without the Holy Spirit, even if this love is in the flesh."[27] And when in the last two paragraphs of this same Sermon he goes on to relativize affectionate love, he does so after asserting once again that "this devotion to the humanity of Christ is a gift, a great gift of the Spirit."

The main point being made by Bernard in his reflection upon the love of the heart and its development into both "rational" and "spiritual" love is that affectionate love is quite essential to the contemplative's experience of the love of God, and that it goes together with the use of "a sacred image of the Godman" as well as with feelings stirred in the heart of "carnal man." This is how Bernard expresses his unwavering appreciation of the love of God's "own humanity":

[26] *On the Song of Songs I*, 151; §5. John 16,7 and Mark 8,33.
[27] *On the Song of Songs I*, 153; §7.

Notice that the love of the heart is, in a certain sense, carnal, because our hearts are attracted most toward the humanity of Christ and the things he did or commanded while in the flesh ... The soul at prayer should have before it a sacred image of the Godman, in his birth or infancy or as he was teaching, or dying, or rising, or ascending. Whatever form it takes, this image must bind the soul with the love of virtue and expel carnal vices, eliminate temptations and quiet desires ... the invisible God ... wanted to recapture the affections of carnal men who were unable to love in any other way, by first drawing them to the salutary love of his own humanity, and then gradually to raise them to a spiritual love.[28]

But it is time now to focus on Bernard's idea of mystical experience as such. A passage from *On Humility and Pride* is the first to call for special attention.[29] It is a concise description of the third and highest degree of the spiritual life, i.e., "contemplation." When the contemplative's soul, the "Bride," is "admitted at last to the King's chamber, for whose love she languishes," this is what happens to her:

> There for a short time, half an hour, while there is silence in heaven, she sleeps sweetly and at peace in that longed-for embrace. But her mind is alert, and it is filled with the secrets of truth on which she will feed in memory when she comes to herself. There she sees things invisible, hears the ineffable, which no man can utter. These things exceed that knowledge which night can give to night, for this is the word that day speaks to day. Wise men speak wisdom to the wise. The spiritual are told spiritual things.[30]

There is a full commentary on this text by Etienne Gilson, who gives an explanation of each of the four main expressions: "for a

---

[28] *On the Song of Songs I*, 152; §6.

[29] *De gradibus humilitatis*. The relevant quotations are taken from Bernard of Clairvaux, *Selected Works*, trans. G.R. Evans (New York: Paulist Press, 1987).

[30] *De gradibus humilitatis*, 118.

short time," "silence," "sleep" and "embrace."[31] It may suffice here to dwell for a moment on the last two, for they evoke most clearly the ecstatic nature of this experience: "embrace" *(amplexus)* and "sleep" *(somnus)*. With regard to "embrace," Gilson points out that it is indeed a scriptural metaphor for ecstasy. The passage in the Bible that Bernard likes to interpret in this way is in the Song of Songs: "O that his left hand were under my head, and that his right hand embraced me! I adjure you, O daughters of Jerusalem ... do not stir up or awaken love until it is ready."[32] As he explains in his *Sermons on the Song of Songs:*

> (In the biblical text) the heavenly bridegroom is plainly shown as passionately defending the repose of his beloved, eager to embrace her within his arms as she sleeps *(servare inter brachia propria dormientem)*, lest she be roused from her delicious slumber (a *somno suavissimo)* by annoyance or disquiet.[33]

God's embrace, therefore, his uniting the soul to himself in perfect, ecstatic contemplation, implies her being put to sleep.[34] In this sleep two aspects can be distinguished, although Bernard is not insistent about this distinction. The first concerns the contemplative's sensibility, and is ecstasy proper: the divine presence proves to be so unusual and strong that the soul is abstracted from her normal sense life. She is not in a position to make any more use of her external senses which are now in suspense. The other

---

[31] See Étienne Gilson, *La théologie mystique de saint Bernard* (Paris: J. Vrin, 1934) 128-129.

[32] See the Song of Songs (Song of Solomon), 2,6-7.

[33] *On the Song of Songs III*, 50; §2. For the original Latin text, I shall quote from *Sermones super Cantica Canticorum 36-38,* eds. Jean Leclercq, C.H. Talbot, H.M. Rochais, in *Sancti Bernardi Opera II* (Rome: Editiones Cistercienses, 1958).

[34] See *On the Song of Songs III*, 52; §5 and §6, "This kind of ecstasy, in my opinion, is alone or principally called contemplation." – "The bride ... sweetly sleeps within the arms of her bridegroom, in ecstasy of spirit" *(suaviter obdormisse, id est in spiritu excessisse)*.

concerns the soul's internal senses: this is the ecstasy of the mind *(excessus mentis)* by which the human spirit is carried away, rather than put to sleep, through being illuminated by God. While still in Sermon 52, Bernard goes on "to explain if I can what this sleep is":

> It is a slumber which is vital and watchful *(vitalis vigilque sopor)*, which enlightens the heart *(sensum interiorem)*, drives away death, and communicates eternal life. For it is a genuine sleep *(dormitio)* that yet does not stupefy the mind but transports it *(non sopiat, sed abducat)*. And — I say it without hesitation — it is a death *(et est mors)*.[35]

It would not be appropriate to analyse at this point every detail of this significant Sermon. However, by studying the salient terms one sees at once how lofty an experience is being offered to the Bernardine mystic: the soul appears equipped with "wings" and wishes to "fly beyond" *(transvolare)*, ready to attain to a super-human state. First, there is the word "death." After confirming that he wishes to "call the bride's ecstasy a death" *(exstasim dixerim mortem)*, Bernard continues throughout paragraph 4 to interpret this mystical death as the contemplative's liberation from the "temptations" that are inherent in the human condition. But when the soul is "drawn out of itself," so as to "transcend the normal manner and habit of thinking," she escapes life's snares, because the "ecstatic soul is cut off from awareness of life" *(excedente quippe anima ... vitae sensu)*. Yet there is still more to this sense of "death." The contemplative's death described so far can be seen as the human way of dying: "humans alone experience this." But, as appears from paragraph 5, there is also for the contemplative the experience of "dying the death of angels." One is called to go even further beyond normal human consciousness, so that

---

[35] *On the Song of Songs III*, 51-52; §3-4.

one gets rid of the desire not only for tangible things, but even "for their images" *(similitudinibus)*. This second way of "going out of oneself" *(excedere)* is marked by "angelic purity". Thus the contemplative achieves the ultimate aim when one "succeeds in flying with purity of mind beyond the material images *(phantasmata corporearum similitudinum)* that press in from every side."

Along with this insistent use of the word "death," Bernard introduces a second key word, namely "rest." While referring partly to the death that liberates from the restlessness that holds those still alive, "rest" is chiefly synonymous with "sleep" and thus points to a state of the contemplative who, like the bride, "sweetly sleeps within the arms of her bridegroom, in ecstasy of spirit."[36]

So far Bernard has based his description of contemplation on two pivotal terms: "death" and "rest." He has shown how, after

---

[36] The thrust of the argument here should not make us overlook the fact that Bernard's idea of the "supreme," ecstatic experience of God is christocentric. This appears clearly in Sermon 8 where, commenting on the first verse of the Song of Songs — "Let him kiss me with the kiss of his mouth" — he comes to describe the "supreme kiss, that of the mouth": "Listen if you will know what the kiss of the mouth is: 'The Father and I are one' ... This is a kiss from mouth to mouth beyond the claim of any creature ... But the kiss of the kiss we discover when we read: 'Instead of the spirit of the world, we have received the Spirit that comes from God' ... But we must make a clearer distinction between the two. He who received the fullness is given the kiss of the mouth, but he who received from the fullness is given the kiss of the kiss. Paul was certainly a great man, but no matter how high he should aim in making the offer of his mouth, even if he were to raise himself right into the third heaven, he would still of necessity find himself remote from the lips of the Most High ... He however who did not count equality with God a thing to be grasped ... does not beg for a kiss from an inferior position; rather on equally sublime heights mouth is joined to mouth, and by a prerogative that is unique, receives the kiss from the mouth. For Christ therefore, the kiss meant a totality, for Paul only a participation; Christ rejoiced in the kiss of the mouth, Paul only in that he was kissed by the kiss" *(Sermons on the Song of Songs I,* 51-52; §7-8). See the comments of Gilson, *La Théologie Mystique de saint Bernard,* 134.

being relieved of the human burden by a twofold dying, the accomplished contemplative is overwhelmed with divine delight in resting. Now, following this growing paean of joy, something like a complaint begins to be heard from paragraph 6 onwards. Here, in its final part, the Sermon lacks semantic signposts comparable to "death" and "rest" in the earlier part, but words such as "disturb" and "trouble" set the tone. There appears a problematic side to the contemplative's rest, as the "restless maidens" of the bride tend to "recall (her) from the sublime company to which she is introduced as often as she becomes ecstatic in contemplation" *(quoties contemplando excedit)*. These maidens, representing the demands of charitable action, prove to be a "disturbance"; they "trouble a person resting in contemplation." That is why they should be "forbidden" to interfere with the bride's sublime experience, because "it is for her to choose both when to be at leisure and when to devote attention to them." For the Bridegroom has judged "that management of those affairs might be safely committed to her discretion." There is, then, no question for Bernard of the contemplative being in a position to dispense with practising the love of one's neighbour. Yet this activity appears rather as an unescapable obligation and a threatening situation. This uneasiness over the disturbing affairs that are integral to the contemplative's earthly existence comes concretely to the fore in the last paragraph of the Sermon where Bernard, the acting abbot, complains about his being too often troubled by his brothers: "There are some sitting here who ... might begin to spare me a little bit more than hitherto, and not intrude so rudely and irresponsibly on my leisure. As they well know, rare is the hour in which I can relax from visitors."

Thus the issue being investigated in this work reappears under a different aspect. Apparently, ecstatic contemplation, "alone or principally called contemplation,"[37] does not fully integrate the

---

[37] See above, note 34.

non-ecstatic aspects of the contemplative's existence. There seems to be no organic unity between the lofty quiet of this angelic state and the lowly restlessness of the human condition. Mystical "death" does not tolerate day-to-day life, and far from enhancing activity the "rest" has rather to be protected from it. The ex-cellence of the *ex-cessus* involves a loss in value of the human and thus of the Humanity.

This conflict between the divine and the human shows itself almost cruelly as the ecstatic suffers the "coming and going" of the Beloved. Ascent into heavenly rest is bound to alternate in arbitrary fashion with descent into earthly restlessness. And, apart from the inconstancy of the Presence, the delightful ascents prove to be short, whereas the regretful descents are painfully long periods. The absence of the Beloved tends to drive the lover to distraction. How is the bride to live her life on earth, when she is filled with nostalgia for the "delicious slumber in the heavenly embrace"? Bernard describes this contemplative dilemma in a moving way: in Sermon 32 he stresses how brief is the period of contemplation, and how changeable the contemplative's condition. No doubt such a person is favoured with feeling the "Word in the guise of a Bridegroom," and at that moment "will experience how sweet divine love is as it flows into his heart. His heart's desire will be given to him." But there is another side to the picture:

> (This fulfilment is) only for a time, a short time. For when after vigils and prayers and a great shower of tears he who was sought presents himself, suddenly he is gone again, just when we think we hold him fast. But he will present himself anew to the soul ... he will allow himself to be taken hold of but not detained, for suddenly a second time he flees from between our hands ... And so, even in this body we can often enjoy the happiness of the Bridegroom's presence, but it is a happiness that is never complete because the joy of the visit is followed by the pain of his departure.[38]

---

[38] *On the Song of Songs II*, 135; §2.

Similarly in Sermon 74 there is a striking passage on the lengthiness of the contemplative's desolation. The first verse Bernard comments on here is "Return, she says," and this is the contemplative question he reads into it: "Who will adequately explain to me the going and returning of the Word?" Later, with a fine sense of paradox, he reflects upon the words Jesus spoke to his disciples, when he was about to depart from them after the resurrection, "a little while and you shall see me":

> Oh little while, little while! How long a little while! Dear Lord, you say it is for a little while that we do not see you. The word of my Lord may not be doubted, but it is a long while, far too long.[39]

To conclude this tentative exploration of Bernard's writings on contemplation, it is worth noting how clearly they illustrate the fallacy of ecstasy. The father of medieval mysticism, who was also the one who put the Godman at the heart of the contemplative's endeavour, does not explain how the Humanity and the human can be part and parcel of contemplation in the strict sense.

Richard of Saint-Victor: "The image of the humility of Christ is set before the eyes"

Among Richard of Saint-Victor's writings on contemplation, three major texts deserve attention here.[40] In the first, currently known as *Benjamin Minor*,[41] he treats of the soul's preparation for

---

[39] *On the Song of Songs IV*, 89; §4. See Song of Songs (Song of Solomon) 2,17 and John 16,17.

[40] For an overview, see Jean Châtillon, "Richard de Saint-Victor," *Dictionnaire de Spiritualité* XIII (1988) c. 612-623.

[41] I will quote from Richard of Saint-Victor, *The Twelve Patriarchs; The Mystical Ark; Book Three of The Trinity*, transl. and intr. Grover A. Zinn. (New York: Paulist Press, 1979) — *The Twelve Patriarchs* and *The Mystical Ark* are

contemplation. He shows how the soul passes through several successive stages so as to finally attain the "summit," that is "ecstasy of mind" *(excessus mentis)*. The introductory motif for *Benjamin Minor* is provided by words from Psalm 67: "Benjamin a young man in ecstasy,"[42] and in the last chapters of the book Benjamin's birth from Rachel is presented as the moment when the soul reaches ecstasy by being led above reason: "Where human reason fails. There Rachel dies, that Benjamin may be born."[43] Richard further specifies the two kinds of contemplation that are to be understood by the death of Rachel and the ecstasy of Benjamin:

> The first is above reason, but not beyond reason; however, the second is both above reason and beyond reason ... In the first, Benjamin kills his mother when he goes above all reason... in the second he goes beyond even himself.[44]

The second important work of Richard of Saint-Victor, *Benjamin Major*, is an exposition of contemplation itself. This is where ecstasy comes into prominence, especially in the final fifth Book. Here, Richard first describes the "three modes" of contemplation or three ways in which a person can perform the act of contemplation:

> The quality of contemplation is varied according to three modes. For now it happens by enlarging of the mind, now by raising of the mind and at another time by alienation of the mind.[45]

---

the titles by which Richard's first two main works, now known as *Benjamin Minor* and *Benjamin Major*, "were commonly referred to by medieval authors." These titles "are accurate reflections of the dominant images in the two works" (p. 7).

[42] Psalm 67,28, according to the Septuagint.

[43] Richard of Saint-Victor, *The Twelve Patriarchs; The Mystical Ark; Book Three of The Trinity*, 140 (chapter 82).

[44] Ibid., 145 (chapter 86).

[45] Ibid., 310 (*Benjamin Major*, Book V, chapter 2).

This "alienation of the mind" (*excessus mentis*) is the subject matter of the remaining chapters of Book V (5-19). Here Richard clarifies "the causes by which ecstasy of the human mind is accustomed to happen." He says that there are three of them, and characterizes them as follows:

> For it is now according to greatness of devotion, now according to greatness of wonder, now according to greatness of exultation, that the mind is completely unable to restrain itself and, being elevated above itself, goes over into alienation.[46]

Not surprisingly, given medieval thinkers' delight in hierarchic distinctions, the third manner of being carried away is considered the highpoint of ecstasy. Here is a description of the most significant characteristics of the alienation of mind caused by the greatness of joy or exultation (notice the repetition of "suspending," "leap," "for a moment," "for a short while;" and in particular "above humanity":

> In this way, when a forceful and unmeasurable joyfulness grows above a human mode, it raises one above humanity, and after raising him up above human things it suspends him in sublime things. We are surely able to see the form of such things daily, even in animals. In their play animals are often accustomed to make a kind of leap and to suspend their bodies in the air for a short while. In this way fishes often leap above the waters when they play in the water, and they go beyond the bounds of their natural habitation when they suspend themselves for a moment in the void. So without doubt when the holy soul is cut off from herself by a kind of internal applause of her dancing, when she is driven to go above herself by means of alienation of mind ... then she seems to have gone beyond the bounds of natural possibility.[47]

---

[46] Ibid., 316 (chapter 5)..
[47] Ibid., 334 (chapter 14).

On reading Richard's enthusiastic evocation of ecstasy in the final part of *Benjamin Major*, one's first impression is that this excursion "above humanity" constitutes the obvious perfection of contemplation. It seems that the contemplative project aims entirely at reaching the ecstatic summit, a sublime *terminus ad quem*. And yet, however fascinating the fish's "leap above the waters," one can hardly fail to notice that this experience is a passing one, and the waters waiting to envelop the flying fish have not changed. In any case, Richard is aware that there is a problem with this sporadic elevation. The accomplished contemplative, far from enjoying anything like a permanent union with the Divine, feels that the gift of ecstasy is often "withdrawn from him." When this happens, he must not accept it passively:

> There is something he ought to do ... to recover this grace ... And so, the soul that is in such a situation ought to recover exultation of the heart in itself by its own meditations.

And so Richard comes to propose what looks, rather paradoxically, like a method for "renewing" the unpredictable divine gift. Referring to the story of Elisha the Prophet who recovered the spirit of prophecy by "having a minstrel brought to him,"[48] he urges the reader to "learn from the example of the Prophet." The contemplative in need ought to know how to restore the soul to "customary delights":

> However, what does it mean to summon a minstrel of this sort except to regain exultation of the heart by provident meditation and to awaken devotion of the heart by recollection of divine kindnesses and promises?[49]

---

[48] Ibid., 339 (chapter 17). See 2 Kings 3,15: "And then, while the musician was playing, the power of the LORD came on him."

[49] Ibid., 341 (chapter 18).

Richard then goes on to describe one way of having the gift of ecstasy "renewed," and he concludes by asserting that this is "effective for the renewing of the mind ... effective especially for the restoration of grace that has been lost."[50]

While following Richard of Saint-Victor's exposition of contemplation in *Benjamin Minor* and *Benjamin Major,* one cannot fail to recognize the Plotinian viewpoint expressed here. The Christian master appears to remain within the perspective on ecstasy proposed by the pagan mystic: the "suspension" of the mind, the "leap" that brings the contemplative for a short while "above humanity," captures one's attention and, by the same token, leaves the Humanity unnoticed. However, Richard has another string to his bow.

His third major work on contemplation, *Of the Four Degrees of Passionate Charity,*[51] was written later than his twofold *Benjamin.* As Clare Kirchberger points out, this is probably "almost his latest work," and in the meantime the spiritual author seems to have learned much in the school of daily life.[52] Originally these *Four Degrees* may well have been a sermon which Richard later developed into a treatise. In fact this lively presentation of the phenomenon of love is a systematic exposition of contemplation.

---

[50] Ibid., 342 (chapter 18).

[51] Richard of Saint-Victor, *De quattuor gradibus violentae caritatis.* I will quote from Richard of Saint-Victor, *Selected Writings on Contemplation,* trans. Clare Kirchberger (London: Faber and Faber, 1957) 213-233. For the original Latin text, I will make use of *Ives: Epître à Séverin sur la charité; Richard de Saint-Victor: Les quatre degrés de la violente charité,* trans. Gervais Dumeige (Paris: J. Vrin, 1955).

[52] Clare Kirchberger, "Introduction" to Richard of Saint-Victor, *Selected Writings on Contemplation,* 45-46, where she suggests that Richard gained a great deal of experience "in the practical way of life which his duties under a non-acting abbot entailed."

The dominant theme in this work is the parallel between human love and the love of God. There are many degrees in each of them, but Richard wants to concentrate on the kind of love which is "above all these degrees," that is, passionate love: "O vehemence of love! O thou violence of charity!"[53] At this stage both loves may develop into passion, but they are also capable of having similar degrees: "I see men wounded, others bound, languishing, fainted, and all for love. Charity wounds, charity binds, makes a man sick, causes him to faint."[54] After describing these four degrees, Richard summarizes as follows: "In the first, love is insuperable, in the second, inseparable, in the third, singular, in the fourth, insatiable."[55] However, the similarity between the two loves does not entail their being simply identical: "These four degrees of love are not grouped in divine love as they are in human love ... In spiritual desires the greater the degree of love, the better; in fleshly desires the greater, the worse."[56]

At this stage any reader of Richard interested in contemplation may well start wondering what he intends by this analysis of love, and the author now provides an answer: these four degrees of love correspond to the successive stages of contemplation which he had previously exposed in the two *Benjamins*. First he renames each of the four degrees. The first, known so far as the degree of "wounded" or "insuperable" love, becomes the degree in which "the soul thirsts for God" *(sitit Deum)*. The second, that of "binding" or "inseparable" love, is now the degree in which the soul "thirsts to go to God" *(sitit ad Deum)*. For the third, "languishing" or "singular" love, the terminology becomes that the soul

---

⁵³ Richard of Saint-Victor, *Selected Writings on Contemplation,* 213.
⁵⁴ Ibid., 213-214.
⁵⁵ Ibid., 220-221.
⁵⁶ Ibid., 221.

"thirsts to be in God" *(sitit in Deum)*, while for the fourth, "faint-ing" or "insatiable" love, the new expression is that she "thirsts in God's way" *(sitit secundum Deum)*. Richard then goes on to indicate the correlation between the different degrees of love and the stages of contemplation, and what he has to say about the last two degrees is something new:

> The soul *thirsts in God*, when in ecstasy she desires to pass over into God altogether, so that having wholly forgotten herself she may truly say: 'Whether in the body or out of the body I cannot tell.' She *thirsts in God's way* when by her own will, I do not mean in tem-poral matters only but also in spiritual things, the soul reserves noth-ing for her own will but commits all things to God, never thinking about herself but about the things of Jesus Christ, so that she may say: 'I came not to do my own will but the will of the Father which is in heaven'.[57]

This arrangement of the different stages of contemplation comes as a surprise, and for several reasons. One is struck in the first place by what appears to be a demotion of ecstasy. The regular summit of contemplation no longer occupies the supreme position. At present it corresponds to the third degree of love and not, as a reader of the *Benjamin Major* might expect, the fourth. Secondly, in this new order an unexpected counter-movement is given prominence just when the contemplative is being ecstatically ele-vated. The continuous upward progress of the soul — "ascending above herself" in the third degree and "lifted up to God" in the fourth degree — turns into a downward movement: "she descends below herself."

After describing in detail the first two degrees, Richard dwells on the last two, and this is where he reveals his final and crucial

---

[57] Ibid., 223-224. Richard first quotes 2 Corinthians 12,2 which is the out-standing scriptural passage to which adepts of ecstasy keep appealing throughout the centuries. Then he paraphrases John 5,30.

insight into the perfection of contemplation. This passage well repays close attention as it provides a highly significant piece of evidence for the theme of this book.[58] This text opens with a paragraph (§38) on "the third degree of love ... when the mind of man is ravished *(rapitur)* into the abyss of divine light." Richard makes it clear now that the divine cause of this rapturous elevation is of a compound nature, therefore bringing about a twofold effect in the human person. On the one hand, there is the impact of the "divine light" with the result that the mind is "altogether unaware of itself" *(penitus nesciat seipsum)* and the soul "is abstracted from itself" *(a seipsa alienatur)*. On the other hand, there is the divine "fire of love" that penetrates the soul to the core, so much so that it "sheds its very self altogether" *(seipsam penitus exuit)*. This is where the heart of Richard's mature view of mystical experience is revealed. God does not just show himself to the contemplative's spiritual eye, fascinating the human mind so strongly that it forgets itself, but he also, at once, touches the ecstatic person's core, and it is only in this way that God causes the soul to lose herself "altogether." And thus the difference between *Benjamin Major* and *The Four Degrees* is immediately apparent.What in the former is seen as the acme of contemplation proves in the latter to be only one of its main aspects: the third degree of contemplation needs the fourth degree of love to bring it to completion.

Richard then (§38) goes on to give an image of the state of the soul in the third degree of love. She resembles iron, which, when put into the fire, undergoes a twofold change. The dark colour turns "hot red" and, moreover, the natural hardness is changed into another "quality": "At last it liquefies entirely and ceases altogether to be itself *(a se ipso plene deficiat)*, changing into another kind of thing" *(in aliam penitus qualitatem transeat)*. So

---

[58] Ibid., 228-231; §38-44.

also, through a comparable fusing, the soul is "altogether changed from its first state." Henceforth "liquefaction" predominates as Richard's pivotal image, for it enables him to present vividly the development of the contemplative beyond the third, ecstatic degree and into mystical configuration with the Humanity.

Richard strengthens his key image by quoting from the Song of Songs — "My soul melted when my beloved spake"[59] — and then (§41) refers to the decisive effects of liquefaction: "There is nothing hard or firm in liquids or liquefied solids." As for human beings, "liquefaction" signifies what may happen to the will. Sick people "depend on the will of others," and contemplatives finally "do nothing according to their own will."

After this explanatory intermezzo, Richard resumes the basic theme of iron liquefying in fire (§42), and goes on to develop it very aptly to represent what happens to the contemplative soul liquefied in the divine fire: the soul is bound to flow down into the human or, as he expresses it further on, she is to be "found in fashion as a man."[60] Before reading this vivid passage one should notice a lexical point that appears in paragraphs 42-44: Richard is playing here with the word *forma*.[61] In this way, with his emphasis in these essential paragraphs on the appearance in mystical union of a "form," he clearly contributes to the solution of the problem being discussed here:

---

[59] Ibid., 229; §40. See Song of Songs 5,6. Richard frequently uses the term *liquefactam* here, and he quotes from the Vulgate, *anima mea liquefacta est*.

[60] Ibid., 230; §44.

[61] Obviously this is clearer in Latin: not only is the word *forma* used seven times, but the word *formula* is used twice, *conformare* thrice, and *informare* twice. *Imago* appears only once, referring to what the metal workers produce, and is translated by Kirchberger as "form," by Dumeige as "figure."

> For just as the metal workers, when the metals are melted *(liquefactis)*, shape any form *(imaginem)* according to their will... so the soul applies herself in this degree to be readily at the beck and call of the divine will ... and adjusts her own will *(voluntatem suam informat)*, as the divine good pleasure requires. And as the liquefied metal runs down easily wherever a passage is opened, so the soul humbles herself spontaneously to be obedient in this way.[62]

Where exactly does the soul descend? Into the human as it has appeared in the Humanity:

> In this state the image of the humility of Christ is set before the eyes *(proponitur forma humilitatis Christi)* so that these words come to her: 'Let this mind be in you, which was also in Christ Jesus: who being in the form of God ... took upon him the form of a servant and was made in the likeness of men and was found in the habit of man; he humbled himself and became obedient unto death, even the death of the cross.' This is the form of the humility of Christ to which every man must conform himself, who desires to attain to the highest degree of perfect charity.[63]

By close attention to the way in which two modern translations of the *Four Degrees* render the original term *forma,* one sees the crux of Richard's view on the Humanity as present in the most advanced contemplation. In this passage, *forma* appears twice: first, there is *forma proponitur humilitatis Christi* — here Kirchberger proposes "image," whereas Dumeige has "modèle" ("l'âme se voit proposer comme modèle l'humilité du Christ"). Further on there is *forma humilitatis Christi ad quam conformare se debet*: in this case Kirchberger (inexplicably) changes "image" to "form," while Dumeige keeps "modèle" ("l'humilité du Christ qui sert de modèle dans lequel doit se couler quiconque veut ..."- notice how *conformare* passes into materialization). But both

---

[62] Ibid., 229-230; §42.
[63] Ibid., 230; §43. Philippians 2,5-8.

these words, "image" as well as "modèle," seem unsatisfactory here: their connotations are too visual. They seem to imply that the *forma* of the humility of Christ takes on a demonstrable shape. Both renderings of Richard's *forma* convey the impression that the mystic in question has something like a vision of Jesus which allows one to look at this image and to model oneself on it.

An initial general objection to this visual interpretation of *forma* is that it suggests a sort of return by the accomplished contemplative to a beginner's meditation on the figure of Jesus, with imitation of this Example. But surely this would be a very unlikely development from the passive "state" of the "liquefied" ecstatic? Is one supposed to progress from the third to the fourth degree of love by leaving behind the imageless and transforming experience of God?

Next, there are several more particular reasons why the *forma* of Richard need not be understood with reference to a representable and model figure.[64] Firstly, as was seen in Chapter 1, the biblical sense of "form"[65] in the Old Testament seems to suggest the contradictory concept of God's self-manifestation without any image whatsoever. Deuteronomy asserts that the people at the foot

[64] There is no need here to investigate the philosophical infrastructure of Richard's teaching. Suffice it to say that attention has been drawn more than once to his Platonism and Neoplatonism. Obviously, if he understood *forma* in this speculative perspective, there is little chance of it referring to the particularity of an image or of an observable model. For a discussion of the sense of "form" (*morphè*) in Philippians 2,5-8, see Joachim Gnilka, *Der Philipperbrief: Auslegung*, Herders theologischer Kommentar zum Neuen Testament X-3 (Freiburg: Herder, 1968) 111-114. It is interesting that the German translation does not use the word "Form." Instead, "in the form of God" is rendered as "in der Daseinsweise Gottes," and "took upon him the form of a servant" is rendered as "Sklavendasein annehmend." Incidentally in Paul's introductory phrase: "Let this (= Christ's) mind be in you" (2,5), "mind" in the sense of a person's disposition makes good sense with the injunction that one is to assume the "Dasein" of Jesus, i.e., his form of life.

[65] See chapter 1 of this study, the text corresponding to notes 14-20.

of Mount Horeb "saw no figure of any kind" (4,12 and 15), while Numbers declares, paradoxically enough, that Moses in his face-to-face encounter with God saw the "very form of the LORD" (12,8). As was shown above, the solution to this difficulty lies in the biblical concept of *kabod,* which evokes the force that emanates from a person. On this interpretation God's "form" is the radiating force of the divine Person.[66] Thus the LORD can be said to "show" his form without the intervention of any figure, to the point that the person who experiences this Presence, "far from looking at God's image, feels his form" (see Chapter 1).

Likewise, in Richard's fourth degree of love, it is God who shows himself *(proponitur)*, with this difference that here the experience of his Humanity completes the experience of his Divinity. Apparently this Humanity manifests itself in the "form of the humility of Christ," not Christ as instancing some observable act of humility, but as *being* sheer, unfathomable humility. But what does the contemplative perceive on entering upon the ultimate stage of spiritual development? The figure of the Man washing his disciples's feet? An image of Jesus dying on the cross? Even if such representations were to appear, they would be quite secondary to the core of the experience taking place at this point: the contemplative now realizes that the "state" into which one enters is nothing other than being actually identified with the Humanity. What has been brought about through the soul's "liquefaction" in the third degree of love — her "running down easily"', or in other words her "humbling herself spontaneously to be obedient in this way" — appears now, in the fourth degree, as a being "in-formed," "con-formed" with the "form of the humility of Christ," that is, with the Humanity.

---

[66] Understandably, some versions of Numbers 12,8 prefer "glory" instead of "form."

Yet another indication that Richard's *forma* is not to be identified with any representation appears in two passages evoking the soul's descent as it attains to the fourth degree of love. The first is the following:

> In the third (degree) the soul lifted up to God passes altogether into Him. In the fourth the soul goes forth on God's behalf and descends below herself.[67]

The second passage presents the descent of the accomplished contemplative as follows:

> Just as the goal to which he ascends by confidence is above man (*supra hominem*), so is the point to which he descends by patience beyond man (*ultra hominem*) ... in the third (degree the soul) passes out into God; in the fourth it descends below itself (*sub semetipsum*).[68]

Evidently, the humility of the mystic at the highest point of his experience is a continuous movement, and one that will never end. Being elevated to immeasurable heights is answered by a sinking away into unfathomable depths. This humility appears as a downward ecstasy: the soul descends "below herself," "beyond man." It becomes clear that the form of the humility of Christ is of the same incompehensible nature, for, as we have seen already, the mystic's descent consists in this form being impressed upon his consciousness. Consequently, there is no question here of the form of the humility of Christ being an image to be looked at and imitated. On the contrary, it is a spiritual act to be unimaginably assumed, and by the same token it appears how the Humanity can be present in perfect contemplation without involving any image-like hindrance to the immediacy of the mystic's experience of God.

To round off this brief encounter with Richard of Saint-Victor, the following quotation illustrates how he summarizes the

---

[67] Richard of Saint-Victor, *Selected Writings on Contemplation*, 224.
[68] Ibid., 232; §47.

paradoxical connection between the loftiness of the third degree and the lowliness of the fourth degree of love:

> Therefore in the third degree the soul is glorified, in the fourth she is humbled for God's sake. In the third she is conformed to the divine light, in the fourth she is conformed to the humility of Christ. And though in the third she is in a way almost in the likeness of God *(in forma Dei),* nevertheless in the fourth she begins to empty herself, taking the form of a servant and begins to be found in fashion as a man.[69]

Bonaventure: "(Francis) passed over into God in ecstatic contemplation"

With regard to Saint Francis of Assisi (1182-1226), the student of Christian mysticism cannot avoid a feeling of frustration. Although known to this day as an incomparably impressive and influential mystic, the founder of the Friars Minor did not leave behind a single piece of mystical writing. Admittedly, among the thirty odd texts dictated or written by him (in rather poor Latin) there are such documents as *The Earlier Rule,* the *Testament* and the (parchment) *Letter to Brother Leo,* that make the spiritual leader's voice heard. And in the *Canticle of Brother Sun,* which helped in the evolution of the Italian language away from Latin, the *Poverello* or "Little Poor Man" sings out his heart. However, this first-hand material is meagre indeed. No wonder, then, that leading authorities on Francis' spiritual way agree that his "greatest and proper work was his life," and that his "mysticism was not put into words but lived."[70]

---

[69] Ibid., 230; §44.

[70] Wolfram Von den Steinen, *Menschen im Mittelalter*, ed. Peter von Moos (Bern: Francke Verlag, 1967) 249; Kurt Ruh, "Zur Grundlegung einer Geschichte

Consequently our knowledge of the *via mystica*, "mystical way," of Francis has come to us through descriptions of his *vita mystica*, "mystical life," as presented by his first biographers.[71] However these *Vitae* fail to record in any strict sense their hero's mystical development. Instead devotional attitudes and ascetical practices intermingle with passive experiences of God, and of course a fair amount of legendary material is added to the complex spiritual elements. Yet this literary tangle does permit the reader to distinguish in the life at least the outlines of Francis' mystical way.[72] Basically this consists in the continuous imitation of Christ in order to attain to an increasingly intimate "conformation with Christ." The *conformitas Christi* is what Francis is aiming at throughout, from the moment when he "strips himself completely naked before all"[73] until, finally, on Mount Alverna, he experiences

der franziskanische Mystik," *Vita seraphica* 61 (1980) 3. See also Francis of Assisi; Clare of Assisi, *The Complete Works*, trans. Regis J. Armstrong, Ignatius Brady (New York: Paulist Press, 1982). In the "Introduction" to this work (p. 5), Regis Armstrong puts it this way: "His actions often spoke louder than his words. He delighted in dramatizing his responses to the actions or thoughts of his brothers or the ideals to which his heart clung. Indeed, the heart of Franciscan spirituality seems to be caught up in the mystery of the human person of Francis ... The Poverello left no lengthy Rule or expositions on the spiritual life; he provided no plan for spiritual exercises or methods of prayer. It is simply the person of Francis of Assisi that captures the heart ..."

[71] Francis' first biographers formed a medieval *vita* from the material gathered by the followers of Francis not long after he died. Thomas of Celano produced two such life stories and Julian of Speyer one.

[72] I borrow here from Kurt Ruh, "Zur Grundlegung einer Geschichte der franziskanische Mystik," (see above, note 71).

[73] This is how Bonaventure describes the initial scene in his *Life of St. Francis* (to which we shall return further on). And he interprets as follows: "Thus the servant of the Most High King was left naked so that he might follow his naked crucified Lord." See Bonaventure, *The Soul's Journey into God; The Tree of Life; The Life of St. Francis,* trans. Ewert Cousins (New York: Paulist Press, 1978) 194; ch. 2, §4. I shall quote Bonaventure from this translation.

Christ's crucifixion in his very own body and soul, so as to be "totally transformed into the likeness of Christ crucified."[74]

Obviously, when a mystic of the stature of Francis focuses so strongly on the *conformitas Christi*, that is, on Christ's form being impressed upon him, he deserves a place in this study, but even more so when this christocentrism is presented as being fully realized by way of "ecstatic contemplation" (on Mount Alverna). The writer who made that connection was none other than Saint Bonaventure (John Fidanza, 1217-1274).

Three features of Bonaventure's teaching on spirituality and mysticism deserve to be mentioned at this point. First, he was a university professor who "was and remained an intellectual of the Paris tradition";[75] thus not only was he informed about the main ideas of the *nobilissimus Plotinus*, but he was also steeped in the Christian tradition: "Grounding himself in Augustine and drawing from Anselm, he brought together the cosmic vision of the Pseudo-Dionysius with the psychological acumen of Bernard of Clairvaux and Richard of St. Victor."[76]

Secondly, for Bonaventure, ecstasy is perfect contemplation,[77] and it is highlighted as such. It is the "goal of all knowing and

---

[74] Bonaventure, *The Life of St. Francis*, 306; ch. 13, §3. Immediately before the vision on Alverna, Francis is made to understand that "just as he had imitated Christ in the actions of his life, so he should be conformed to him in the affliction and sorrow of his passion" (see p. 304; ch. 13, §2).

[75] Ewert Cousins, "Introduction," to Bonaventure, *The Soul's Journey into God; The Tree of Life; The Life of St. Francis*, 6.

[76] Ibid., 2.

[77] For a detailed explanation, see Titus Szabo, "Extase, B: Mystique chrétienne, IV: Chez les théologiens du 13e siècle," *Dictionnaire de spiritualité* IV/2 (1961) c. 2120-2126. Bonaventure mainly uses two expressions to indicate ecstasy: *excessus mentis* and *alienatio mentis*. He distinguishes "ecstasy," which plunges the human spirit into darkness, from "rapture," which brings about an anticipated beatific vision: *nec est idem ecstasis et raptus*. See col. 2124.

operating," and by means of it "one knows through real experience." So ecstasy comes to be presented as the "common rule"
(*lex communis*) of the spiritual life, that is, the normal acme of
prayer.[78] Thus, in *The Soul's Journey into God*, Bonaventure
asserts that on Mount Alverna, where Francis "passed over into
God in ecstatic contemplation, (he) became an example of perfect
contemplation ... so that through him, more by example than by
word, God might invite all truly spiritual men to this kind of passing over and spiritual ecstasy."[79]

A third feature of Bonaventure's view of contemplation is that
this highly appreciated scholar and organizer — he was the "second founder" of the Friars Minor, being their Minister General for
seventeen years — wanted to integrate faithfully the Poverello's
humble way with the high points of earlier spiritual tradition.

The main point at issue here is the way in which Bonaventure
combines ecstasy and the Christ-centered spiritual life of St Francis.
This can best be seen in *The Life of Saint Francis* (*Legenda
Maior*)[80] and *The Soul's Journey into God* (*Itinerarium mentis in
Deum*). In the *Life*, the phenomenon of ecstasy recurs constantly.
Quite early Bonaventure introduces the highly contemplative figure of brother Giles, who "was raised to the height of exalted contemplation ... and he was often rapt into God in ecstasy ... so that
he seemed to live among men more like an angel than a human

---

[78] Titus Szabo, "Extase; Chez les théologiens du 13ᵉ siècle,"c. 2125.

[79] Bonaventure, *The Soul's Journey into God,* 112-113; ch. 7, §3.

[80] Bonaventure took to writing this *Life* at the request of the General Chapter
of Narbonne in 1260. He completed it in 1263. The main purpose was to reduce
the trilogy of Thomas of Celano — First Life, Second Life and Miracles of
Francis — to "one good legend." So, Bonaventure composed his *Legenda
Major*, that is, the *Life of Saint Francis*. For the sense of 'legenda', see Cousins,
"Introduction," to Bonaventure, *The Soul's Journey into God*, 37-38. Bonaventure started writing down the *Itinerarium* in 1259, prior to the *Life*.

being."[81] As for Francis himself, his love for Christ is presented as essentially ecstatic. He "longed to be totally transformed into Jesus Christ crucified by the fire of ecstatic love." And when he received Holy Communion, "he was often rapt in ecstasy as if drunk in the spirit."[82] The most vivid description of Francis as an ecstatic is to be found in chapter 10 of the *Life*. Bonaventure first asserts that "many times he was lifted up in ecstatic contemplation so that, rapt out of himself ... he was unaware of what went on about him." Then he goes on to report what happened to Francis in Borgo San Sepulcro — his ecstasy seemed to turn him into "a lifeless corpse" — and he concludes: "That this happened to him often was confirmed by the repeated experience of his companions."[83]

But before turning to the penultimate chapter of the *Life*, where the ecstatic tendency culminates, if only to coincide with the figure of the Crucified, a counter-tendency has to be borne in mind. Bonaventure's emphasis on ecstasy does not entail that he portrays the Poverello as solely rapt to the angelic heights. For example, just before describing the spectacular ecstasy in Borgo San Sepulcro, he reports that the founder used to show his friars how "to be zealous in prayer":

> For whether walking or sitting, inside or outside, working or resting, he was so intent on prayer that he seemed to have dedicated to it not only his heart and body but also all his effort and time.[84]

Clearly Francis is shown here as favoured with the gift of continuous prayer, but this prayer appears to consist of different

---

[81] Bonaventure, *The Life of St. Francis*, 201; ch. 3, §4. This is part of the new material Bonaventure added to the work of Thomas of Celano and Julian of Speyer. See Cousins, "Introduction," to Bonaventure, *The Soul's Journey into God*, 39 n. 74.

[82] Ibid., 263-264; ch. 9, §2.

[83] Ibid., 273-274; ch. 10, §2.

[84] Ibid., 273; ch. 10, §1.

moments, that is, of different manners of being in close touch with God. It is not as if Francis was elevated all the time in ecstatic contemplation, because, among other things, he was "working." One wonders whether the activities of the Poverello's life indicated by "walking," "being outside," "working," were or were not included in his contemplative experience. Did they not belong to his perfection? And if they did, what was the link that made his continuous but diverse prayer into an organic whole?

Two chapters later in the *Life*, the same issue — whether and how the "opposites coincide" in the accomplished contemplative's experience[85] — is presented with narrative power. Francis is shown as struggling with a problem he proposes to his friars for resolution: "What do you judge better? That I should spend my time in prayer or that I should go about preaching?" And Bonaventure goes on to present Francis as describing prayer in this way:

> Finally, in prayer we address God, listen to him and dwell among the angels as if we were living an angelic life; in preaching we must think, see, say and hear human things adapting ourselves to them as if we were living on a human level, for men and among men.[86]

The opposing claims of action and contemplation appear in the typical fashion already familiar from earlier presentations of the ecstatic view of contemplation. Once again the question arises

---

[85] The "coincidence of opposites" is recognized as essential to Bonaventure's mentality: "It permeates all his thought: his philosophy, theology and spirituality." And "the coincidence of opposites is found ... throughout his thought and can be seen graphically in his interpretation of Francis as the humble, simple poor man who is wondrously exalted by God." (See Cousins, "Introduction," to Bonaventure, *The Soul's Journey into God*, 17-18, 22). Could Bonaventure have failed to be aware of the coincidence of opposites in the case of working/resting in contemplation? One might also ask if this "exaltation" of the "humble" one should be considered the "coincidence" or rather the disappearance of opposites.

[86] Bonaventure, *The Life of St. Francis*, 291-292; ch. 12, §1.

whether there is a solution to this conflict between the longed-for angelic, and the burdensome human, condition. Francis knew, by reflecting upon Christ who in fact went through all those human experiences, what option to take: "I interrupt my quiet and go out to labor."[87]

However, Bonaventure's *Life of St Francis* does not seem to clarify the issue it raises: must the perfect contemplative's life be divided into two, the active and the contemplative life? And yet Bonaventure is quoted as saying in a sermon: "The part of those who are active is good, that of contemplatives better, but the best is that which has both together."[88]

It is appropriate now to consider how Bonaventure rounds off his presentation of Francis as the exemplary contemplative (*Life*, chapter 13 "On the sacred stigmata"). Once again the Poverello is introduced as "dividing" his time so that "he expended part of it in working for his neighbor's benefit and devoted the other part to the peaceful ecstasy of contemplation."[89] Then Bonaventure relates what happened to Francis when he had retired for a long period of prayer on Mount Alverna:

> On a certain morning about the feast of the Exaltation of the Cross,[90] while Francis was praying on the mountainside, he saw a Seraph with six fiery and shining wings descend from the height of heaven. And when in swift flight the Seraph had reached the spot in the air near the man of God, there appeared between the wings the figure of a man crucified, with his hands and feet extended in the form of a cross and fastened to a cross. Two of the wings were lifted above his head, two were extended for flight and two covered his whole body.

---

[87] Ibid., 293; ch. 12, §1.

[88] "Bona est pars activorum, melior contemplativorum, sed optima, quae habuit utrumque simul." (Sermon 6, *De Assumptione Beatae Mariae Virginis*).

[89] Bonaventure, *The Life of St. Francis*, 303; ch. 13, §1.

[90] September 14, 1224.

> When Francis saw this, he was overwhelmed and his heart was flooded with a mixture of joy and sorrow. He rejoiced because of the gracious way Christ looked upon him under the appearance of the Seraph, but the fact that he was fastened to a cross pierced his soul with a sword of compassionate sorrow.[91]

This passage in the *Life of St. Francis* may well surprise one. At the high point of this ecstatic contemplative's development there is a visionary experience. The person shown so far as exemplary in prayer because of his going beyond anything particular finally appears to be seeing things and trembling with emotion. The Unseen has taken the liberty of making himself visible as Christ: "Christ looked upon him under the appearance of a Seraph."

What is most striking in this visionary scene is the presence of contrasting elements: the sharp particularity of the "figure of a man crucified" clashes with the vague elusiveness of "a Seraph," while the fettered hands and feet of the man painfully conflict with the freely flying wings of the Seraph. It is precisely this contrast that evokes in the visionary's heart "a mixture of joy and sorrow." As Bonaventure explains "so unfathomable a vision":

> The weakness of Christ's passion was in no way compatible with the immortality of the Seraph's spiritual nature.[92]

And he states that the purpose of this imaginative experience was

> that (Francis) was to be totally transformed into the likeness of Christ crucified, not by the martyrdom of his flesh, but by the fire of his love consuming his soul."[93]

[91] Bonaventure, *The Life of St. Francis*, 305; ch. 13, §3. This vision — in Celano's version — was mentioned above. See chapter 2, note 5.

[92] Further on, Bonaventure puts it this way: "You were shown at the same time the sublime vision of the Seraph and the humble figure of the Crucified, inwardly inflaming you and outwardly marking you." (See Bonaventure, *The Life of St. Francis*, 313; ch. 13, §10).

[93] Ibid., 306; ch. 13, §3. And this is how the meaning of the vision came to be realized: "When the true love of Christ had transformed his lover into his

In his *Life of St. Francis*, Bonaventure succeeds in uniting the mystical way of Francis with the earlier spiritual tradition by presenting a christocentric view of ecstasy, and he will have more to say on this in *The Soul's Journey into God*. But first the end of the Alverna story deserves attention: "The angelic man Francis came down from the mountain, bearing with him the image of the Crucified, which was ... engraved in the members of his body."[94] One wonders what happened to the perfection of Francis' contemplation after he had descended from the ecstatic heights.

The occasion for Bonaventure's composition of *The Soul's Journey into God* is significant. In September-October 1259, the seventh Minister General of the Franciscan order went on a kind of pilgrimage to Mount Alverna in order to meditate on what had happened there to the founder some thirty-five years earlier. Evidently, Bonaventure was "searching out his Franciscan roots." He felt the need to face "Francis' ideal, both for his own life and for guiding the Order in its difficult attempt to embody this ideal."[95]

Bonaventure must have been particularly sensitive to the distance that separated Francis from his followers with regard to their contemplative experience: in fact the individual "mystical way" *(via mystica)* of the Poverello, with its climax in the vision and stigmatization of Alverna, was quite inimitable. Even the "mystical life" *(vita mystica)* modelled by the first biographers on Francis' original way had proved too personal to multiply. It was

image and the forty days were over" (p. 307). The "consuming of the soul" *(incendium mentis)* not only affected the heart but also the body in the form of Francis' stigmata: "As the vision disappeared, it left in his heart a marvelous ardor and imprinted on his body markings that were no less marvelous. Immediately the marks of nails began to appear in his hands and feet just as he had seen a little before in the figure of the man crucified" (p. 306, §3).

[94] Ibid., 307; ch. 13, §5.

[95] Cousins, "Introduction," to Bonaventure, *The Soul's Journey into God*, 19.

a clear insight into this problem that came to Bonaventure as he reflected on Francis' vision of the six-winged Seraph in the form of the Crucified. He feels called upon to transform Francis' mystical "way" into a mystical "theology," and to show a teachable Franciscan way to those who in fact are not Francis and never will be. Such is the intuition embodied in *The Soul's Journey*. The author recalls his sudden inspiration as follows:

> While reflecting on this (Francis' vision), I saw at once that this vision represented our father's rapture in contemplation and the road by which this rapture is reached.[96]

These words imply that the mystical theologian is about to process the experience of the mystical Poverello in a speculative way.[97] The original Christ-centered vision is now seen as "symbolizing" that to which every person intent on contemplation can attain:

> The six wings of the Seraph can rightly be taken to symbolize the six levels of illumination by which, as if by steps or stages, the soul can pass over to peace through ecstatic elevations of Christian wisdom.[98]

Thus, Bonaventure's reading of the Seraph becomes a proposal for a program of six meditations that are supposed to lead readers gradually up to the summit of ecstatic experience.[99]

Clearly, in *The Soul's Journey*, Bonaventure appears predominantly as the speculative thinker displaying his capacity to draw on different philosophical and theological sources. Indeed, no less a scholar than Emile Bréhier concluded that Bonaventure's

---

[96] Bonaventure, *The Soul's Journey into God*, 54; Prologue, §2.

[97] Bonaventure used to designate the Franciscans as "*speculativi*" and Francis as "*ecstaticus*".

[98] Bonaventure, *The Soul's Journey into God*, 54; Prologue, §3.

[99] This aspect of *The Souls' Journey* has been highlighted by Kurt Ruh in his "Zur Grundlegung" (see above, note 71).

"itinerary" is Platonic and more particularly Plotinian: the conversion away from things, first to self, then to things divine, and finally up to ecstasy, "and this way has been adopted by Christianity, not discovered."[100] Such a criticism has been proved to be too severe, but it does shed light on a crucial point. This masterpiece of Christian spiritual writing is pervaded with pagan as well as christianized (Neo)platonism, so that Duméry, while appreciating Bonaventure's creative power, considers his thought to be "Pseudo-Dionysian, Neoplatonic by its sense of transcendence, its theory of the image or the vestige, which replaces that of participation." Thus, the *Journey* can be seen to be "a mixture of philosophy and mysticism,"[101] and therefore it comes as no surprise to find the centuries-old theme of ecstasy strongly revived in this spiritual itinerary, summarized as follows:

> The *homo viator,* the Christian, sets out on his journey by the act of faith; he goes on by the meditation of the philosopher, by the considerations of the theologian; he achieves his course by the ecstasy of the mystic.[102]

---

[100] Quoted in Saint Bonaventure, *Itinéraire de l'Esprit vers Dieu,* trans. Henry Duméry (Paris: J. Vrin, 1978) 15 n. 17. Duméry reacts to Brehier's statement by asserting that "here 'adoption' was a re-creation."

[101] Henry Duméry, "Introduction" to Bonaventure, *Itinéraire de l'Esprit vers Dieu,* 13, 10. See, for instance, chapter 7, §5, where Bonaventure inserts a passage from Dionysius, *De Mystica Theologia.* For a thorough discussion of the philosophical, especially the Neoplatonic, elements in the *Journey,* see Werner Beierwaltes, *Denken des Einen: Studien zur Neoplatonischen Philosophie und Ihre Wirkungsgeschichte* (Frankfurt am Main: Vittorio Klostermann, 1985). See especially "Aufstieg und Einung in Bonaventuras 'Itinerarium'." Beierwaltes also gives a detailed exposition of Bonaventure's use of the "coincidence of opposites" (see pp. 410 ff, especially p. 414, where Beierwaltes points out how the *coincidentia oppositorum* "culminates in a christological ... reflection: Christ is the unity of opposites par excellence").

[102] Duméry, "Introduction" to Bonaventure, *Itinéraire de l'Esprit vers Dieu,* 11.

Duméry rightly claims that *The Soul's Journey* was meant to present the Christian contemplative way. However important Bonaventure's speculative-ecstatic interests, there is no doubt that the keynote of this work is Christian and, moreover, Franciscan, which amounts to saying that the *Journey* is intended as a Christocentric spiritual program. From the outset, Bonaventure shows his fidelity as a Franciscan teacher: "except through the Crucified," there is no entering upon "divine contemplation that leads to mystical ecstasy."[103] One can hardly imagine a more christological prelude, and yet it is especially in the final chapter of the *Journey* that Bonaventure makes his unwavering dedication to the Godman abundantly clear. There he asserts that the ecstatic climax of the entire itinerary is solely to be reached through Jesus Christ, the Mediator. Christ is not only the "way" and the "door," but the achievement: he is the one who — as the Mercy Seat — stands at the end of the mystical path, at the point where all sensing and thinking falters:

---

[103] Bonaventure, *The Soul's Journey into God*, 55 (Prologue), §3. The whole passage deserves to be quoted: "The six wings of the Seraph, therefore, symbolize the six steps of illumination that begin from creatures and lead up to God, whom no one rightly enters except through the Crucified. For *he who enters not through the door, but climbs up another way is a thief and a robber.* But *if anyone enter* through this door, *he will go in and out and will find pastures* (John 10,1-9). Therefore John says in the Apocalypse: *Blessed are they who wash their robes in the blood of the Lamb that they may have a right to the tree of life and may enter the city through the gates* (Apoc. 22,14). It is as if John were saying that no one can enter the heavenly Jerusalem by contemplation unless he enter through the blood of the Lamb as through a door. For no one is in any way disposed for divine contemplation that leads to mystical ecstasy unless like Daniel he is *a man of desires* (Dan. 9,23). Such desires are enkindled in us in two ways: by an outcry of prayer that makes us *call aloud in the groaning of our heart* (Ps. 37,9) and by the flash of insight by which the mind turns most directly and intently toward the rays of light."

> It now remains for our mind ... to transcend and pass over not only this sense world but even itself. In this passing over, Christ is the way and the door; Christ is the ladder and the vehicle, like the Mercy Seat placed above the ark of God.[104]

Given the scope of this inquiry into the position of the Humanity in mystical contemplation, the last chapter of *The Soul's Journey* deserves special attention. For this is where the strong emphasis on ecstasy as the final goal of the journey has to be reconciled with the conviction that the experience of the Crucified constitutes its completion. A long-standing and broad-based spiritual tradition is supposed to harmonize with the fresh mystical event on Mount Alverna. Obviously this raises a problem. If the contemplative's perfection involves ecstasy, it seems quite impossible that there should also be any perception of the Godman. The ecstatic "passing over into God" is due to the "height of our affection" being "totally transferred and transformed into God." Therefore, contemplation, strictly speaking, is something that happens to the undivided core of the soul, beyond the range of its faculties: "all intellectual faculties must be left behind." This experience of God must be utterly passive and image-less,[105] and consequently one presumes that it must also be at the expense of Jesus, even if the *Journey* can culminate in focusing on Christ. The task now will be to trace both the ecstatic and the christological threads in the finale of *The Soul's Journey* and to see to what extent Bonaventure succeeds in intertwining them.

The suggestion that the entire itinerary ought to lead to ecstasy returns almost obsessively. For example, chapter six ends as follows:

---

[104] Ibid., 111; ch. 7, § 1. For the "Mercy Seat" — the "*propiciatorium* ," the "cover of reconciliation" — see Exodus 25,21: "It is there that I shall meet you" says the LORD.

[105] Ibid., 113; ch. 7, §4.

> Nor does anything more remain except the day of rest on which through mystical ecstasy the mind's discernment comes to rest from all the work which it has done.

Here "rest" is used as a synonym for "ecstasy": there is a terminus to the journey that yields undisturbed peace and quiet. In chapter seven it is confirmed again and again that "ecstasy" and "rest" go together; thus, when the soul has passed through the previous six considerations, "we arrive at peace, where the true man of peace rests in a peaceful mind as in the interior Jerusalem." And, at last, the mind "may reach the sabbath of rest."[106]

But there is a still quieter rest than rest, viz. death, a variation on the theme of rest which appears in the next paragraph. Yet here, for the first time, the contemplative's ecstasy is presented as a Christ-experience: "and with Christ he rests in the tomb, as if dead to the outer world." This restful dying with Christ is bliss, for by now this person is "experiencing ... what was said on the cross to the thief who adhered to Christ: *Today, you shall be with me in paradise.*"[107] In this way, the two crucial elements of the *Journey's* ending are quietly made to converge and, in the masterly passage that crowns Bonaventure's work, they are fused together:

> Whoever loves this death can see God because it is true beyond doubt that *man will not see me and live.* Let us, then, die and enter into the darkness; let us impose silence upon our cares, our desires and our imaginings. With Christ crucified let us pass *out of this world to the Father* so that when the Father is shown to us, we may say with Philip: *It is enough for us.*[108]

---

[106] Ibid., 110; ch. 7, § 1. Already in the first paragraph of the Prologue, Francis' sense of peace is placed in the perspective of ecstasy: "At the beginning and end of every sermon he announced peace; in every greeting he wished for peace; in every contemplation he sighed for ecstatic peace" (p. 53).

[107] Ibid., 111, ch. 7, §2.

[108] Ibid., 116; ch. 7, §6. Bonaventure quotes Exodus 33,20; John 13,1 and 14,8.

One has to recognize that Bonaventure has succeeded in christianizing the soul's ecstasy-oriented journey. The contemplative's experience of passing out of this world and over into God is understood as the communion with Christ crucified. Mystical ecstasy now appears as a person's partaking of the Person who, *being* the Son, *is* ecstasy throughout. Christ's existence has concretized spiritual ecstasy without in any way arresting its transcending drive: the Godman is tangibly the "passover."[109] In the inconceivable figure of the Crucified, the contemplative experience of the human mind's "dying" rides to anchor.

This christological presentation of perfect contemplation may be most enlightening, but so far it leaves the Humanity in the shadows. Admittedly, an important passage of the final chapter of *The Soul's Journey* remains to be considered. It is the description of Francis' experience on Mount Alverna: the revelation of paradise made by Christ to the good thief[110] has also been made to Francis; in his case, however, "paradise" has been realized already in this life by way of ecstasy, Christ-centered ecstasy; and this was the exact moment when Francis passed over into God:

> *Today you shall be with me in paradise.* This was shown also to blessed Francis, when in ecstatic contemplation on the height of the mountain — where I thought out these things I have written — there appeared to him a six-winged Seraph fastened to a cross, as I and several brothers heard in that very place from his companion who was with him then. There he passed over into God in ecstatic contemplation.[111]

But evidently even in this description the Humanity of Jesus does not get a place. Bonaventure's christianizing ecstasy seems to fall

---

[109] Ibid., 112; ch. 7, §2.
[110] See above, note 107.
[111] Bonaventure, *The Soul's Journey into God*, 112; ch. 7, §2-3.

short of humanizing it. And this rather frustrating conclusion is confirmed by the way in which (at long last!) he connects Francis' "perfect contemplation" with the rest of his life as a man: he "became an example of perfect contemplation as he had previously been of action." The preponderance of contemplation (being with Christ "on the height of the mountain") over action (being "conformed" with Jesus in the lowliness of daily life) is striking. And consequently the connection between these two aspects of a person's spiritual life can be understood at best as a succession of opposites, not as their coincidence. At the end of Bonaventure's *Life of St. Francis* we are told that "the angelic man Francis came down from the mountain." The vision on Mount Alverna happened in 1224 and Francis died in 1226. One is left with the question: how did the Poverello — the accomplished contemplative — live out the non-ecstatic aspects of his life, after he had "come down"?[112]

Concluding Reflections

The results of this examination of three leading figures in medieval spiritual literature with regard to the role of the Humanity are not very satisfying. The representative texts considered

---

[112] The point being made here surfaces in the following comment: "While *The Soul's Journey* contains significant Christological material, the emphasis is on the mystical Christ, who as the crucified figure in the midst of the Seraph's wings is the gateway and door into mystical consciousness ... In *The Soul's Journey* we do not find the human Christ, the historical Jesus as described in the Gospels, who was born humble and poor in a manger, who wandered about preaching and healing, who suffered and died on Calvary, with his body bleeding and broken ... This picture, however, is presented in *The Tree of Life*, where Bonaventure meditates on Christ in the concrete details of his life as a man." See Cousins, "Introduction," to Bonaventure, *The Soul's Journey into God*, 13-14.

show Bernard and Francis, both known as champions of the God-man, apparently unable to integrate the felt presence of the Man with their mystical experience of God.[113] However Christ-centered the spirituality of Bernard and Francis may be, when all is said and done the prominence of ecstasy eclipses the Humanity. As for Richard of St. Victor, known as an exponent of the ecstatic tendency, he is the one who at least shows the possibility for the Humanity to be present in the highest contemplation. In his view, the third degree of love, that makes the mystic ascend ecstatically into the divine, is to be brought to completion by the fourth degree that has the mystic descend into the human.

Does this conclusion mean that medieval spiritual literature lacks writings that show in a plausible way how the Humanity can actually be part and parcel even of the most advanced mystical experience? And, moreover, is Christian mysticism as such doomed to remain on the thorns of the dilemma Ecstasy-Humanity? In reply to this last question, the outlines of an interesting post-medieval development can be mentioned here, even if not discussed in detail. It concerns two complementary points.

---

[113] One must always beware of a common misunderstanding in reading mystical texts. The enterprise has much in common with that of anyone engaged in research on writings supposed to reflect human, and in particular personal, experience. On the one hand, one has to acknowledge that — at least in a text like Bernard's *Sermons on the Song of Songs* — the expression is integral to the experience: a pure, language-free experience is not a human experience. On the other hand, one has to remember that one can never grasp the full actuality of the (spiritual) life represented, however carefully one may try to read a text. At times one may forget that, as the French put it so well, "la realité dépasse la fiction." In this particular case we should not jump to the conclusion, after considering the *Sermons* or *The Soul's Journey into God,* that the spiritual life of Bernard and Francis split into active and contemplative moments, or that in their prayer Christ became actually detached from Jesus. What one can say, however, is that the texts describing their experiences do not show the coincidence of the Divinity and the Humanity as mystically perceptible.

On the one hand, writers began to prune descriptions of ecstasy of certain alienating psychosomatic elements. As has already been shown,[114] Gregory of Nyssa († 394), was the first Christian mystical author to concentrate without reticence on ecstasy as part of a person's religious experience. He was careful to relativize the function of psychological ecstasy, which he considered to be an occasional epiphenomenon that in itself lacks religious significance. For Gregory the primary sense of ecstasy is ontological: the human creature receives existence continuously from the Creator, so that for a human being *to be* is already *to be beyond* oneself. With regard to the second, contemplative sense of ecstasy (based on the first), Gregory emphasizes that ecstasy is the spiritual event of God's presence, while acknowledging that it may have psychological repercussions. This critical appraisal of the visible and tangible — not to say spectacular — aspect of ecstasy, did not always prevail through the centuries. Especially from the fourteenth century onwards, growing importance is attached to perceptible elements.[115] And this tendency continues to increase, reaching its peak in the sixteenth and seventeenth centuries. By then, "when one mentions ecstasy, one thinks less of a particular degree of the spiritual life ... than of an extraordinary phenomenon which is at once psychological and supernatural."[116] However, this is also the period when a reaction began to set in, recuperating Gregory of Nyssa's thoughtful approach to ecstasy. By the seventeenth century, "theologians and the majority of the authentic contemplatives grow cautious and come to feel suspicious

---

[114] See above, at note 8.

[115] See Szabo, "Extase: Chez les théologiens du 13e siècle," c. 2131; Baumgartner, "Extase," c. 2136-2137.

[116] Ibid., col. 2138. Teresa of Avila is mentioned here as an exception to this rule. For more information about Teresa's experience and interpretation of ecstasy, see col. 2151-2160.

about this phenomenon and the vocabulary it is accompanied by."[117]

On the other hand, while the exterior and ephemeral facets of ecstasy are being relativized, there also emerges a more comprehensive concept of ecstasy. If the essence of ecstasy consists in going beyond oneself, and consciously so, there is no reason to restrict the soul's outgoing to her upward movement into the divine. Ecstasy may be just as well a matter of leaving one's self by descending into the human.

The first significant figure who should be mentioned at this point is the Italian Jesuit Achille Gagliardi (1537/8-1607). In his most influential work, known as the *Brief Compendium*,[118] the double development — both pruning and broadening the concept of ecstasy — is very striking. On the one hand, Gagliardi strongly advocates the *estasi pratica,* which concerns the will and thus covers all aspects of a person's life. On the other hand, he is suspicious of the ecstasy that may occur in contemplation and mainly concerns the intellect: this kind of ecstasy is "dangerous ... and full of occasions for curiosity and possessiveness (*proprietà*)."[119] According to Gagliardi, the contemplative's desolation — "deprivation of the divine help" — is a "lively and eminent imitation of Christ our Lord."[120] This lack of the felt presence of

---

[117] Ibid., col. 2138.

[118] First published in French in 1591, the *Breve Compendio* did not appear in Italian before 1611. It was particularly influential in the French spiritual literature of the seventeenth and eighteenth centuries. It is greatly indebted for its sources to the Flemish mystical authors of the fourteenth and the fifteenth centuries.

[119] Achille Gagliardi S.J., *Breve compendio di perfectione cristiana e "vita di Isabella Berinzaga"* (Florence: Libreria Editrice Fiorentina, 1952) 97.

[120] Ibid., 87: "sottrazione del concorso divino"; "e una viva et alta imitatione di Cristo nostro Signore."

God is "to suffer the divine more certainly than when in ecstasy."[121]

Next there is Francis of Sales (1567-1622), champion of the "ecstasy of action," which appears in one's "work" and comes about by one's "operation,"[122] and a few decades later, also writing in French but in Quebec, the Ursuline Marie de l'Incarnation (1599-1672); she distinguishes ecstasy, strictly speaking, from the subsequent "ecstatic condition" which may last for months and even for years. This is a selfless disposition which does not entail any abstraction from the senses while implying a renewed willingness to practise the virtues and perform works of charity. Here Marie's experience ties in with the "ecstasy of action" of Francis of Sales. She even gives preference to this embodiment of ecstasy: her sisters "should look for and desire these ecstasies of actions, and not the ones that have appeared in the prayers of some saintly souls."[123] This broadening of the notion of ecstasy so as to extend to the human world allows for the Humanity to be really integral to the accomplished contemplative's experience.

It appears then that the sense of ecstasy did develop after the medieval period and thus allow for the Humanity to have its proper place in mystical experience. But what is one to say about the contemporaries and immediate successors of Richard, Bernard and Bonaventure? The following chapters will show that the issue of the Humanity in Christian mystical experience was clarified most convincingly in the thirteenth and fourteenth centuries by the two leading figures in the Flemish tradition: Hadewijch and Jan van Ruusbroec. But here, by way of concluding this chapter, some

---

[121] Ibid., 91: "questo è patir divino, più sicuro, che con estasi." — See also p. 97: "what those mystics call *pati divina*."

[122] See Baumgartner, "Extase," c. 2143: "extase de l'action, (qui est) en l'oeuvre (et) se fait par l'opération."

[123] Ibid., c. 2147.

words of the great medieval English master, author of *The Cloud of Unknowing,* deserve to be quoted as he explains what is for him the "perfection" of the contemplative "exercice" or "work":

> Some people believe that this work is so difficult and awesome ... that it can be achieved only very seldom, and this during the time of rapture ... But there are some who are so refined by grace and in spirit, and so familiar with God in this grace of contemplation, that they may have the perfection of it whenever they will, in their ordinary state of soul: whether they are sitting, walking, standing or kneeling. And at the same time they have the full command of all their faculties, bodily and spiritual, and can use them if they so wish: not without a certain hindrance, but one not hard to overcome.[124]

[124] *The Cloud of Unknowing,* ed. James Walsh (New York: Paulist Press, 1981) 257-258; ch. 71.

CHAPTER IV

HADEWIJCH:
"TASTING MAN AND GOD IN ONE KNOWLEDGE"

So far we have not been very successful in finding a mystical account that establishes unmistakably that the Humanity is integral throughout to the experience of God. Admittedly, in Chapter 2 it was shown from Julian of Norwich that even a strong sensory appearance of the Passion need not be a hindrance to a mystic experiencing simultaneously the presence of the Divinity. And Maria Petyt made us appreciate how she was able to perceive in an imageless way the presence of the suffering Man. However, in Chapter 2 we also had to admit that the great Teresa of Avila, so well known for her Christ-centered mysticism, did not succeed in explaining how the experience of the Humanity is part and parcel of what she calls "perfect contemplation": she failed to satisfy our expectations. In Chapter 3, we found that this was also the case with two other renowned mystical champions of the God-man: Bernard of Clairvaux, in his *Sermons on the Song of Songs*, and Francis of Assisi, as presented in Bonaventure's *Life of St. Francis* and *The Soul's Journey into God*. Both appear to have been misled into giving excessive importance to "ecstasy," which prevented them from giving the Humanity the place, which they admitted it deserves, in the experience of the accomplished mystic. But Chapter 3 also brought the good news that Richard of Saint-Victor, who seems initially to have thought of ecstasy as the perfection of contemplation, later left a remarkable piece of Jesus-centred mystical writing in his *Four Degrees of Passionate Charity*.

He shows how one attains to the height of contemplation of the divine by finally descending into the human, while "the image of the humility of Christ is set before the eyes."

The overall impression may be that the scrutiny of mystical works in search of the Humanity does not yield a definite solution to the riddle of Christian mystical experience. But this would be premature: many significant texts concerned with the role of the Humanity in mystical experience remain to be considered, in particular, what is probably the richest and most illuminating source, Flemish mystical literature.[1] In the first place, the work of a mysterious female figure, Hadewijch, deserves our attention. This will allow us to consider the question of the Humanity from a fresh point of view. Although she was herself a visionary and ecstatic, she does not focus primarily on the problem of images, visions and ecstasy. Instead she draws attention in the first place to what she sees as the distinguishing mark of mystic union, and then from that basis she provides a solution to the "riddle."

Hadewijch: a highly educated beguine[2]

A great deal of mystery surrounds the figure of Hadewijch, as no hard historical evidence is available about her. Lacking any

---

[1] It is good here to note that the term "Flemish" means in fact "Brabantine." So-called "Flemish" mysticism appeared in the medieval duchy of Brabant which was much larger than the modern Belgian province of Brabant: it stretched from 's Hertogenbosch (nowadays in the Netherlands) as far as Nivelles (nowadays in the French-speaking part of Belgium) and thus included such cities as Antwerp, Mechelen (Malines), Louvain and Brussels. This Brabantine mysticism flourished from the thirteenth till the sixteenth-seventeenth centuries and, obviously, has to be distinguished from Rhineland mysticism. Its most prominent figures are Hadewijch (thirteenth century) and Jan van Ruusbroec (fourteenth century).

[2] For an extensive treatment of the historical and mystical aspects of Hadewijch, see Paul Mommaers, *Hadewijch: Schrijfster-Begijn-Mystica* (Averbode: Altiora, 1989).

definite information regarding the date or place of her birth and death, one has to make educated guesses about the place or region where she lived. Her literary output, which was known and highly appreciated by Ruusbroec and his companions in the fourteenth century, disappeared later on, until it was rediscovered in 1838 in the Royal Library of Brussels. Thus, all that we know about the historical Hadewijch has to be gathered from indications in her writings and from information now available about the socio-cultural context. At present there are reasons to assume that Hadewijch lived in Brabant in the middle of the thirteenth century.

Despite the gaps in our knowledge it is clear that three talents were strongly blended in this probably noble lady: she appears to have been at once a creative writer, a leading beguine, and an original mystic. As a prose writer, Hadewijch left her *Letters* and the *Visions*, as a poet, *Poems in Stanzas* and the *Poems in Couplets*. Especially in the *Poems in Stanzas* the author shows herself to be a woman of culture. On the one hand, she successfully transfers the poetic techniques of the French troubadours, with all their refinement and complication, into her native Brabantine language. On the other hand, she takes up the main themes of courtly love lyrics, but reshapes them according to her own mystical experience. The basic theme of those southern singers of love was that a man's real, that is, unremitting love for his *domna,* "mistress," consists in his desiring her without this desire ever being satisfied.[3] Evidently, this could produce startling expressions of the experience of the transcendence of the beloved. And among the passages from Hadewijch's work that leave a lasting impression, there are precisely those where she describes her ceaselessly renewed desire for the Beloved. However, there is a substantial difference here

---

[3] This is why they felt that love and marriage cannot coexist: "Entre mari et femme le véritable amour est impossible," as Marie de Champagne is supposed to have declared in 1174.

between her desire and the unending desire of courtly love. For the troubadours "otherness" makes itself felt in the absence of the human beloved and/or her remaining at a distance: *Amor de lonh,* "Love from afar." Hadewijch experiences Otherness in the inexhaustible presence of the divine Beloved. So, in place of the high but frustrated desire of the troubadour, the desire of the mystic is one that comes to be fully satisfied without ever being fulfilled.[4]

In addition to being steeped in courtly culture, Hadewijch had learning as well.[5] She could deal with theologians and spiritual authors who obviously wrote in Latin, in the same way as she did with the troubadours. The best ascertainable evidence of this is the translation she made of a text of William of Saint-Thierry. She renders the original correctly while managing to incorporate it into her own mystical thought.[6] But the most impressive proof of Hadewlijch's intellectual capacity is to be found in her eighth *Vision.* Here she presents on the visionary scene a "fighting cock"

---

[4] *Begherte,* "desire" is a key word for Hadewijch. For a thorough study of this theme, see Rob Faesen, *Begeerte in het werk van Hadewijch* (Louvain: Peeters, 2000).

[5] In Hadewijch's time a woman was by definition officially considered unlettered. So much so that there came to exist a most paradoxical cultural phenomenon: the "Illiteraten Literatur," as Herbert Grundmann has named it. See chapter 2 of this study, note 4.

[6] William of Saint-Thierry was from Liège (Belgium), but went to live in France, first as a Benedictine, later as a Cistercian. He was a close friend of Bernard of Clairvaux and a very influential author. Brabant mysticism took up some of his mystical themes such as "love itself is knowledge" (*amor ipse notitia est*). The passage in question is about the "two eyes of the loving soul: love and reason." Hadewijch's translation appears in Hadewijch, *The Complete Works,* trans. Mother Columba Hart, The Classics of Western Spirituality (New York: Paulist Press, 1980) All references to Hadewijch will be taken from *The Complete Works.* Hereafter cited as CW. References to *The Complete Works* will identify the source from which the quotation is drawn. In this case, the text is taken from CW: *Letter* 18, lines 80-129.

(kimpe), viz., a scholastic "champion" of the spiritual life. She may well have had in mind no less a person than Abelard (1079-1142), who had become famous as the irrefutable master of a new, rational theology, based on Aristotelian principles.[7] The conclusion of Abelard's line of thought, "following the strict counsel of the intellect," as Hadewijch describes her champion's reflection, was that the real union between God and humanity appeared to be absolutely impossible, sheer wishful thinking for men and women endowed with feeling. Clearly, the contrast between Abelard's theological theory, which presented God as utterly unreachable, and the religious experience of his mystical contemporaries could hardly have been more blatant. No wonder, then, that a violent conflict developed between, on the one hand, Bernard of Clairvaux and William of Saint-Thierry, and on the other, Abelard and his followers. Hadewijch entered this debate, which had been persistent, almost a century later and in her own style. In her eighth *Vision* she presents the champion as the spiritual guide who had been able to lead her "upward," climbing the mountain of mystical experience, "and yet not to the end." Although he could travel up that mountain along the first four ways, he could not reach the fifth and highest way. And with considerable cunning, the mystic, the woman of affection, brings on the thinker, the lucid man, to explain in person the reason why:

> But the Beloved gave you (Hadewijch) the fifth way; you have received it where I am not. For when I lived as man, I had too little love with affection, and followed the strict counsel of the intellect. For this reason I could not be set on fire with the love that creates such a great oneness, for I did the noble Humanity great wrong, in that I withheld from it this affection (115-122).

---

[7] In this context the accepted adage was: *quidquid recipitur ad modum recipientis recipitur,* "whatever is received, is received to the measure of the recipient."

A few points deserve to be noted here regarding Hadewijch's personality as a writer. She was creative enough to launch a new literary genre: the mystical love lyric. But this does not mean that her main aim as a writer was to give expression to her own emotional life as such, or to present her mystical experience as something highly individual. Recent research has shown convincingly that the *Poems in Stanzas* were meant to support and uplift a "group";[8] the *Visions* were intended as guidelines for the "friends"; and the *Letters* were to convey the leader's teaching and sympathy. It appears moreover that Hadewijch was proud of her native, vernacular language:

> Words enough and Dutch enough can be found for all things on earth, but I do not know any Dutch or any words that answer my purpose. Although I can express everything as far as this is possible for a human being, no Dutch can be found for all I have said to you, since none exists to express these things, so far as I know.[9]

There are indications enough in Hadewijch's writings to establish that she was a beguine and, moreover, the leader ("mistress") of a small group of beguines. Beguines, at least in Hadewijch's days, were, to put it briefly, those women who wished to live a form of religious life that would tie in with the way of life of Jesus' first apostles, while dispensing with the prevailing customs and structures of the Church. Therefore, not only did they not want to enter

---

[8] The *Poems in Stanzas* are songs that were certainly meant to be sung by the group of "friends," who probably also danced to this music.

[9] CW: *Letter* 17, 115-122. Unlike Hadewijch, Mechtild of Magdeburg, who expresses her feelings beautifully in German, speaks of her verbal impotence as a mystic in the following way: "Nun gebricht mir mein Deutsch, Latein kann ich nicht." See Mechtild von Magdeburg, *Das flieszende Licht der Gottheit,* ed. Margot Schmidt, Menschen der Kirche in Zeugnis und Urkunde, N.F. 3 (Einsiedeln: Benziger Verlag, 1955) 89.

into marriage, they also did not want to enter a monastery.[10] Their aim as women and as religious was a renewed "apostolic" life, but they were also breaking with the existing social structures. The beguines appeared to form an in-between class, a *Zwischenstand,* as German scholars put it. It is no wonder, then, that before long they came to be suspected and persecuted, and Hadewijch mentions more than once her real and public hardships. In Letter 29, she tells her friend "to cast away from you all alien grief, and to grieve for my sake as little as you can. What happens to me, whether I am wandering in the country or put in prison — however it turns out, it is the work of Love" (9-14).

"I constantly wished to know ...: 'What is Love? And who is Love?'"

As a mystic, Hadewijch excelled in what is known as "love mysticism" *(minnemystiek).* Thus in the first instance the experience granted her consisted in perceiving the presence of the "unheard-of" Reality as "Love" *(Minne).* For Hadewijch the *Minne* she perceived as an all-penetrating force (in answer to *"What* is love?") was unmistakably the God of her Christian faith (in answer to *"Who* is love?") manifesting himself to her. This was the Beloved she met in feeling Love. Consequently, mystical experience is represented in Hadewijch's oeuvre as a tangible love-relationship that joins together God and the human person. So strong is the transforming power of this interplay between the Beloved and the lover that they become one through their mutual loving.

---

[10] In 1273 a German bishop put this as follows: "They flee the obedience of the priests as well as the constraint of the marriage yoke and they do not have themselves bound to a religious order." See Grundmann, *Religiöse Bewegungen im Mittelalter,* 336.

Hadewijch, like all mystics, is preoccupied in the first place with this union of the human and the divine; and like all those who write as mystics, she offers a description of that union. The core of Hadewijch's literary work consists in what might be called a phenomenology of the "being-one" of two personal entities. What strikes the reader immediately is that the author succeeds in presenting this phenomenon as a special reality: the being-one envisaged by her is essentially a compound reality. In her view different aspects (or "moments," in the non-chronological sense of the word) make up the mystic's experience of being united with the Other. However perfect this experience may be, it is indelibly composed of different and, what is more, contrasting, feelings.

In order to evoke the two main moments that constitute the being-one, Hadewijch employs words that strike home for any reader alive to expressions of personal love. On the one hand, there is the term *ghebruken*, "to enjoy,"[11] which indicates the mystic's feeling of satisfaction: she is absorbed in the pleasurably liberating aspect of being united with the Other. On the other hand, there is the term *ghebreken*, "to fail,"[12] which refers to the mystic's feeling of dissatisfaction: she is aware of falling short in the face of the Other with whom she is one. These are the two contrasting key terms in Hadewijch's description of mystic union. But she does not merely juxtapose them. She makes *ghebruken*

[11] The word *ghebruken* can be translated as "to have fruition." However, the disadvantage of "fruition," which is currently used in spiritual literature, is precisely its spiritualizing ring.

[12] *Ghebreken* can be rendered correctly by "to fail," but it is a versatile word, apparently much to Hadewijch's taste. Depending on the context, it means either "to fall short" (because one is not able "to content" the Other and to receive enough of Him), or "to miss," "to lack" (because the Other is felt to be absent or utterly different).

and *ghebreken* sing a duet the reader cannot possibly miss.[13] Throughout her writings they continually respond to each other, so much so that it is clear, visually as well as audibly, how the experience of being-one comprises two quite different feelings.

Before investigating the role for Hadewijch of the Humanity in mystic union, it is important to notice how these two aspects of being-one relate to one another. However strong and permanent the contrast between *ghebruken* and *ghebreken,* they complement each other intrinsically. Far from indicating a succession of exaltation and depression, or a construction made up of loose component elements, these opposites appear as interacting elements of an organic unity. For Hadewijch there can be no "enjoying" independent of "failing," and "failing" is essentially connected with "enjoying."[14] Moreover, these two contrary feelings intensify each other within the mystic's single experience of the being-one.

[13] Hadewijch has selected a pair of words that are euphonious, and the poet-singer knows how to make them echo one another, e.g. *dat ghebreken van dien ghebrukene dat es dat sueste ghebruken,* "the incompletion of this blissful fruition is yet the sweetest fruition" (CW: *Letter* 16,17-18).

[14] The interrelation of *ghebruken* and *ghebreken* is not presented in abstract terms. Hadewijch describes it with poetic force, as in the following two passages: "Sometimes Love so enlightens me that I know what is wanting in me — that I do not content (*niet ghenoech en ben*) my Beloved according to his sublimity; and sometimes the sweet nature of Love blinds me to such a degree that when I can taste and feel her it is enough for me; and sometimes I feel so rich in her presence that I myself acknowledge she contents me" (CW: *Letter* 11, 40-47). "Lightning is the light of Love, which shows her in one flash and confers grace in many things, in order to show who Love is and how she can receive and give — in the sweetness of clasping, in the fond embrace, in the sweet kiss, and in heartfelt experience when Love actually speaks: 'I am the one who hold you in my embrace! This is I! I am the all! I give the all!' But after that comes the thunder. Thunder is the fearful voice of threat: and it is retraction; and it is enlightened reason, which holds up before us the truth, and our debt, and our failure to grow up (*scout ende onghewassenheit*) in conformity with Love, and our smallness compared to Love's greatness" (CW: *Letter* 30, 155-167).

And so radical is this interrelation that the distinguishing mark of the accomplished mystic — of the "grown-up," as she puts it — is precisely her being enabled to sense these contrary feelings "at once": "Consolation and ill treatment both at once, / this is the essence of the taste of Love." In this way the mystic's final delight is not simply a rapturous "enjoying"; for her this is "a matter for jubilation: / How Love knocks down / and seizes / at one stroke."[15]

Up to this point the study of Hadewijch has brought out the main features of her description of mystic union. This "phenomenology" from the pen of a medieval love mystic can be heard to ring so true that it must appeal to a wide audience. Her highlighting of the organic structure of mystical being-one can hardly fail to strike all those interested in mysticism as an extensive phenomenon appearing in both East and West alike.[16] And all those who reflect upon the possibility for humans to live a real and lasting union in love are bound to be startled when Hadewijch insists so strongly that any authentic being-one of persons *is* an interplay of "enjoying" and "failing."

But it may come as a further surprise to find that this same concept of mystic union, which has such a universal validity, is at once utterly Christ-centred. In fact our account of Hadewijch's

---

[15] CW: *Poems in Stanzas* 31, 25-26 and 5, 32-35.

[16] In passing it is worth noting that there is much more *bhakti* (personal, loving devotion) than is usually appreciated in the East, not only in Hinduism but also in Buddhism. My impression is that Hadewijch gives confident expression to what appears elsewhere more hesitantly. Still, in her sense of the unassailable transcendence of the One, who "alone suffices to himself and is Love (*hem selven allene ghenoech es*)," she is second to none. The question, "Who you are in your incomprehensibility?" is always present, and so is the mystery of that "reaching out to me who am unreachable (*mi te gherijnne die ongherijnlec ben*)." See CW: *Letter* 16, 65-67; *Vision* 6, 35-36 and 8, 42-43.

description of her experience, however accurate, has resulted from a process of abstraction. We have distilled, so to speak, a general, Christ-less phenomenology, highly valuable in itself, from a particular, Christocentric description of mystical experience. We have identified the flower of Hadewijch's mystic plant, but not seen its supporting stem. It is time therefore to look at the way in which the contrast and interplay between *ghebruken* and *ghebreken* actually appear in Hadewijch's work.

"To be God with God"

On closer acquaintance one realizes that for Hadewijch the word "God" is not the abstract term it presumably is for most present-day readers. When she speaks of being-one with God, we tend to think in terms of "God," whereas she is imagining "Christ" or "the Trinity"'. Again when she gives the name "Love" to the divine, she obviously refers to the Love that has united the three Persons from all eternity and which, when the time had come, appeared in the Godman. For Hadewijch to be one with God/Love means to be one with Christ and thus, automatically, with the Holy Trinity. So, in the opening lines of the first *Vision,* the mystic's "enjoying" is very specific: the author reports how she felt possessed by a single, fierce desire, "And that desire which I had inwardly was to be one with God in fruition *(een te sine ghebrukeleke met gode)*." At first sight this may seem to be in the pattern of the phenomenology mentioned earlier on. But now Hadewijch goes on to describe how this longing for union with God is answered in reality: it is on receiving Holy Communion, viz. Christ "in the shape of the Sacrament,"[17] that the mystic's exalted

---

[17] Compare the account given by Hadewijch in CW: *Vision* 7: "Then he gave himself to me in the shape of the Sacrament, in its outward form, as the custom

desire "to be one with God in fruition" is to be fulfilled, and her "God" is unmistakably the Godman:

> When I had received our Lord, he then received me to him, so that he withdrew my senses from every remembrance of alien things to enable me to have joy in him by being one with him *(sijns te ghebrukene in enecheiden)*.[18]

The desire to which Hadewijch gives expression here is probably not strange to most readers. Apparently human beings are innately inclined to "be one" with what they consider the ultimate reality — whether called the absolute, the divine, the "no-thing," or God. In addition, people tend spontaneously to imagine this "being-one" as a final state of undisturbed bliss, and the terms used by Hadewijch here can be easily appropriated: presumably there will be a "oneness" *(enecheit)*, when the One will absorb everyone, liberating each at last from the self, and this dispossessed home-coming will be sheer "enjoying" *(ghebruken)*. In short, Hadewijch's desire for the God who is "Love" *(Minne)* bears a strong similarity to a very natural religious dream: to pass once and for all to a "beyond," one where the reality of the human condition will be surpassed.

Hadewijch's description of the desire that drives her seems to hold great promise. However, a different, more sober tone makes itself briefly heard: "For this I was still too childish and too little grown-up."[19] These warning words gradually become more frequent, but this does not alter the fact that the mystic has seen her

is; and he gave me to drink from the chalice, in form and taste, as the custom is" (70-74). It is worth noting that the "great" mystic is not afraid to mention "shape," "outward form," "taste," "custom."

[18] CW: *Vision* 1, 8-9 and 15-16. In the second passage I have altered Hart's translation of *sijns te ghebrukene in enecheiden* which reads: "to have joy in him in inward togetherness with him."

[19] CW: *Vision* 1, 9-10.

initial desire abundantly fulfilled. Obviously, given that "God," for Hadewijch, refers to the Godman, her desire to "have joy in him" (*ghebruken*) implies that she wishes to attain to joyful oneness with both the Divinity and the Humanity. This longing for a twofold *ghebruken* is made perfectly clear in a passage from Vision 7 (to which we shall return):

> I desired that his Humanity should to the fullest extent be one in fruition with my humanity (*Sine menscheit ghebrukeleke mitter miere*) ... I wished he might content me interiorly with his Godhead, in one spirit, and that for me he should be all that he is, without withholding anything from me (*met siere godheit in eneghen gheeste ghenoech ende al ware dat hi es*). (28-31)

With regard to this fruition of the Humanity, it should be enough to note here that the Man emerging in this passage is the incomparably graceful and lovable human person in his glorified state.[20] In Vision 7 Hadewijch describes the Humanity in her forthcoming pleasure-filled union as follows:

> Looking like a Human Being and a Man, wonderful, and beautiful, and with glorious face, he came to me as humbly as anyone who wholly belongs to another. (67-70)

As sample texts, three passages deserve to be quoted where Hadewijch puts into words how her desire to "be one with God in fruition" was fulfilled. First there is the very short Letter 9. Here Hadewijch writes as the spiritual guide of kindred souls; she wants to spur her addressee on to strive continuously after *Minne*. Therefore she evokes her own delight at experiencing "oneness" with God, and clearly Hadewijch's *ghebruken* of God is linked to her feeling joyfully united with the Man:

---

[20] More will be said about this in Chapter 6. It may be of interest to look again (see Chapter 2) at the way in which Teresa of Avila describes the Humanity "impressing" itself upon her.

> May God make known to you, dear child, who he is, and how he
> deals with his servants, and especially with his handmaids — and
> may he submerge you in him! Where the abyss of his wisdom is, he
> will teach you what he is, and with what wondrous sweetness the
> loved one and the Beloved dwell one in the other, and how they
> penetrate each other in such a way that neither of the two distin-
> guishes himself from the other. But they abide in one another in
> fruition *(si ghebruken onderlinghe ende elc anderen)*, mouth in
> mouth, heart in heart, body in body, and soul in soul, while one
> sweet divine Nature flows through them both, and (being in each
> other, they are both one and they remain completely one) — yes,
> and remain so forever.[21]

The second passage, that shows how Hadewijch's looking for *ghebruken* has been answered, is taken from Vision 6. After describing her visionary experience of Christ as the "unknown Power and
great almighty Lord," which occurs as she is still "in the spirit,"
she goes on to evoke what happened to her when she had come
"out of the spirit." In this text it is the mystic's fruition of the
Divinity that becomes prominent:

> And as ... I recognized my awe-inspiring, my unspeakably sweet
> Beloved, I fell out of the spirit — from myself and all I had seen in
> him — and, wholly lost, fell upon the breast, the fruition, of his
> Nature, which is Love *(die ghebrukeleke borst siere naturen der
> minnen)*. There I remained, engulfed and lost, without any compre-
> hension or other knowledge, or sight, or spiritual understanding,
> except to be one with him and to have fruition of this union *(een te
> wesene met hem ende dies te ghebrukene)*. (79-81)

And finally, from Vision 7, a third text may give us some idea of
what Hadewijch means by *ghebruken*. This is the only passage in

---

[21] This is the whole of *Letter* 9. The final phrases (between brackets) can be
read in two ways. Hart's translation is less daring: "And they are both one thing
through each other, but at the same time remain two different selves ..." (*Ende Si
beide een dore hen selven, Ende al eens beide bliven, Ja ende blivende*).

Hadewijch's oeuvre that expresses — and with great beauty — the sensuous aspect of her being united with the Humanity:

> After that he came himself to me, took me entirely in his arms, and pressed me to him; and all my members felt his in full felicity, in accordance with the desire of my heart and my humanity. So I was outwardly satisfied and fully transported. Also then for a short while, I had the strength to bear this; but soon, after a short time, I lost that manly beauty outwardly in the sight of his form. I saw him completely come to nought and so fade and all at once dissolve that I could no longer distinguish him within me. Then it was as if we were one without difference *(een waren sonder differencie)*. It was thus: outwardly, to see, taste, and feel, as one can outwardly taste, see, and feel in the reception of the outward Sacrament. So can the Beloved, with the loved one, each wholly receive the other in all full satisfaction *(ghenoechten)* of the sight, the hearing, and the passing away of the one in the other. (74-94)

"To live as human beings with his Humanity"[22]

It is in the first Vision that one finds what seems to be the most significant text of all on the position of the Humanity in mystical experience. As we have seen, this Vision opens with Hadewijch's description of her desire "to be one with God in fruition." Further on it appears that on this occasion also her wish was fulfilled. However, this elevated feeling of fruition is mentioned only to be followed at once by a downward swing:

[22] The texts used as headings here and in the previous section are from *Letter* 6: "People wish to live with God in consolations and repose, in wealth and power, and to share the fruition of his glory *(in siere ghebrukeleker glorileecheit te sine)*. We all indeed wish *to be God with God,* but God knows there are few of us who want *to live as human beings with his Humanity (god met gode wesen ...mensche met siere minscheit wille leven)* (227-230).

And my Beloved gave himself to me, both in spiritual understanding of himself and in feeling. But when I saw him, I fell at his feet, for I divined that I had been led toward him the whole way, of which so much was still to be lived (259-264).

This recalls the brief warning words from the first paragraph of this Vision: "For this I was still too childish and too little grown-up." It begins to dawn on the visionary that the enjoyable union with God that has been conferred upon her so far is only a partial experience of the human person's unity with God. The object of Hadewijch's initial longing — "to be one with God in fruition (*ghebruken*)" — is seen to be the limited religious concept which (as suggested above) she shares in some way or another with many people. She has been spoiled by *Minne*, rather like a child by its mother; now she has to learn how to "grow up," that is, to let her experience of mystic union reach completion. The words "so much was still to be lived" do not imply that the delightful oneness with God was just a mirage, nor that she must first try hard to lead a meritorious life of prayer and virtue in order to attain to the full being-one. Hadewijch has indeed been mystically united with God through being raised to enjoy the Divinity and the glorified Humanity, but she still has to realize this high gift at the lowly level of human existence.

After concentrating in a few brilliant lines what is probably the core of her own mystical experience and of her teaching, Hadewijch goes on to expand this by having Christ speak extensively to the visionary (from line 265 to the end of the Vision). It is Christ in person who allows the visionary a clear insight into what is meant by "so much was still to be lived." He will bring home to this "noble" mystic, who had always wished to enjoy him without any restriction,[23] that for her an essential part of the divine "totality"

---

[23] Jesus will point to "the urging of your noble nature, which makes you desire me in my totality (*na die fiere nature die di mine gheheelheit heyschet*)"

had been left in the dark, eclipsed by the shining fruition of the Divinity and the glorious Humanity. With a tinge of irony Christ is ready to fill in the mystic's image of "all that he is," demystifying at once the aura of superhumanity that so far has shrouded both mystic union and his own Humanity. The first steps in the lesson Christ is to teach her are expressed by Hadewijch as follows:

> If you wish to be like me in my Humanity (*mi gheliken inder menscheit*), as you desire to possess me wholly in my Divinity (*inder gotheit als te ghebrukene van mi*), you shall desire to be poor ... (289-291)

It is significant that the basic contrast already familiar from Hadewijch's general phenomenology — "to have joy in" / "to fail"[24] — reappears here, but with two alterations. On the one hand, "to fail" (*ghebreken)* is replaced by "to be like" (*gheliken*), and on the other, this "to be like" is connected with Christ's "Humanity," while "to have joy in" (*ghebruken*) is linked to Christ's "Divinity." To fully appreciate Hadewijch's mystic view of the Humanity it is important to notice that "to be like" replaces "to fail." This semantic shift illustrates how the real human Humanity of Christ is given its rightful place in the mystic's experience of being united with God.

As we have seen in her general account of mystic union, Hadewijch was granted the gratifying feeling of *ghebruken* ("to enjoy") coupled at once with the frustration of *ghebreken* ("to fail"). The sense of failure was brought home to her mainly in two ways: by her impotence to "content" Love and by her suffering at the absence of Love. There is ample evidence in her writings that Hadewijch found it a real struggle to recognize the "failing" as

(297-298). We have seen already in *Vision* 7 that, for Hadewijch, God "should be all that he is, without withholding anything from me."

[24] The original text uses a striking chiasmus at this point: *gheliken* responds crosswise to *ghebruken* and so do *menscheit* and *gotheit*.

part and parcel of mystic union. How could her feeling of the absence of Love be compatible with the experience of their being one? How could she combine her awareness of a "debt" that could never be repaid with her sense of definite unity? It now becomes clear that Hadewijch was able to accept "failing" with all her heart only by understanding it as part of her being tangibly united with Jesus. This perception of the Humanity seems to have dawned on her in two stages. First, she saw that Christ had lived through the same experience of distress: in fact, he was the one who suffered complete "failing." But she also came to realize that for herself and kindred souls to feel their "failing" was precisely their being actually "like him in the Humanity" (*gheliken inder menscheit*). Consequently there was no need for them (but neither was it a problem) to "meditate" on the life and passion of the Man. By living their condition of "failing" they were actually being identified with his earthly Humanity. Thus the painful core of the love mystic's experience, where "to fail" is essential to the being-one, could be realized. *Ghebreken* crystallized into *gheliken*. With the certainty that the Man was the very embodiment of "failing," the mystic could experience within her own spiritual need that she was being united with the Godman, that is, God in person.

Hadewijch elucidates her teaching with the words she has Jesus speak to herself in Vision 1. This intervention was occasioned by the mystic's dissatisfaction with her "exile" (*ellende*), her feeling banished from the enjoyable divine presence. She had grown impatient with this situation:

> Now you have complained of your misery (*ellende*) and of the fact that you did not receive from me what you needed, according to your desire. (341-344).

Initially, Hadewijch had given vent to her irritation by asking that the Beloved should finally appreciate her distress. Central to the answer given by Jesus is a striking statement (worthy of a twentieth-century christology "from below"): "I lived merely as a human being." The message is immediately clear: whether mystic or not, one must live the human condition to the full, religious desolation included:

> You are young in days, and you want me to recognize the sore pain of your body, and the fidelity of your handiwork, and your new will always overflowing with charity for others, and the desires of your heart, and the languishing of your senses, and the love of your soul. All this I do recognize. But recognize also on your side that I lived merely as a human being *(ic leefde suver mensche),* and that my body suffered sore pain, and that my hands worked faithfully, and that my new will overflowed with charity for men through the whole world, upon strangers and upon friends, and that my senses languished, and that my heart desired, and that my soul loved. (310-322)

Yet Hadewijch appears to have persisted with her complaint. Appealing to a sort of christology "from on high," she employs an *ad hominem* argument: this Man, being the Godman, must have found it "easy" to live the human condition. Was he not, as the Son, in a position to raise himself to joyful oneness with the Father, and thus to alleviate by means of that consolation the desolation of his "living merely as a human being"?

> You have said to me at times that it was easy for me to live as a human being *(Ic hadde goed mensche leven)* ... But I make known to you a hidden truth concerning me, perceptible however for one who knows how to understand it: this is, that never for a single instant did I call upon my power to give myself relief when I was in need, and never did I seek to profit from the gifts of my Spirit, but I won them at the price of sufferings and through my Father ... before the day when my hour came of my full-grownness *(volwassenheit).* (325-340)

Finally Jesus indicates to the mystic, who is still intent in "childish" fashion on the gratifying aspect of the being-one, how to

"grow up." By accepting to "live in exile" (*ellendich leven*) —
the situation which necessarily goes together with her being a
human person (*mensche*) — she will herself discover the "consolation" (*troest*) that is not simply feeling consoled by "having
joy" in the Divinity. United with the Humanity through her living
the "human condition" (*menscheit*), she will have certainty of the
Father even without feeling certainty:

> And I ask you also, when were you forsaken by my Father in any
> state of soul, so that my Father was not always with you as he was
> with me and I with him, while I lived as a human being (*doen ic
> mensche leefde*)? Since, then, you are a human being, live in exile
> as a human being (*Nadien dattu mensche best, soe leve ellendech als
> mensche*). I wish that on earth my life in you should be so fully
> lived in all virtues that you may in no point fail me in myself ... But
> feel yourself as a human being in all the hardship proper to the
> human condition, except sin alone (*Maer ghevoelt u mensche in
> allen dien ghebreken die ter menscheit behoren sonder sonde
> allene*). All the suffering that belongs to the human race I experi-
> enced while I lived as a human being, except sin alone (*All die pine
> die ter menscheit behoren die becorde ic doen ic mensche leefde
> sonder sonde allene*). I never cheered myself by my inner power,
> except with the consolation that I was certain of my Father (*sonder
> met troeste dat ic seker was van minen vader*). (346-364)

Hadewijch's view on the position of the Man in mystic union was
the result of her growing awareness that the "failing" (*ghebreken*)
she suffered *vis-à-vis* the Divinity was her being "like" (*gheliken*)
the Humanity. This insight was for her of key importance, and
therefore was presented in a vision as the explicit "command" of
the Beloved; such was her (medieval) way of authentifying her
experience and teaching. In Letter 6 Hadewijch rephrases what
has been taught in Vision 1 in the following way:

> We must be continually aware that noble service and suffering in
> exile (*ellendich wesen*) are proper to the human condition; such was

the share of Jesus when he lived on earth as a human being (*doen hi minsche levede*). We do not find it written anywhere that Christ ever, in his entire life, had recourse to his Father or to his omnipotent Nature to obtain joy and repose (*ghebruken van rasten*). He never gave himself any satisfaction, but continually undertook new labors from the beginning of his life to the end. He said this himself to a certain person who is still living, whom he also charged to live according to his example and to whom he himself said that this was the true justice of Love: where Love is, there are always great labors and burdensome pains. (86-99)

It is illuminating now to return to the beginning of Vision 7 where Hadewijch expresses her desire to "have joy" (*ghebruken*) in the Humanity as well as in the Divinity. This passage looks back to the opening lines of Vision 1 about the mystic's longing to "be one with God in fruition" (*ghebrukeleke*). Yet in the meantime Hadewijch seems to have learnt the lesson she was taught by Christ himself later in Vision 1. Her initial hunger for *ghebruken* has not been blocked, but now it appears as immediately connected with *gheliken* ("to be like"): she wants to "have full fruition of my Beloved" together with the capacity to "content him fully in every virtue" and to "give satisfaction in all great sufferings." One can see that this urge to "content" (*ghenoegh doen*) is part and parcel of Hadewijch's general phenomenology, but here it materializes for the mystic into her being identified with the poor Humanity. The "most perfect satisfaction" consists in living the way of life of the Man, and it is only by so "growing up" with him that one may expect to "be God with God."[25] In the following passage the word *ghenoegh*, linked to *doen* and *sine* (meaning "to content," "to satisfy"), recurs with an almost obsessive frequency:

---

[25] Compare with the quotation in note 22.

I desired to have full fruition of my Beloved, and to understand and taste him to the full. I desired that his Humanity should to the fullest extent be one in fruition with my humanity, and that mine then should hold its stand and be strong enough to enter into perfection, until I content him (*ghenoech ware*), who is perfection itself ... and in all things to content him fully in every virtue (*ghenoegh te doghene in elker doghet*). To that end I wished he might content me (*ghenoegh ware*) interiorly with his Godhead, in one spirit, and that for me he should be all that he is without withholding anything from me. For above all the gifts that I ever longed for, I chose this gift: that I should give satisfaction (*ghenoech ware*) in all great sufferings. For that is the most perfect satisfaction (*ghenoech doen*): to grow up in order to be God with God. For this demands suffering, pain, and misery (*ellende*), and living in great new grief of soul: but to let everything come and go without grief, and in this way to experience nothing else but sweet love, embraces, and kisses. In this sense I desired that God give himself to me, so that I might content him (*ghenoech te sine*).[26]

"Tasting Man and God in one knowledge"

Between the first and the seventh Vision, Hadewijch's desire to be one with God appears to have developed: by incorporating the earthly Humanity, the visionary has been enabled to "grow up." In fact, the whole *Book of Visions* displays a process of ascent. Hadewijch gradually emerges as Love's elect reaching

---

[26] CW: *Vision* 7, 21-41. — Hadewijch often plays with *ghenoechte,* to feel "satisfaction," and *ghenoeghen/ghenoegh doen,* to give "satisfaction." So, in *Letter* 13: "We must do without the satisfaction of Love in order to satisfy Love" (*ghenoechten van hare ontberen omme hare ghenoegh te doene*) (38-39). And in *Letter* 23: "Live thus exclusively for holy Love out of pure love, not because of the satisfaction you might find (*omme uwe ghenoechte*) by communing with his love in your devout exercises, but in order to devote yourself to God himself in the works that content Love (*die Minnen ghenoeghen*). (4-8)

mystical maturity, to the point that Vision 14, which concludes the whole series, represents her full-fledged experience of God. And what strikes one most at the end of the *Book* is the Christ-centered character of Hadewijch's highest state. Far from being absorbed by a purely divine "beyond," the ecstatic visionary finally concentrates upon the Godman, his poor human Humanity included. Hadewijch seems to prepare the reader — or more likely the listener in her day — for the great finale of Vision 14. Thus in the last lines of Vision 11, she describes what she had longed for from the outset — "consolation," "the perfect pride of love," "rich repose":

> Hence I never felt love, unless as an ever-new death — until the time of my consolation came, and God granted me to know the perfect pride of love; to know how we shall love the Humanity in order to come to the Divinity (*de menscheyt ter gotheit minnen*) and rightly know it in one single nature (*in eenre naturen*). This is the noblest life that can be lived in the Kingdom of God. This rich repose God gave me, and truly in a happy hour. (194-203)

Further on, at the end of Vision 12, Hadewijch at last sees herself as the "veritable bride of the great Bridegroom," and this implies that she has been granted the "certainty of being received, in this form (of the bride), in my Beloved, and my Beloved also in me" (172-174). Everything is ready now for the Humanity-centred climax of this mystical career as shown in the last two Visions, 13 and 14.[27] In Vision 13 Hadewijch is shown the "Countenance of God," and the end is in sight: on either side of the Countenance (the "six wings") "are the veritable attributes of the mighty Godhead, in the perfection of which no one can himself participate

---

[27] In fact the last two Visions form a whole, and the central visionary image can be reduced to its essentials: "the Countenance" and "the throne." "The Countenance had six wings" is a reference to Isaiah 6,2 and Revelation 4,8.

unless he wishes to live God and Man" (*god ende mensche pleghen*). (41-44)

The opening lines of Vision 14 correspond to those of Visions I and 7. Hadewijch is "continually in great desire and in the madness of love." However, she now receives from God "some new strength" while she sees a throne that "signifies a new state of power." One would expect her to become very "strong" by being nourished with a divine substance, and, indeed, she does receive strength from "his own Being." But the new gift, that apparently crowns her mystical life, is described as follows:

> But the new power he then gave me, which I did not possess previously, was the strength of his own Being (*van sijn selves wesen*), to be God with my sufferings according to his example and in union with him, as he was for me when he lived for me as Man. That was the strength to endure, as long as the fruition of Love was denied me: really to endure the arrows Love shot at me.[28]

Now the sense of the throne that was shown to Hadewijch is clear to her: it "was the loftiness of the life of union to which I was chosen." (21-22)

With the next stage in the development of Vision 14 the central point of Hadewijch's ultimate mystical experience is reached. In the midst of the throne she sees the figure of Christ, "the Creator of our love, the Master of justice, who passes judgment on love in her adherents with final sentence" (74-76). Thus the Godman in person is the decisive touchstone for the love-mystic's experience. God's own Face is only to be enjoyed by those who have the "undivided taste" of Jesus Christ:

---

[28] CW: *Vision* 14,11-20. The original text is beautifully phrased in Flemish: *ene cracht van sijn selves wesene hem god te sine met minen doeghene na heme ende in heme, ghelijc dat hi mi was doe hi mensche levede te mi.*

The Countenance, which he had at that moment, was invisible and inaccessible to the sight for all creatures who never lived human and divine love as one single reality: (*menscheleker ende godleker minnen in enen wesene*), and who could not grasp or feed in the undivided taste of the single nature (*in ere naturen smake onghesceden*). (77~82)[29]

Hadewijch now realizes that she has found her destiny. She has attained to the fullness of the God-experience for which she had been chosen: "that I might taste Man and God in one knowledge (*mensche ende god in eenre const smaken*), what no man could do unless he were as God, and wholly such as he was who is our Love." (162-165) Her last Vision ends with the words:

The Voice said to me: "O strongest of all warriors! You have conquered everything and opened the closed totality, which never was opened by creatures who did not know, with painfully won and distressed Love, how I am God and Man (*hoe ic god ende mensche ben*)! O heroine, since you are so heroic, and since you never yield, you are called the greatest heroine! It is right, therefore, that you should know me perfectly." (173-179)

To conclude this study of Hadewijch, we can return to Letter 6. Shortly after the text already quoted,[30] there is a passage that expresses with exceptional force her Christ-centered experience. First there is the usual antithesis: on the one hand, the mystic has "to fail" (*ghebreken*), which materializes as "to be like" (*gheliken*) the labouring and suffering Humanity, and on the other hand, the mystic has "to enjoy" (*ghebruken*), referred to here with the verb "to rejoice" (*jubileren*):

With the Humanity of God you must live here on earth, in the labors and sorrow of exile, while within you must love and rejoice (*jubileren*) with the omnipotent eternal Divinity in sweet abandonment.

---

[29] Hart's translation has been slightly altered in the light of the original text.
[30] CW: *Letter* 6, 86-99: the new passage is *Letter* 6, 117-121.

This rhythmic sentence sheds light once more on the contrast that is essential to Hadewijch's experience of being one with God through her living the Godman. Next, the skilful writer can suggest the experiential integration of contrasting feelings with a single phrase: "For the truth of both is one single fruition" (*ghebruken*). Hadewijch plays here with the term for *ghebruken* used earlier in the sentence: in place of the word her readers expected to find (viz., *ghebruken*), she used the term *jubileren,* "to rejoice." It is as if she were saying: "As long as I was 'childish', I identified the real being-one with the pleasurable *ghebruken* or *jubileren*. Now, having 'grown up', I realize that this real being-one, which I keep calling *ghebruken,* for it is the only 'fruition' I finally value, lies hidden in a compound experience as the 'truth' of both 'rejoicing' with the Divinity and 'failing' with the Humanity."[31]

[31] In Hadewijch's day mystical *jubilus* was a well-known phenomenon. Note that this "jubilus of the heart" is comparable to the "jubilus of the lips," found in Gregorian chant. Hadewijch uses the verb *jubileren* ("to rejoice") several times, presumably in a broad sense when she mentions "those we had chosen to rejoice (*jubileerne*) with us in our Beloved" (*Letter* 5,19), or, as we have seen, in a mystical sense, when she evokes poetically the coming together of "failing" and "enjoying." (See above, the text corresponding to note 15). Ruusbroec's fine description of the mystic's jubilation deserves to be quoted here: "And in the meeting with the light, lust and delight are so great that the heart cannot bear it, but bursts forth for joy, through the voice; and this is called jubilating or jubilation, that is a joy which cannot be expressed in words" (*The Spiritual Espousals, Opera Omnia* III, b492-496). However, "to jubilate" often had a pejorative ring as it also referred to the affectation and self-consciousness of those who, to use Hadewijch's terminology, enjoyed the pleasurable aspect of God's presence "in a childish way." For more on this point, see Paul Mommaers, *Hadewijch*, IV, 2: "The community of women and the authorities." (See above, note 2).

CHAPTER V

THE ROLE OF THE INTERMEDIARY

The figure of the Godman is recognized to be the "image of the invisible God" (Colossians 2, 9), acting as the "one mediator between God and man" (1 Timothy 2,5). However, a question arises (as was seen in chapter I) concerning the merits and demerits of the image, especially with regard to the mystic's awareness of the invisible Other. Ruusbroec interconnects image and intermediary, subsuming the first, specific kind of "means" under the second. If the "secret friends" (i.e., well-advanced contemplatives) are not able to reach the ultimate experience proper to the "hidden sons," the reason is that their mind is beset "with images and intermediaries," literally "they are imaged and mediated" (*verbeelt ende vermiddelt*). Thus, the secret friends keep feeling "distinction and otherness" (*onderscheet ende anderheit*) in their union with God.[1]

Julian of Norwich on "using means"

Julian of Norwich, as was shown earlier (chapter 2), is a mystic who successfully integrates imaged and imageless awareness of God. In Chapter 6 of the Long Text, she tackles the question of the intermediaries. As it stands, this chapter is not a mystical report, but Julian's reflection upon "how we usually pray," occasioned

---

[1] Ruusbroec, *The Sparkling Stone, Opera Omnia* X, 328-329. For the way in which Ruusbroec's works are cited, see chapter 1, note 10.

by the experience described in the first three paragraphs of the previous chapter, namely, the "spiritual vision of his familiar love."[2] In this vision, the paradoxical nature of any intermediary strikes her as she reflects on the appearance of "all that is made." On the one hand, there is the ontological contradiction proper to all creatures and seen so suggestively in the hazelnut: "I wondered how it could last ... 'It lasts and will last forever'." On the other hand, there is the mystic's feeling that she is to become one with God beyond everything that is not God: "for until I become one substance with him (*for till I am substantially vnited to him*) ... until I am so bound to him that there is no created thing between my God and me (*that ther be right nought that is made betweene my god and me*) ... until all that is made seems as nothing, no soul can be at rest (*till [the sowle] is noughted of all thinges that is made*)."[3]

This reflection of Julian, which does not appear in the Short Text, has already begun in the last paragraph of the previous chapter, and is obviously linked with what precedes. The soul's coming to God in a "bare" way ties in with there being "no created thing between my God and me," while the insight that his goodness "includes all his creatures," though he "surpasses everything endlessly," springs from the appreciation of the frail hazelnut's

---

[2] As in Chapter 2 (see note 1), the modern English translations of Julian's texts will be taken from Julian of Norwich, *Revelations of Divine Love*, trans. E. and A.C. Spearing, and references to the original texts will be taken from *A Book of Showings to the Anchoress Julian of Norwich*, eds. E. Colledge and J. Walsh. Here, too, as in chapter 2, references to the so-called "short text" will be indicated by ST, while references to the so-called "long text" will be indicated by LT. Julian's account here of her experience of God's immediate presence may be significantly compared with Hadewijch's explanation of the difference between whatever image of God we may have and what God really "is." See Hadewijch, CW: *Letter* XII, 31-38 and *Letter* XVIII, 82-91.

[3] LT ch. 2, p. 42 and ST ch. 6, p. 10-11; Colledge and Walsh (eds.), *A Book of Showings to the Anchoress Julian of Norwich*, 300: 19-30.

permanence. Thus, when Julian, in chapter 6, considers the problem of the intermediaries, her views are founded on the particular experience she has described in chapter 5.

She begins chapter 6, then, with the criticism: "Usually ... we pray indirectly" (*we use ... to make menie meanes*).[4] This is a

---

[4] Throughout chapter 6 Julian keeps repeating the word *meanes*. One wonders why, despite the principles laid down in the "Translator's Note," pp. XXXVIII-XXXIX, this key word is not rendered consistently by "means." The result is that the author's talent to catch and hold the reader's attention is weakened: one loses the impact of the repetition of such an ambivalent word as "means" — means being a help to come into contact with something else, but also, to some extent, an obstacle, hampering as an 'in-between'. Piers Plowman expresses the positive aspect of the "means": "crie Crist merci, / And Marie his moder to beo *mene be-twene*" (A. Passus VIII, 182-184). In the translation Julian's phrase, "*we use ... to make menie meanes ,*" is replaced by "we pray indirectly;" again, her expression, "*if we made all the meanes that hart maie thinke* " is changed into "if we approach him through all the intermediaries that heart can devise." Why has the word "means" been replaced here by the academic term "intermediaries"? The tenor of the note that accompanies "intermediaries" may provide the answer: "she is careful to add that he (God) is not displeased by prayers directed to his Humanity, to the saints etc. — a necessary addition at a time when the Church was persecuting Lollards" (see note 6, p.183). Does this give a fair inkling of Lady Julian's way of being and writing? As will be shown shortly, this genuine mystic clearly connects her reflection upon the use of "means" (in chapter 6) with her experience of the reality of all creatures (in chapter 5). As Colledge and Walsh point out, Julian here "describes her own devotional life; and we can see how closely she followed the patterns prescribed and recommended in the *Ancrene Riwle*" (Part I, pp. 77; see the quotations from the *Riwle*, pp. 77-78). As A.C. Spearing himself shows in his Introduction (pp. XXIII-XXVI), "Julian was a theologian," and as a genuine theologian she openly expresses the contradiction between her mystical experience and the teaching of the Church regarding universal salvation. (See especially chapter 32 of the Long Text, with the phrase "I shall keep my word in all things and I shall make all things well," p. 86.) One can hardly imagine the daring theologian-writer of chapters 32-33 or chapter 50 being so pusillanimous as to write chapter 6 because she felt it was a "necessary addition at a time when the Church was persecuting Lollards," unless one presupposes that Julian and all mystics must be unorthodox or outside the Church. A.C. Spearing gives the impression that he wants to depict

short-sighted procedure, for we should rather address God directly, and ask him to answer our prayers himself "through his own goodness." Seeing that "all the intermediaries (*all the meanes*) that heart can devise ... are diminishing," we should reach out without any means to "his own goodness." After referring in this way to the concept of an intermediary, Julian goes on to exemplify it, mentioning four such particular means: for instance, "we pray to him by the love of the sweet Mother who bore him ..." Julian further indicates that there are in fact "a great many excellent means," but concludes that the "chief and principal one (*principalle meane*) is the blessed Humanity (*the blessed kynde that he toke of the maiden*)." However, by making more explicit the problematic concept of the intermediary by referring to sacrosanct Christian items, she suggests where the solution lies. No reader can fail to notice that in the enumeration of the different means she keeps repeating one phrase: "from his goodness." Displaying her gift for rhetoric, Julian brings home to us that whatever we receive, and by whatever means — even the noblest intercessor — it flows from the Source itself. She resumes with the masterly phrase: "For

Julian as such: she "repeatedly affirms her acceptance of the Church's teachings, and by leaving the nature of the great deed (of universal salvation) mysterious, she avoids head-on conflict with orthodoxy" (see p. XXV). My views on this surprising interpretation of Julian's view on intermediaries were confirmed when I came across Barbara Newman's *From Virile Woman to Woman Christ: Studies in Medieval Religion and Literature* (Philadelphia: University of Pennsylvania Press, 1995). She comments as follows on Julian's sense of universal salvation (pp. 132-133): "Because the voice of Julian-the-visionary proclaims this consoling message, and because modern readers prefer inner authority to that of Holy Church, it is easy to interpret the protestations of Julian-the-believer as heresy insurance, proof against real or imagined prosecutors. Indeed, if we accept the revisionist dating of the Long Text proposed by Watson, persecution of Lollard anchoresses was actually taking place as Julian composed her book. Yet it would be dangerously anachronistic to assume that it was only her 'even Christians', and not also herself, that she needed to assure of her orthodoxy."

in his goodness God has ordained a great many excellent means to help us (*For the meanes that the goodnes of god hath ordeineth to helpe vs be full faire and many*)."

Thus the hazelnut of chapter 5, which evidently belongs to "all that is made," reappears in the form of the means. The answer to the problem of the intermediary is to be found in seeing Reality as essentially differentiated. Everything created is "included" in God, as are the "many excellent means" he has "ordained," and thereby the attitude of the praying person towards the intermediaries is clarified: "Therefore it pleases him that we should seek and worship him in these intermediate ways (*seke him ... by meanes*) while understanding and knowing that he is the goodness of all." Julian completes her reflection upon the intermediary with a touching picture of the creatures God has made "in his own likeness," so as to be the primary means by which to reach him: "for as the body is clad in the cloth, and the flesh in the skin, and the bones in the flesh, and the heart in the chest, so are we, soul and body, clad in the goodness of God and enclosed in it."

On the issue of the intermediary, Julian of Norwich presents succinctly both the question and the answer, the latter being what one would expect from a mystic who wants to strengthen the prayer of the ordinary Christian. Obviously, the mystics have a lot more to say about the role of the intermediary in their own experience of God, as will be seen in relation to Jan van Ruusbroec, who made the interplay of prayer "with intermediary" and "without intermediary" a key theme of his writing. However, before examining this mystic's approach, it is important to recall that the phenomenon of mediation is something specifically human, which has constantly provoked reflection, especially in modern times. Far from being an esoteric matter, the problem posed by the mystics on mediation and the intermediary will be seen to have a genuine human interest.

Mediation in classical and modern reflection

The very first point to be kept in mind is that human existence is intrinsically linked to mediation. In the face of reality, human beings always and everywhere make use of signs, which do much more than point to things: they represent them. Language is obviously the most comprehensive and subtle reproductive means at our disposal, for words can signify everything, even the objects pointed at by other kinds of signs. The power to symbolize can be shown to be the distinguishing human characteristic, and the one gift by which men and women stand supreme. But it is precisely this unique human capacity that entails a crucial anthropological condition: there is no immediate natural relation between a human being and the world, nor between human beings themselves. The inter-medium of symbols, especially of a system of signs that constitutes language, is necessarily present.[5]

As long as conventional signs are being used spontaneously, they appear to be intimately connected with the things they represent. Even if in a mediated way, we feel able to signify the real world and our real selves, and so does any speaker who consciously intends to refer to a particular thing through a general word and who "does things with words." However, it is at this point that the limitation of human signifying activity in its grasp of reality shows itself. The classical way of posing the problem still has meaning today: given that we represent the existing thing with signs that are necessarily abstract, surely we fail to capture its particularity, its *being this one thing*?

The ambivalence of any signifying intermediary soon becomes obvious and doubts arise as to its soundness. On the one hand, one

---

[5] See Emile Benveniste, *Problèmes de linguistique générale* (Paris: Gallimard, 1966) 24-31.

is tempted to focus on the fact that a "means" sits unavoidably between the real thing and our knowing it, so much so that the mediation as such appears as a hindrance to actual contact. On the other hand, there remains the apparently unavoidable fact that when we use a mediating sign in the ordinary way, that is, intending the thing it represents, we do not feel hampered or frustrated in our contact with reality.

Such, in broad outline, is the classical way of reflecting upon the role of the intermediary. In addition, modern thinking has dramatically sharpened the question by shifting the focus from knowing things to knowing human minds. Since Descartes, our signifying as a reliable means to mutually express ourselves has come under suspicion. The notion that one person could be really in contact with another person by an exchange of signs has been seen by many as the uncritical illusion par excellence. For them the human ego is by nature a hidden reality, and must remain so. A graphic passage from Descartes' *Second Meditation* criticizes the conviction that through perceptible intermediaries one can know another human being as human, as "having a soul."[6] When a philosopher looks out of the window and watches people walking by in the street, he does not see any signs that may enable him to say "this is a person": "But what can I 'see' besides hats and coats, which may cover automata? I judge that they are men."[7]

---

[6] The picture of the human self as a hidden reality is older than Descartes. A typical statement, that seems to express a very modern point of view, is that we are not able fully to "reveal ourselves": "We stand, as it were, behind the wall of the body, sheltered from the eyes of others in the recesses of our mind; but when we wish to reveal ourselves we come forth, with speech as the gateway, in order to show our inner selves." Gregory the Great, *Morals on the Book of Job*, II, 8; quoted by Fergus Kerr, *Theology after Wittgenstein* (Oxford: Basil Blackwell, 1986) 80.

[7] René Descartes, *Philosophical Writings*, trans. / eds. Elizabeth Anscombe, Peter Thomas Geach (Edinburgh: Nelson, 1959) 73-74.

Many other influential thinkers question if mediation is the appropriate way to know a person's mind. This is not the place to discuss them. However, a contemporary of Descartes (1596-1650), namely, Blaise Pascal (1623-1662), does deserve special attention.[8] When he discusses the phenomenon of our loving another person, his mistrust of interpersonal encounter by way of intermediaries may leave an even more powerful impression than the doubts of Descartes. Pascal argues that such love can only prove self-love. We may well intend the other one's self through his or her "qualities,"[9] but we do not reach it for it is an altogether different thing.

---

[8] According to his Memorial, Pascal had been granted a life-changing mystical experience in the night of 23 November, 1654. It was recorded on a piece of parchment which he had sewn inside the lining of his clothes so as to carry it always with him: "Fire / God of Abraham, God of Isaac, God of Jacob, not of philosophers and scholars./ Certainty, certainty; feeling, joy, peace./ God of Jesus Christ ... The world forgotten and everything except God ... / Joy joy joy tears of joy!"

[9] Robert Musil, *The Man Without Qualities* (London: Picador Pan Books, 1979), a twentieth-century masterpiece, presents a mysticism without God, which appears only in Book III. Ulrich, the "man without qualities," has spoken of the present-day mysticism which occupies him and his sister Agathe: "There is absolutely no need to be a saint in order to experience something of the kind." Agathe exclaims: "'Love your neighbour' does not mean love him on the basis of what you and he are. What it means is a sort of dreamlike condition!" (*The Man Without Qualities*. Book Three, pp. 111 and 112). Later, in the posthumously edited additions to the novel arranged by Adolf Frisé in *Der Mann ohne Eigenschaften* (Hamburg: Rowolt Verlag, 1952), Musil dwells on this theme, and he has Agathe and Ulrich discussing the sense of "Love your neighbour as yourself." It is introduced in §41 by way of a reflection upon the impossibility for people to actually "feel with the others": "You see, although one must love one's neighbour as oneself ... It is absolutely unbearable not to be able to really share in the being one loves, and it is also absolutely simple. This is how the world is made up." In §51 Musil tackles more thoroughly the question of our loving each other: "But what does one finally love in a human being when one does not know it at all?" In §53 he goes on to specify the problem: "You'll love your neighbour without knowing who he is, that's where the relations between

We are in a dilemma. Either we approach the other person by means of body or spirit, and become enmeshed in their fleeting beauty or passing intelligence, or we try to touch the "substance" of the other person's soul directly, and we clasp something "abstract," being left without any means to know *who* this "substance" is.[10]

Readers of mystical texts may well feel sympathy with the misgivings of classical and modern thinkers on the subject of mediation. The moving descriptions of "immediate" encounters with God, which at times are said to happen when one switches from "imaged" to "imageless" experience, or from knowing "with intermediary" to knowing "without intermediary," seem to imply a depreciation, if not the rejection, of all "means." Such an interpretation does not do justice to the far broader view of the mystics, but initially it is worth considering what two contemporary thinkers have to say on mediation.

love and reality are tested ... What the other person says, thinks or is really, wouldn't that play any role?" — "For its apparition and continuation love does not depend on anything essential. One loves someone in spite of everything and because of nothing." Finally, in §59, Musil points to the only way of actually carrying out the commandment in question. One needs to enter the "new condition" of mystical experience: "Love him without knowing him, before knowing him, although knowing him ... This is how a seemingly banal commandment, when it is taken literally, belongs to the realm of ecstasy!" It would be interesting to show how the fallacy of ecstasy (see chapter 3) reappears in Musil's modern, post-Christian mysticism.

[10] "But what about a person who loves someone for the sake of her beauty; does he love her? No, for smallpox, which will destroy beauty without destroying the person, will put an end to his love for her. And if someone loves me for my judgement or my memory, do they love me? Me, myself? No, for I could lose these qualities without losing my self. Where then is this self, if it is neither in the body nor the soul? And how can one love the body or the soul except for the sake of such qualities, which are not what makes up the self, since they are perishable? Would we love the substance of a person's soul, in the abstract, whatever qualities might be in it? That is not possible, and it would be wrong. Therefore, we never love anyone, but only qualities." (Pascal, *Pensées*, trans. A.J. Krailsheimer (Harmondsworth: Penguin Books, 1966) 245, nr. 688 (323).

Appreciating Mediation: Michael Polanyi

Polanyi has argued that normally the intermediary does not constitute a hindrance to real contact: in the case of language one may speak of its "transparency." This pure conductivity can be accounted for by our "two kinds of awareness."[11] The person who makes use of a particular means in order to reach something else, displays a "subsidiary" awareness of the means as well as a "focal" awareness of the object intended. Consequently, the intermediary is not felt as a distracting in-between, for it hardly appears at all. Mediated contact proves to be actual contact. One of Polanyi's illustrations of this point runs as follows: "Think of how a blind man feels his way by use of a stick, which involves transposing the shocks transmitted to his hand and the muscles holding the stick into an awareness of the things touched by the point of the stick." Thus the blind man himself is really touching things. Polanyi exemplifies his view on mediation — how we use linguistic means to reach the meaning they convey — by reporting a "homely episode": reading a letter that has just arrived, he is not aware of its being written in a foreign language, and it is only at the moment that he passes it on to his son, who "understands only English," that the presence of this particular medium dawns on him. The normal interplay between subsidiary and focal awareness can be disturbed if the reader's attention becomes concentrated upon the words as such instead of their meaning. Whenever such a shift occurs, the mediating signs "become slightly opaque and prevent my thought from passing through them unhindered to the things they signify."

[11] This is the heading of the subdivision in Michael Polanyi, *Personal Knowledge* (London: Routledge and Kegan Paul, 1958) 55-57, referred to in this paragraph.

The two kinds of awareness, which go together harmoniously as long as the mind's intending movement prevails, prove to be "mutually exclusive"[12] as soon as the reflective movement takes over. In this context, Polanyi uses the term "self-consciousness," and we saw in Chapter 1 how both the philosopher Jean-Paul Sartre and the mystic Maria Petyt alerted us to the nature of "reflection" as a secondary and restricting act of consciousness.

One can see, in general lines, how Polanyi counterbalances the tendency to discard mediation. This line of thought enables him to shed light on a point of particular interest to students of mystical texts. These abound in references to the body as the locus of the most personal religious experience. For Polanyi, the body effectively signifies the person. Starting from the way in which we make use of instruments, he first points out that the body is the "basic instrument" of which we are only subsidiarily aware.[13] He then goes on to present this subsidiary body-awareness as part and parcel of our existence as human beings, so much so that our personal identity is intrinsically connected with the instrumental body:[14] the body takes first place as "expressing," in the strong

[12] See, for this expression and the next, Polanyi, *Personal Knowledge*, 56. In *The Study of Man*: The Lindsay Memorial Lectures 1958 (London: Routledge and Kegan Paul, 1959) 30, Polanyi formulates this point as follows: "If you shift your attention from the meaning of a symbol to the symbol as an object in itself, you destroy its meaning. Repeat the word 'table' twenty times over and it becomes a mere empty sound. Symbols can serve as instruments of meaning only by being known subsidiarily while fixing our focal attention on their meaning."

[13] "We use instruments as an extension of our hands and they may also serve as an extension of our senses. We assimilate them to our body by pouring ourselves into them ... we never attend to our body as an object in itself. Our body is always in use as the basic instrument of our intellectual and practical control over our surroundings." See Polanyi, *The Study of Man*, 31.

[14] Polanyi, *The Study of Man*, 31: "And, of course, our body is more than a mere instrument. To be aware of our body in terms of the things we know and

sense of "realizing," the human person. The possibility then appears of knowing another human being's inner self without any need of some unmediated access to the hidden "substance of the soul," which Pascal declared to be "impossible." According to Polanyi, the "mind of man is known" in the same way as we "know a face":[15] "A man's mind can be known only comprehensively, by dwelling within the unspecifiable particulars of its external manifestations. This conception of the mind ... will allow us to attribute to the mind of another person the same faculties of comprehension we use in comprehending it ... He and I may be mutually comprehending each other, by dwelling within one another's external mental manifestations."[16]

Prescinding from Mediation: The "fundamental unity" of different spiritual ways

At this point, a general observation concerning the intermediaries in religious experience seems appropriate. Nowadays the existence of different world religions is a striking fact that cannot be ignored. Each religion proposes for its believers a particular way to realize its doctrines. But equally striking is a widespread

do, is to feel alive. This awareness is an essential part of our existence as sensuous active persons ... every time we assimilate a tool to our body our identity undergoes some change; our person expands into new modes of being."

[15] To know a face is the example par excellence of knowing through subsidiary awareness: one knows "from" a wealth of particulars that are mostly unspecified. And this knowing concerns recognizing a face "among a thousand, indeed a million," as well as recognizing the "moods of the human face." See Michael Polanyi, *The Tacit Dimension* (New York: Doubleday and Company, 1966) 4, 5.

[16] Polanyi, *The Study of Man*, 33-34. For a more detailed presentation, see *The Tacit Dimension*, 15-16.

tendency to open-mindedness, which takes for granted the fundamental unity of what seem to be divergent paths. It appears that one and the same train of thought, or chain of feelings, can be recognized in different forms, all of which render insignificant, not to say null, all mediation. Again and again one original Experience is evoked as the meta-point upon which, even if unconsciously for the most part, the different spiritual ways converge and within which they coincide. This all-founding Experience is absolute, in the original sense of utterly detached ("absolved"). By belonging to a pure beyond, it is rigorously ineffable or "apophatic," and can thus be the implicit meeting place of different explicit beliefs. And as a matter of fact several traditions are indeed saying things with regard to the unsayable: for instance, they may objectify the Experience by naming it "God" or even addressing it "our Father."

For those who hold the unifying view that unmediated experience occurs in the blank minds of spiritual experts, this multiplicity of expressions and practices poses a problem: from where does it come? Is it from some unique nowhere, that has absorbed individual consciousness? What is the meaning of all that lively variety in relation to the self-contained, still point of the original Experience? In general the answer to this kind of question runs as follows: all the theory and praxis of different spiritual traditions is an epiphenomenon. It is the fruit of human reflection upon the Ungraspable; it is the way in which people try to make significant the Beyond which otherwise would remain irrelevant to them. What various religions and spiritualities say and do is their particular and fallible way of giving an understandable shape and desirable appearance to the one Experience.

In the present context a few remarks may suffice. In the first place, this unifying view cannot do justice to any intrinsic connection between the unsayable and what human beings say about it, between the motionless and people's spiritual motions. According to this theory, the entire religious and contemplative picture/construct does not really matter. Everything that can be considered an intermediary has no ultimate value.

Secondly, this view seems founded on an acute awareness that there is an unavoidable difference between a spiritual experience and its expression. As such this insight is correct and all-important, but it has a misleading twist that casts all mediation in an artificial role, as if one were filling a garden with useless trees and flowers, or providing a training ground with futile exercises, all of which need to be transcended ruthlessly in order to plunge into the depth of experience. In fact those contemplatives who take intermediaries seriously, i.e., as integral to the ultimate experience, are the first to recognize the value of deep experience. Jan van Ruusbroec, who is the mystical champion of mediation, has this to say of such experience:

> And here is the enjoyable passing-over, an engulfment flowing away into essential bareness where all divine names and all modes and all life-giving ideas which are depicted in the mirror of divine truth fall without exception into this simple namelessness, without modes and without reason.[17]

Finally, it may help to take into account an empirical investigation into this question.[18] J.M. van der Lans carried out a psychological experiment in order to show that "without a religious frame of reference, without a religious tradition, without myths

---

[17] Ruusbroec, *Opera Omnia* III, c211-215.

[18] Presented by Walter Van Herck in *Religie en metafoor: Over het relativisme van het figuurlijke* (Leuven: Peeters, 1999), 51-54. This investigation is contained in J.M. van der Lans, *Religieuze ervaring en meditatie: Een godsdienstpsychologische studie*, Psychologische mongrafiën (Deventer: Van Loghum Slaterus, 1980).

and rites, religious experiences are impossible." Two groups of test subjects were involved in the experiment. Both were taught in the same way how to meditate, but one group was also being instructed about the sense of this practice: its spiritual nature and religious purpose was explained to them; the experiences to which it may lead were noted and linked to their real lives. The result was that the same meditation procedure yielded different experiences depending on the presence or absence of a pre-meditation religious instruction, and van der Lans was in a position to conclude that "religious experiences will not appear in a person who has no religious frame of reference" (which does not imply that these experiences will necessarily appear when such a frame of reference is present).

Appreciating Mediation: Ludwig Wittgenstein

Wittgenstein is another contemporary thinker who may help us to approach the issue of the intermediary in mystical experience with sensitivity. In his discussion of mediation in human knowing he makes three steps which deserve particular attention. First, Wittgenstein shows that in fact no intermediary can be pinpointed in cases where we usually assume there is one.[19] A favourite example of this illusion appears when we apply a rule: as "following a rule is analogous to obeying an order," one does not need first to call to mind the rule in order to be able to apply it, since "I obey the rule *blindly*."[20] There simply is no interior intermediary that represents the rule and shows me how to use it.

[19] For this point I am drawing on Van Herck, *Religie en metafoor*, 111-124.

[20] Ludwig Wittgenstein, *Philosophical Investigations,* transl. G.E.M. Anscombe (Oxford: Basil Blackwell, 1967), §206 and §219. (Hereafter cited as PI).

But for our present purpose, with regard to the non-existent intermediary, the way in which Wittgenstein clarifies the phenomenon of "seeing-as" is even more telling. He distinguishes two kinds of "seeing-as." There is, on the one hand, an instantaneous "seeing-as" in the case of aspect-dawning and aspect-change. And there is, on the other hand, the "continuous seeing" of an aspect.[21] In both these kinds a mysterious addition appears, and a question arises as to the origin of this extra perception. There is a strong temptation to posit a mental intermediary. "Seeing-as" would then be explained as a subjective performance: I remodel some mediating interior picture which faithfully represents objective reality. Seeing a thing "as something else" would simply result from interpreting a reproduction that might be read in another way, and this theory is only one step away from the idea that "seeing-as" is the projection of one's personal view upon reality. Wittgenstein rejects this mentalist view of the phenomenon of "seeing-as." There is, he argues, no intermediary in our mind that has to be interpreted in order for us to have this new perception of the thing we see. What we perceive in "seeing-as" is not a secondary reality attached and ontologically inferior to a primary one: the lines

---

[21] Aspect-dawning or noticing an aspect: "I contemplate a face, and then suddenly notice its likeness to another. I see it has not changed; and yet I see it differently" (PI, 193e). — One should bear in mind that Wittgenstein is concerned here with clarifying human experience, not with establishing its psychological causes: "We are interested in the concept (of aspect-dawning) and its place among the concepts of experience" (P.I., 193e). The well-known example of aspect-change is the figure of the duck-rabbit which "I can see as a rabbit's head or as a duck's" (PI, 194e). And generally speaking, "a change of aspect is the expression of a *new* perception and at the same time of the perception's being unchanged" (PI, 196e). According to Wittgenstein, "seeing-as" is our normal way of perceiving: we constantly see things as being something else. Thus "we *regard* the photograph, the picture on our wall, as the object itself (the man, the landscape, and so on) depicted there" (PI, 205e; see also 203e).

and color-patches of a face are by no means more real than the smile. And the way we perceive this "more" must not be thought of as the result of a mediation: our perception of the smile, even of its kindness or haughtiness, is unmediated.

The most important point here in Wittgenstein's treatment of the problem of "seeing-as" is his clarification of its immediacy. He brings out a more general anthropological riddle that has to be borne in mind in any confrontation with the particular questions of mystical experience. First he argues that "seeing-as" and the immediacy it implies are integral to the human condition: "seeing-as" is the human way of being in the world, so much so that an "aspect-blind" individual cannot be considered properly human.[22] Then he explains the crucial paradox that this immediacy, characteristic of "seeing-as," implies. This natural, spontaneous way of perceiving something as also being something else is in fact an acquired ability. This seemingly innate capacity is actually taught us: we take it in from an early age and go on developing and adjusting it — the architect learns to see the plan as the house. Consequently, the immediacy of "seeing-as" disappears and the latter becomes mediate when we lack the proper technique for "seeing-as" or when, for whatever reason, its spontaneous practice gets stuck.

With regard to religious experience in general, this analysis of Wittgenstein may prevent us from brushing aside as pure "projection" the opinion of those who see traces of God in particular things and events. Similarly in the case of mystical experience, it may make one think of appeal to the intermediary more as a capacity or attitude which is proper to any person who desires to

---

[22] See the striking passage in PI, 213e-214e which starts as follows: "Could there be human beings lacking in the capacity to see something *as something* — and what would that be like?"

"see" God, rather than as an accidental screen suspended between the mystic and God, which could and should be removed, for instance, by psychological means. It may also remove the need to oscillate between two seemingly contrasting opinions on mystical reports: "these are just the product of some mediating interpretation" (implying that they do not come from God), or/and "here are immediate experiences" (implying that they come from God).

Wittgenstein proposes another important step with regard to mediation: it consists in demystifying the widespread idealization of unmediated encounter.[23] Mystics too seem at times to refer to a contact between humans that would obviate all intermediaries: for example, Hadewijch mentions the possibility of "speaking with the soul" (*metter zielen spreken*), and tells her addressees that to explain the highest way "nothing can be said by reason, unless one speaks with inspirited soul to inspirited soul" (*met ghegheester zielen te ghegheester zielen spreken*).[24] Commenting on Wittgenstein's considerations on "thought-reading," Fergus Kerr describes the ideal in question as follows: "In effect, souls dream of being wordlessly transparent to one another ... a longing to communicate in some more direct way than by using symbols."[25]

[23] For the presentation of Wittgenstein's views in the following paragraphs, I shall draw unashamedly on Fergus Kerr, *Theology after Wittgenstein* (Oxford: Basil Blackwell, 1986).

[24] See CW: *Letter* 28, 92 and *Letter* 22, 130-131. For more details, see Paul Mommaers and Frank Willaert, "Mystisches Erlebnis und sprachliche Vermittlung in den Briefen Hadewijchs," *Religiöse Frauenbewegung und mystische Frömmigkeit im Mittelalter* (Köln: Böhlau Verlag, 1988).

[25] Kerr, *Theology after Wittgenstein*, 44. Wittgenstein: "What would we mean by 'reading thought'? Language is not an indirect method of communication, to be contrasted with 'direct' thought-reading. Thought-reading could only take place through the interpretation of symbols and so would be on the same level as language. It would not get rid of the symbolic process." See *Wittgenstein's Lectures, Cambridge,* 1930-1932, ed. Desmond Lee (Oxford: Blackwell, 1980) 25.

This same idealizing tendency affects our view of self-knowledge as well. We think we are basically self-transparent, able to know our inmost self directly. Yet, as Kerr puts it, "I discover myself, not in some pre-linguistic inner space of self-presence, but in the network of multifarious social and historical relationships."[26] He refers to four suggestive paragraphs of the *Philosophical Investigations* which emphasize that "there is no 'inner experience' which does not have conceptual links with other people's experience."[27] And on our twofold desire to transcend mediation — to know another and to know oneself directly — he summarizes: "The craving for unmediated encounter either with my own states of consciousness or with the objects that confront me has to be resisted."[28]

At this point one needs to be careful: in the wake of Wittgenstein's clarification of idealized, unmediated self-awareness and self-disclosure, one might be tempted into ascribing to him a fashionable view of the human self which he did not hold.[29] While drawing attention to the problems of mediation, he did not intend to do away with the inner life or to deny the possibility of its being communicated. What he did want to do was to put immediate self-knowledge in its proper place, to show that it is neither primary nor independent. Immediacy presupposes mediation, and in this

[26] Ibid., 69.

[27] Ibid., 75. Wittgenstein: "An 'inner process' stands in need of outward criteria" (P.I., 580). "An expectation is embedded in a situation, from which it arises" (581) — "What is a *deep* feeling? Could someone have a feeling of ardent love or hope for the space of one second — *no matter what* preceded or followed this second? — What is happening now has significance — in these surroundings" (P.I., 583).

[28] Ibid., 73.

[29] Iris Murdoch, *The Sovereignty of Good* (London: Routledge and Kegan Paul, 1970) 15, contains the following observation: "But ... while Wittgenstein remains sphinx-like in the background, others have hastened to draw further and more dubious moral and psychological conclusions."

situation "moments of self-transparence" are possible indeed. Kerr refers those who feel that Wittgenstein "wants to eliminate the interior life altogether" to a little dialogue in the *Philosophical Investigations*,[30] and he comments as follows: "The voice that protests on behalf of the reality of the inner life is itself impelled to appeal to its *visibility*. When we think of someone as 'deep', or as having 'inner strength', or 'inner resources', we should automatically fill it out with stories about that person's style of life, or remarks about the character in his or her face, and the like."[31]

Before referring to one more insight of Wittgenstein, it is worth mentioning how the praxis of the mystics appears to fit in with the findings of the philosopher. Despite the difference of world-view and in most cases the historical distance, there is a certain correspondence or bridge between them in the tendency to de-idealize and de-mystify. For instance the mystics would agree in practice with the import of the passages from the *Philosophical Investigations* quoted above (in note 27). No matter how exceptional and personal is the "inner process" to which they attest, the "surroundings" undeniably count for them. Why do these people, who keep saying they cannot "say" it, constantly want to speak and write about it? It is not simply for the sound psychological reason that if they did not communicate, they would go mad. The main reason for their wanting to express themselves, to bring out the inner self, is that they are aware of the need for such experience to "have conceptual links with other people's experience," as Kerr put it. Mystics feel the need to test the authenticity of

---

[30] "'But you surely cannot deny that, for example, in remembering, an inner process takes place?' — What gives the impression that we want to deny anything? When one says 'Still, an inner process does take place here' — one wants to go on: 'After all, you *see* it'" (PI, §305).

[31] Kerr, *Theology after Wittgenstein*, 90. See also p. 148 with the quotation from PI, §587.

their experience; can one be sure that the "deep feeling," however self-evident, comes from God? Usually their guideline is the saying of Jesus: "you can tell a tree by its fruit" (Matthew 12,33); what "precedes and follows" matters very much for them.[32] However, these mystics would have appreciated the fact that the critical philosopher does not deny the possibility of what for them is sheer fact: the immediacy of their meeting the Other.

To some extent Wittgenstein's third step repeats the paradox enunciated by the first: the immediacy of mediated experience. In this case, however, he focuses on the body as the unalloyed intermediary yielding direct knowledge of the soul. A phrase from the *Philosophical Investigations* provides a striking summary of his analysis: "The human body is the best picture of the human soul."[33] Once more the philosopher alerts the student of mysticism: bodily feelings very often appear as integral to mystical experience (as was seen, even if to a limited extent, in Chapter 4), and bodily posture plays an important role in contemplative prayer.[34]

Initially, Wittgenstein helps one to put aside the concept of the "metaphysically generated body" (Kerr's expression), that is, the body seen from the perspective of a supposedly transcendent human spirit. Such an idea of the body, "derived from the thought of the immateriality and invisibility of the soul, displaces our

---

[32] Ruusbroec continually uses such combinations as *vore gaen ende na comen*. For instance, speaking of mystical "rest," he points out that "the grace of God and our active love must precede and follow" (*Opera Omnia* III, b1923-1924).

[33] PI, 178e. On the same page: "My attitude towards him is an attitude towards a soul. I am not of the *opinion* that he has a soul."

[34] For more details on both these points, see Paul Mommaers and Jan Van Bragt, *Mysticism Buddhist and Christian: Encounters with Jan van Ruusbroec*, Nanzan Studies in Religion and Culture (New York: Crossroad, 1995) 151, 221.

experience of the whole living man or woman. This picture of the body gets in the way of our conversation with one another."[35]

Not surprisingly, the effect of this metaphysical view of the human being appears most clearly and painfully in a certain attitude to the face, which "becomes a veil, a mask that needs to be manipulated from behind."[36] But Wittgenstein, reacting against this soul-less, "portrait" concept of the face, points out that we "*see* emotion," and we do not "see facial contortions and make inferences from them (like a doctor framing a diagnosis) to joy, grief, boredom. We describe a face immediately as sad, radiant, bored, even when we are unable to give any other description of the features ... Grief, one would like to say, is personified in the face."[37]

In Chapter 1 we saw the importance of the divine Face as a basic theme in the Bible, and also how the Face of Jesus appears as the primary Icon in Christian contemplation. Here one may note that both Hadewijch and Ruusbroec, among other mystics, emphasize in their descriptions of mystical union this most fascinating "means" of personal encounter. For them the core, the "nature," of the divine as well as of the human being, really appears in the "face." In Letter 6 Hadewijch invites her friends to

---

[35] Kerr, *Theology after Wittgenstein*, 46.

[36] Ibid., 46. Kerr enlarges as follows: "We have to *decide,* on *every* occasion, whether to reveal our thoughts ... The face is *always* under the control of the will ... the face is naturally blank until the soul behind it deliberately allows itself to show through" (p. 80). See also p. 107 on Wittgenstein's imagining "a people with totally expressionless faces": "These people will have nothing human about them."

[37] Ibid., 137. Perhaps the best summary remark by Wittgenstein on the human face is his rhetorical question: "Do I *believe* in a soul in someone else, when I look into his eyes with astonishment and delight?" See *Remarks on the Philosophy of Psychology,* vol.1, eds. G.E.M. Anscombe and G.H. von Wright, trans. G.E.M. Anscombe (Oxford: Basil Blackwell, 1980), §268.

love the Divinity not merely with devotion but with unspeakable desires, always standing with new ardour before the terrible and wonderful countenance in which Love reveals herself (*dat eyselike anschijn van wondere, daer de Minne haer selven al in openbaert*) and engulfs all works. Read in that most holy countenance (*ute dien anschine*) all your judgements and all you have done in your life.

And in Letter 20 she writes:

The eighth nameless hour is that the nature of Love in her countenance is most mysterious to know (*dat der Minnen nature in haer anschijn es alre wonderleecst te kinnnenne*). What one is, is usually best revealed by one's countenance (*de anschijn pleghen nochtan alre openbaerst te sine*). In Love, however, this is what is most secret; for this is Love herself in herself.[38]

Ruusbroec, who points out that "we must be turned towards God ... with a bare countenance" (*met eenen bloten anschyne*), writes in one of his most striking descriptions of the mystical meeting between the divine and the human person:

These two spirits, that is, our spirit and God's Spirit, flash and shine each into the other, and each shows the other its face (*elc toent den anderen sijn aenschijn*) ... Each exacts of the other that which he is (*dat hi es*), and each offers and invites the other to that which he is (*dat hi es*).[39]

---

[38] Hadewijch, CW: *Letter* 6, 130-137 and *Letter* 20, 81-85. In the ninth nameless hour: "And the more deeply Love wounds him at whom she rushes, the more gently, with the dignity of her countenance, she engulfs this loved one within herself (*soe si metter werdicheit van haren anschine dien si mint sachtere in hare selven verdrinket*). See also, especially, CW: *Vision* 13.

[39] Ruusbroec, *The Sparkling Stone*, Opera Omnia X, 798-799 and III, b1346-1349. "Face" renders the Middle Dutch word *aenscijn*. It is the part of the body where the eyes are located, and the eyes shine from within outward: note in Ruusbroec's passage "shine each into the other."

Jan van Ruusbroec on the role of the intermediary

The theme of the intermediary leads to the heart of the spiritual teaching in the work of Jan van Ruusbroec. It will also show, as if from within the mystic's most advanced experience, how the Humanity of Christ can be permanently at the center of his being one with God.

The gist of his teaching is that the intermediaries reappear, or rather revive, in mystic union. This may well come as a surprise. For the mystic-to-be is supposed to expect complete immediacy. He or she has to let go of the ways of knowing and existing that belong to one's ordinary human condition. The mystic, instead of actively approaching by means of images the God who is felt as distant — as the unknown "Object" — has to be willing to be unified with an Other in a passive and imageless way, and even to feel "annihilated."[40] This crucial transition from the non-mystical to the mystical life inevitably gives the impression that what properly belongs to one's humanity — images and other means, activity, the self — this is all wiped out or at least pushed out of the way. At first sight, the mystic's insistence on immediacy may lead one to think that in mystic union the human person with all one's inherent attributes and qualities has to disappear. The doubt may arise whether the experience of the mature mystic does not reveal that the God believed to be "philanthropic,"[41] is in reality an abyss that swallows not only our own being but the Humanity of Christ as well.

[40] See Paul Mommaers and Jan Van Bragt, *Mysticism Buddhist and Christian*, 49-69, "The chief marks of mystical experience."

[41] See Paul's letter to Titus, 3-4, "the kindness and generosity (*philanthropia*) of God our saviour."

"Meeting" as the unchanging centre of the whole spiritual life

For Ruusbroec there is a "natural" or, one might say, a structural relation between God and the human being. The latter is necessarily and permanently "suspended" in the divine Being. Man is essentially God's image, and can never lose this fundamental likeness: believers and unbelievers, sinners and saints alike, they are all ontologically joined with God. At the same time there is a "supernatural" or "accidental" link between God and humans,[42] but these terms can give rise to misunderstanding. Nowadays "supernatural" has an ethereal tone; it seems to refer to some unnatural reality that is detached from, and foreign to, what human beings are by nature. And "accidental" seems to suggest something of external or of secondary importance. Ruusbroec certainly did not understand these words in this sense. For him the "supernatural" *is* the natural, but lived by the human person in a particular way, or rather "possessed" by him or her, as he usually puts it. And for him the "accidental" is what actually counts most, for what takes place "above nature" gives its ultimate sense and splendour to what we have "in nature."

Ruusbroec's favourite term in the context of the "supernatural" is "meeting" (*ontmoet*). This is the term that is used when there is something happening between God and the human person which does not as such belong to their natural, necessary relationship. "Meeting" suffuses the structural link with unexpected life: it is brought about by God's grace evoking human faith; it consists in the "accidental" mutual movement of divine and human persons, which suddenly enriches their "essential" relation.[43]

---

[42] Ruusbroec's expression is *toevallich ende overnatuerlijcke*, and he says, for instance, that "we have nothing of ourselves, neither in nature nor above nature" (*Opera Omnia* III, b1237-1238 and 1469).

[43] I am summarizing here the substance of what I have explained at greater length elsewhere. See "Introduction" to volumes I, III, VIII and X of the *Opera Omnia* and *Mysticism Buddhist and Christian*.

One general remark will be in order here. The "meeting" Ruusbroec has in mind is not essentially a contemplative, let alone a mystical, phenomenon. Every ordinary Christian meets God from the moment she or he comes to believe in him and to trust in him by an act of faith.[44] It is precisely this pre-contemplative, often hardly felt, "meeting" that necessarily lies at the root of every further, maybe highly contemplative, development of the spiritual life. Ruusbroec the mystic is adamant on this point: one will never be a mystical "son of God" without being at the same time, like any believer, a "faithful servant of the Lord." Even the most elevated experience requires this common foundation: "But you should know that all faithful and good men are the sons of God."[45] Just a brief scan of *The Spiritual Espousals* is enough to see how "meeting" is always at the centre of the spiritual life:

> For all our inward spiritual seeing ... and all our virtuous going-out ... all tend towards the meeting and union with Christ our Bridegroom, for he is our eternal rest and the end and reward of all our labor.[46]

This passage shows not only that "meeting" is the aim of all inner and outer practice, but that far from being two successive or separate moments, "meeting" and rest are really combined. This point is also prominent on the last page of *The Spiritual Espousals*:

> And this is the active meeting (*werkelijc ontmoet*) of the Father and of the Son, in which we are lovingly embraced ... Now, this active meeting and this loving embrace are, in their ground, enjoyable and without mode.[47]

---

[44] It should be clear that I am not making theological statements here that would exclude non-Christians from meeting God. I am trying to determine this medieval mystic's view of the relationship between God and human beings; see *Mysticism Buddhist and Christian*.

[45] *The Sparkling Stone, Opera Omnia* X, 378-379.

[46] *Opera Omnia* III, b1387-1390.

[47] *Opera Omnia* III, c204-208. On the idea of life within the trinitarian God as the "model" of the mystic's experience, see the "Introduction" to the *Little Book of Enlightenment,* in *Opera Omnia* I, p. 41-42.

Clearly, even in the most advanced mystical experience "meeting" is not excluded. It is not after or beyond "active meeting," but in its "ground" that ultimate rest, "enjoyable and without mode," is to be found.

Describing the phenomenon of meeting

Ruusbroec explains the basic structure of "meeting" in a neatly arranged passage in *The Spiritual Espousals,* where he proceeds in three steps:[48] he begins with a general definition:

> You know well that every meeting is a gathering of two persons who come from different places which are opposed to and separate from each other.

Then he goes on to specify this starting-point within a common religious perspective:

> Now Christ comes from above as a lord and a generous giver who can do all things; and we come from below as poor servants, unable to do anything ourselves, but needing everything.

Finally, as a mystic who sees the contemplative path as a "turning inward," he readjusts the former perspective: "Christ comes from within outwards, and we come to him from without inwards."

To look more closely at the way in which the phenomenon of "meeting" is organized, Ruusbroec gives a lead in the concluding passage of this section of the *Espousals:*

> And this meeting ... occurs in two manners, that is, with intermediary and without intermediary.[49]

These words raise the key question concerning mediation: to what extent is the intermediary more than just a provisional means in

---

[48] *Opera Omnia* III, b1390-1396.
[49] *Opera Omnia* III, b1396-1398.

relation to immediacy? Is "meeting without intermediary" the summit in any human way of knowing, detached far above anything involving intermediaries?

Ruusbroec has certainly made plain the difference between mediate and immediate experience. But there is another revealing sentence in *The Spiritual Espousals* that brings the two together and also shows how he understands mediation as it appears in meeting:

> For God gives, in one bestowal, Himself and His gifts; and the (human) spirit, in each inward-turning, gives itself and all its works.[50]

This is, in a nutshell, Ruusbroec's crucial insight about "meeting" and mediation: it is in one "gift"[51] that God gives himself and his gifts. However, the mystic further clarifies this compound self-giving of God, which provokes a similar response in the human person. He does this in a developed description in the first book of *The Spiritual Espousals,* where he is dealing with "meeting" in the pre-mystical, "active" life:

> We should also rest upon the One and in the One whom we intend and love (*meynt ende mint*), more than upon all his messengers which He sends, namely, his gifts. The soul should also rest in God above all the enrichments and the presents that it can send by its messengers. The messengers of the soul are intention, love and desire; these bear all good works and all virtuousness to God. Above all this, the soul should rest in its Beloved above all multiplicity.[52]

---

[50] *Opera Omnia* III, b1942-1944.

[51] The original Middle Dutch text has a stronger sound than the modern translation(s): *god ghevet in eere* (in one) *ghichten hem selven ende sine gaven.*

[52] *Opera Omnia* III, a809-814.

In this passage it is striking that the "supernatural" relationship of "meeting" is very dynamic. There is no suggestion that it is a terminus or a turned-in state. "Meeting" is movement. It is the interplay of two beings "coming" towards each other. The chapters devoted to "meeting" in the different books of *The Spiritual Espousals* have as their motto: "The Bridegroom comes." For Ruusbroec the ultimate reality, in the sense already indicated, is this lively interplay, generated from a reciprocal giving-and-receiving.

Each partner in the "meeting," as well as the bond that unites them, is a compound reality. As the divine and the human "go out to meet" (to use Ruusbroec's own expression), they appear to consist of different layers. There is in both of them a depth which nevertheless is such that it manifests itself — makes itself *present* — in what each gives to the other, that is, in what they do for or to one another. God himself comes through his gifts, the human person responds through his or her presents. Briefly, these two beings are persons who dwell in their reciprocal offerings.[53]

Obviously, a materialistic interpretation of these offerings is out of place here. The gifts are not some sort of precious objects exchanged by partners who have first produced them for their own sake; from the outset these gifts benefit from the spiritual dynamism given by "intention."[54] God's gifts are valuable for being

---

[53] An image of the self-revealing (literally "ex-pressive") gesture of the believer making an offering to the deity or of the lover presenting flowers to the beloved — with out-stretched arms — comes to mind here. Such an image is appropriate as something similar appears, for instance, in *The Sparkling Stone,* where Ruusbroec describes how the meeting of the human being with God is to take place: "In our approach to God we must carry ourselves and all our works before us as an eternal offering to God, and in the presence of God we shall forsake ourselves and all our works, and dying in love we shall pass away" (*Opera Omnia* X, 422-425).

[54] "The single intention is end and beginning and enrichment of all virtues" (*Opera Omnia* III, b1536-1537). In the passage analyzed here, intention is also

his "messengers" and human presents are meant to be borne by the human messengers of "intention, love, and desire."[55] The link that actually joins the divine and the human in "meeting" is not the gift as such but the *giving* of the gift, the *act* of mutually reaching out to each other in the interchange of gifts.

Thus intention (*meynen*, to "intend") is what binds the partners together, and the chief feature of this living link is immediately obvious: it is made up of different moments[56] corresponding to the different layers that constitute the partners. Intention involves both activity and rest. In its first moment it is occupied with receiving and offering the gifts, in its second it pays attention to their several sources. And just as the appearance and the depth of each partner form one and the same reality, so action and rest go together in one single act. Ruusbroec uses a graphic word to suggest how intention integrates these two moments: intention "passes through" (*doregheet*) itself and all things:

supposed to be single: "We should not set forth two ends in our intention" (b804). — Intention and intentionality have already been mentioned in chapter 1 of this study. The focus here will be on the human side of "meeting," as it appears in this passage; this should not be taken to imply a toning down of the similarity and reciprocity between the divine and human partners. For a suggestive and daring passage where Ruusbroec evokes this correspondence, see the "storm of love" text quoted below (note 64).

[55] In this text of Ruusbroec, the strong, ancient and medieval sense of "messenger" is to be understood. The messenger actually and fully "re-presents" the person who sends, and should be considered the image of the sender, in the ontological sense mentioned above (see chapter 1, note 22: *L' image: Fonctions et usages des images dans l'Occident mediéval*). Thus the messenger's presence is supposed to be effective, not simply passing on a message but performing it. On listening to the messenger's message, one hears the master's voice and not just the words.

[56] "Moments," not in a temporal sense but in the descriptive/phenomenological sense of aspects/dimensions.

> The single intention offers God praise and honor and all virtues, and it goes beyond and passes through itself, all the heavens, and all things, and it finds God in the one-fold ground of its very self.[57]

By this passing through any gift or activity, the human person reaches "the One we intend."[58] This implies on the one hand seeing through the particular character of all gifts and passing "above all multiplicity," and on the other, recognizing the limited range of all activity and therefore accepting to become passive and willing to rest.

This description of "meeting" occurs in the first book of the *Espousals*, which deals with the pre-mystical, "active life." This explains why there is only a slight hint here of "resting in the Beloved" and of the passivity that goes with it.[59] More has to be said to fill in this initial picture of "meeting," but already two important points concerning Ruusbroec's view of the intermediary have appeared. First, the *presents* one offers, that is, the practice of particular virtues as well as the inner attitude that inspires them, "all good works and all virtuousness," belong to the domain of the "intermediaries" or "means," and to this same intermediate domain belongs the *activity* one develops in intending the One. Secondly, the mediated and the immediate are intimately connected: *together* they make up the organic structure of "meeting."

---

[57] *Opera Omnia* III, b1537-1539.

[58] "For to be intent on God means to see God spiritually" (*Opera Omnia* III, a779).

[59] Earlier in the *Espousals* the person who has not yet reached the "inner life" — concentrating on "outward modes" — is characterized as follows: "He does not feel that he is resting in God above all virtues. And therefore he possesses One whom he does not know" (*Opera Omnia* III, a732-734).

Being mystically one with God is a compound phenomenon

One of the most striking features in Ruusbroec's description of mystic union is his insistence that it consists of different aspects: one can even arrange in contrasting columns a series of his quasi-synonymous terms and their opposites. Among these correlated terms the most inclusive pairs have an abstract ring: "union" (*eninghe*) as opposed to "unity" (*enecheit*); "with intermediary" (*met middel*) as opposed to "without intermediary" (*sonder middel*). However, there are many concrete, descriptive terms too that can be classified in the "union/with intermediary" column or in the "unity/without intermediary" column: for instance, "working" (*werken*) and "active" (*werkelec*) on the one hand, "resting" (*rasten*) and "enjoyable" (*ghebrukelec*) on the other.

Before examining in detail some texts, a caveat is needed: this type of text demands close attention to words, rather than a search for "deep" mystical substance. Gradually it should become clear how certain words form significant phenomenological chains, without one having to probe consciously for mystical depth. Take, for instance, the leading term in the first text to be analyzed: "union." Apart from any reference to mystical experience, and even without the accompanying adjective "living," the word "union" itself indicates movement or progress; it signals an ongoing development, especially in relation to its counterpart "unity," which indicates rest and completion. By slowly savouring Ruusbroec's words, equivalent expressions soon catch one's attention. For instance, "otherness" (*anderheit*) seems to be connected with "union": partners on being moved to union necessarily feel they are different from each other. Similarly, the word "(God-)like" (*ghelijc*) belongs to the same semantic chain: insofar as the human partner is aware of resembling the Other, he or she at once senses a distance in being one and a tendency to bridge the gap, which is a way of feeling the characteristic incompleteness of union.

Another point to remember is that the descriptive passages to be considered now do refer indeed to the mystical experience of being one, which is a completely passive phenomenon. The presence of terms that suggest activity — such as, to mention the most obvious, "active" (*werkelec*) — should not mislead one into thinking they indicate a non-mystical appendage to the truly mystical experience. If such were the case, union would have to be considered as falling outside the area of what is properly mystical being-one, and one would overlook a key element in Ruusbroec's teaching. One would fail to see from within the mystic's own experience, so to speak, how the intermediaries fare in the human being one with God.

To start with, a passage from *The Mirror of Eternal Blessedness* reveals the many terms referring in different ways to the same feeling as "union" and "with intermediary":

> The living union that we feel with God is active (*werkelec*) and always renews itself between us and God. In that we mutually kiss and touch, we feel otherness (*anderheit*) that does not let us be quiet in ourselves. For though we are above reason, we are not without reason. And therefore we feel that we touch, and are touched; love, and are loved, and are always renewing and turning back into ourselves, going and coming as the lightning of heaven. For much as we incline and strive in love, it is swimming against the current: we cannot break through our createdness nor pass beyond it.[60] And

---

[60] According to Ruusbroec, mediation as it appears in mystical experience, that is, as integral to the spiritual phenomenon of being one with God, is based on the ontological fact of man's createdness (a consideration that appeared earlier in this chapter when reference was made to Julian of Norwich's insight into the sense of "means"). As reason teaches that no created being can contain uncreated Being, a human being can receive God only in a mediated way, that is, reduced to one's own created measure. However, in the mystical experience of

therefore his touching and our hidden inner striving are the last intermediary (*middel*) between us and God, where we become united (*vereeneghen*) with him in mutual meeting in love ... And therefore we always remain standing above reason in our selfhood: unimaged, gazing, striving in incomprehensible richness. In our works we always remain (God-)like (*ghelijc*) in the purity of our spirit. For we feel that we contemplate and strive in an Other (*in een ander*) than what we ourselves are: through this we are (God-)like. But in his works we are wrought by his Spirit, and undergo the transformation (*ghedooeghen de overforminghe*) of his resplendence and his love. There we are above likeness, the sons of God by grace.[61]

This elaborate description speaks of the aspect of *union*, except for the last two sentences, where the phrase to "undergo the transformation" is a set expression referring to *unity*. But these two moments of being one are not only different; they are opposites: for instance, in *The Sparkling Stone* Ruusbroec writes, "poor and rich, hungry and replete, working and at rest, are contraries indeed," and in *The Twelve Beguines*, "unity in love (*eenheit in minnen*) cannot become otherness (*anderheit*), and otherness cannot become unity; thus they are both divided in one spirit."[62] And yet, both these aspects are integral to the phenomenon of being one; both appear in one and the same human spirit. There ought then to exist an intimate connection between them, unless one assumes, despite the mystic's assertions to the contrary, that his experience is simply a succession of instantaneous exposures:

being one with God, this unbridgeable difference appears as caused above all by God's inexhaustible abundance: "For a created vessel cannot contain an uncreated good; this is why there is an eternal, hungry avidity here, and God overflows everything, but (is) always uncontained (*vloeyt al over in een ontbliven*)," (*Opera Omnia* III, b1321-1324).

    [61] *Werken* III, p. 207,1-208,3.

    [62] *Opera Omnia* X, 489-490 and *Werken* IV, p. 198, 27-30.

union and unity must be organically related, excluding any gradual, smooth transition from one to the other. If there is a passage,
it is bound to take the form of "dying."[63] In the following text this
crucial point is driven home with three expressions: the human
spirit "exhausts its activity," is "reduced to nothing," and "fails
in all its activity":

> And the more inner and nobler (the spirit) is, the more quickly it
> must exhaust its activity (*hem uut werket*), being reduced to nothing
> in love (*te nieute in minnen*), and then it falls back into new activity.
> And this is the life of heaven. The voracious spirit always imagines
> that it is eating and swallowing God, but by God's touch it is itself
> constantly being swallowed, and it fails in all its activity (*faliert in al
> sijn werken*), and itself becomes love, above all activity.[64]

[63] See the passage from *The Sparkling Stone* quoted in note 53. When Ruusbroec wishes to refer to the human being's felt transition into God, the verb that
appears again and again is "to die." For example, in *The Sparkling Stone*, "And
therefore it is all unfathomable in which the spirit has to die to its own self in
bliss and return to life in virtues at love's command and touch" (*Opera Omnia*
X, 774-776).

[64] *Opera Omnia* III, b1364-1369: the words *hem uut werket* might be rendered more literally by "it overworks, overspends, outdoes itself." Although not
directly relevant, it is worth quoting here the famous passage from *The Spiritual
Espousals* which speaks of the "storm of love" and where Ruusbroec shows how
union develops into something beyond itself: "In this storm of love, two spirits
contend: the Spirit of God and our spirit. God, through the Holy Spirit, inclines
Himself towards us, and thereby we are touched in love. And by God's operation
and the faculty of loving, our spirit presses into and inclines itself towards God,
and thereby God is touched. From these two, there arises the strife of love: in the
depths of the encounter and in that innermost and most intense visit, each spirit
is wounded the most by love. These two spirits, that is our spirit and God's
Spirit, flash and shine each into the other, and each shows the other its face. This
makes each spirit continually crave for the other with love. Each exacts of the
other that which he is, and each offers and invites the other to that which he is.
This makes the lovers flow away (into each other). God's touch and His gifts, our
loving craving and our giving in return, keep love steadfast. This flowing out and
flowing back cause the fountain of love to overflow. Thus God's touch and our

There is one more significant expression in the passage that should not be overlooked. The spirit that exhausts its activity also "falls back into new activity" (*in nuwe werken*): the word that matters is "new." The self-transgression of the mystic's inner activity does not entail its disappearance. On the contrary, the activity is again and again intensified. Ruusbroec's key word here is *vernuwen,* "to renew," which appears twice in the description of union quoted above, each time accompanied by "always."[65] If it is borne in mind that union requires some sort of intermediary, it is clear how for Ruusbroec the mediation of union is not wiped out by its transition into the immediacy of unity. On the contrary, the intermediary is constantly renewed:

> And the more inner gifts He gives, and the more subtly He moves (us), the more inner and lustier is the practice of the spirit ... And this is in constant renewal (*altoes in een vernuwen*). For God always gives new gifts, and our spirit always turns inward again ... and in this meeting it always receives a new (and) higher (gift) (*een hogher nuwe*). And thus one is constantly growing into a higher life. And this active meeting is entirely through intermediary. For the gifts of God and our virtues and the activity of our spirit constitute that intermediary.[66]

love's craving become one single love. Here a person is so possessed by love that he must forget himself and God, and he knows nothing but love. Thus the spirit is burned up in the fire of love, and it goes so deeply into God's touch that it is overcome in all its craving and is reduced to nothing in all its acts; and it must exhaust its activity, and it becomes itself love, above all devotedness, and it possesses the innermost (core) of its created being, above all virtues, where all creaturely works begin and end. This is love in itself, foundation and ground of all virtues" (*Opera Omnia* III, b1340-1359).

[65] See the text that goes with note 60.

[66] *Opera Omnia* III, b1507-1515.

Ruusbroec's skill as a writer can be appreciated in another passage where he plays with different tenses of the verb *berren*, "to burn," to help his reader "see" union and unity as well as the transition between them:

> Our spirit becomes like oil bubbling in the fire of the love of God. So long as the oil is foaming and crackling and bubbling, there is still un-likeness (*onghelijc*). But when the fire has consumed and burned up all un-likeness, the oil becomes pure and hotter than hot, and it is still and immobile like the fire ... The greatest heat is where our spirit is burning (*berrent*), and hotter than hot when it burns up (*verberrent*) and undergoes the transformation by God. But where it has been burnt up (*verberrent es*) and is one spirit with God, there it is idle, essential love.[67]

For a final description of unity a passage from *A Mirror of Eternal Blessedness* deserves to be quoted. It describes how this aspect of the mystic's being one with God appears

> where we are one with God above all practice of love in an eternal enjoyment (*ghebruken*), that is: above working and enduring, in a blessed being empty (*een salegh ledegh sijn*), above union with God, in unity where no one can work than God alone. For his work is he himself and his nature. And in his working we are inactive and transformed (*ledegh ende overformt*), and one with him in his love ... There we feel no difference (*onderscheet*) between us and God, for we are, above ourselves and above all order, breathed out (of ourselves) into his love. There is no demanding, nor desiring, giving, nor taking; but a blessed essential empty being (*een salegh ledegh wesen*), crown and essential reward of all holiness and all virtue.[68]

---

[67] *Werken* IV, p. 102,26-103,8.
[68] *Werken* III, p. 215,12-30.

With intermediary and without intermediary: one single experience

From Ruusbroec's account the mystic's experience of being one with God requires that two different, indeed contrasting, aspects go together. In addition, his texts have shown not just the coexistence but the incessant interplay of these opposites. Yet one may still wonder whether it is really a single experience that the author has in mind. Does the advanced mystic feel union and unity at the same time, and does he or she know God at once with and without intermediary? Is this being one with the Beloved the integration of working and resting?

First, one unmistakably affirmative answer which uses the terminology of working/resting:

> For in one now, in one instant, love acts and rests in its beloved. And the one is reinforced by the other. For the higher the love, the more the rest; and the more the rest, the more inner the love. For the one lives in the other. And he who loves not, rests not; and he who rests not, loves not.[69]

But Ruusbroec also articulates the nucleus of his teaching on mediation using the most obvious terms: with/without intermediary, as in what may be the key sentence of the whole *Spiritual Espousals*[70]:

> Now understand: God comes without cease within us, with intermediary and without intermediary, and demands of us enjoyment and

---

[69] *Opera Omnia* III, b1709-1713.

[70] *Opera Omnia* III, b1932-1934. For a detailed discussion of this passage and its focal role in the *Espousals,* see my article, "Une phrase clef des *Noces Spirituelles*," in *Jan van Ruusbroec: The Sources, Contents and Sequels of his Mysticism*, eds. P. Mommaers and N. De Paepe, Medievalia Lovaniensia, series I, studia XII (Leuven: University Press, 1984).

activity, and that the one should not be hindered by the other, but rather always fortified.

The use of chiasmus in this sentence shows almost visibly how the Divine and the human are bound up with each other in their being one in an inextricably twofold way: human activity responds to God's affecting the person with intermediary, while human enjoyment responds to God's being present without intermediary. Just as working and resting "live the one in the other," so mediation and immediacy are mutually "fortified." Ruusbroec goes on to portray the mystic at the height of the "inner life":

> Therefore, the inner person possesses his life in these two modes, that is in resting and in activity. And in each, he is whole and undivided, for he is wholly in God where he rests in enjoyment, and he is wholly in himself, where he loves with works. And he is admonished and bidden by God at every moment to renew both rest and activity.[71]

These passages leave no doubt that the author wishes to bear witness to the felt paradox of union and unity inextricably going together in one single experience; similarly he highlights not just the permanence but the ceaseless "renewal" of the intermediaries. He could hardly be more explicit, and yet there is another, perhaps even more striking way in which he underlines this same message. In a passage from *The Seven Rungs* the mystic's being one with God is shown as a kind of triangle, and the two aspects already mentioned are referred to by another pair of contrasting terms: "to go inward" (*ingaen*) and "to go outward" (*uutgaen*). Here these are used to express the one constant, "to remain united" (*gheëeneght bliven/ bliven altoes een/ gheëeneght bliven*):

---

[71] *Opera Omnia* III, b1935-1939.

Even if the spirit loses itself and if its activity fails as it achieves enjoyment and blessedness, it is always renewed in grace, charity, and virtuousness. Thus the going inward into idle enjoyment (*ingaen in een ledegh ghebruken*) and the going outward into good works (*uutgaen in goeden werken*), and always remain united with God's Spirit (*altoes gheëeneght bliven*): this is what I mean. For just as we blink our eyes open and closed so quickly that we are not aware of it happening, so, too, we die in God and live from God, and yet always remain one with him (*bliven altoes een met gode*). So, too, we shall go outward into our sensitive life and go inward with love and cling to God and remain one in God without moving (*in god gheëeneght bliven sonder beweeghen*).[72]

Not surprisingly, the second book of *The Spiritual Espousals* ends with the following characterization of the "inward life":

> And thus we shall be eternally indwelling and always flowing out and without cease returning in again.[73]

By way of summary

Ruusbroec's teaching on the question of mediation emphasizes two main points. Firstly, the experience of being one with God as

---

[72] *Werken* III, p. 269, 12-23. The triangular structure of being one with God is seen most clearly in the *Little Book of Enlightenment,* where the central theme is the organic relation between, on the one hand, "with intermediary/without intermediary" and on the other, "without difference": "And so they are united to God by intermediary, without intermediary, and also without difference" (*Opera Omnia* I, 337-338). Note the key passage: "With God they will ebb and flow, and will always be in repose, in possessing and enjoying. They will work and endure and rest in the super-essence without fear. They will go out and in (*ute gaen ende in gaen*) and find nourishment within and without" (438-440). For more details, see the Introduction in *Opera Omnia* I.

[73] *Opera Omnia* III, b2216-2218.

lived by the full-fledged mystic does not obliterate the intermediaries.[74] On the contrary, they are constantly "renewed": from being the means used by the person "working" his or her way towards God they have changed into expressions indicating the feeling of "resting" in God. It is now within the being-one with the divine that the mystic rediscovers what being human means, "admonished" to be more and more oneself while remaining one with the Other. Secondly, this general picture of mystic union makes it abundantly clear that Ruusbroec, precisely in his capacity as a world-class mystic, may be able to truly explain the permanent role of the Humanity of Christ, "the one mediator between God and men."

[74] *En passant*, a most interesting argument *e contrario* appears in almost all the works of Ruusbroec. In his view the big mistake of the adepts of "natural contemplation" or "going inward without grace" is precisely that they want to get rid of all intermediaries, of everything genuinely human: "They say that they live above all modes modeless (*boven all wise wiseloes*), and that they are as inactive as when they were not; and that they have neither knowledge nor love, will nor desire, nor any practice of virtues, but they are empty of all (*alles leedegh*)" (*Werken* III, p. 193,10-15). For an extensive treatment of Ruusbroec's appreciation and critique of "natural contemplation," see *Mysticism Buddhist and Christian*, Part III.

CHAPTER VI

**RUUSBROEC:
THE WAY FROM HUMANITY TO DIVINITY**

For Ruusbroec the sole objective foundation of a person's becoming one with God, both in the ordinary and in the mystic sense, is the saving fact of the incarnation of the divine Word: "Christ, the solid rock, is his foundation."[1] And the corresponding subjective basis is faith in Jesus, the Son of God: "For no one comes to the Father except through the Son and through his passion and death, which he endured in love. Those who wish to ascend in any other way are deceived."[2]

Thus the first step for all "good persons"[3] on the way to God consists in considering and following Jesus. This means that one meditates upon the figure of the Man and tries to become like him, inwardly and outwardly:

In order for us to follow Him in virtues according to our strength, it now behooves us to consider in Christ our Bridegroom the modes

---

[1] *Opera Omnia,* III, a450-451.

[2] *Werken,* III, p.132,18-21. This is not the place to comment on Ruusbroec's apparently exclusivist statements, but see Mommaers and Van Bragt, *Mysticism Buddhist and Christian,* 213-217.

[3] This is how Ruusbroec designates the ordinary faithful, and, as will be seen, he repeats constantly that the mystic too should always be such a "good person." Here the word "ordinary" indicates not a lack of earnestness, but of experience. Good persons take faith seriously, so without any exceptional religious feelings each "puts the glory of God first in all his works." See the "three points that make up a good person" in *The Sparkling Stone* (*Opera omnia,* X, 6-24).

that he practiced within and the works that He wrought without, which are: virtues and works of virtue.[4]

Jesus is prominent in the first instance as the outstanding model upon which all who desire to approach God need to mirror themselves. He is indeed God's own "mirror and his image ... him you shall bear in your hands, before your eyes and in your heart."[5] However, Jesus is not just the model for all "good people" to imitate. As soon as a person turns to him in faith, the Godman "dwells" and "lives" in him or her. He "works within" the faithful, he "acts on" them so as to incline them to live in the same way as he did: "If then Christ lives in you and you in Him, follow Him in works and in enduring."[6] Through this active union with the Son, every ordinary Christian becomes a "son of God," and the mystic will, in addition, become conscious of the sonship. Ruusbroec's clearest explanation appears in the following passage from *The Sparkling Stone*:

[4] *Opera Omnia*, III, a176-179. This passage from the *Spiritual Espousals* is followed by a long meditation on Christ's humility, charity, patient endurance and suffering.

[5] *Werken*, III, p. 142,4-8. It is worth noting here that Jesus is also presented as the model for the sort of mystical experience that Ruusbroec proposes. After describing, in *The Spiritual Espousals*, the deficient mystical experience of those who "contemplate without grace" or "in a natural manner" and only reach "emptiness," he goes on: "But Christ, God's Son, who, according to His Humanity, is the rule and the head of all good people, as to how they ought to live ... His soul was and is united and blessed in the divine being. But He could not — nor ever shall — come to this emptiness (*ledicheit*) ... And therefore, enjoyment and activity (*ghebruken ende werken*) constitute the blessedness of Christ and of all His saints, and this is the life of all good people, each one in the measure of his love" (*Opera Omnia*, III, b2196-2207). For more information on Ruusbroec's treatment of "natural" mysticism, see Mommaers and Van Bragt, *Mysticism Buddhist and Christian*, chapters 10 and 12.

[6] *Werken*, III, p. 232,13-15.

> But you should know that all faithful and good people are the sons
> of God. For they are all born out of the Spirit of God and the Spirit
> of God lives in them, and he moves and impels everyone in particu-
> lar, according to his ability, towards virtue and good works in which
> he is pleasing to God. But because they have turned towards God in
> different degrees and because their practice is different, I call certain
> people faithful servants, others secret friends, and still others hidden
> sons. Yet they are all servants and friends and sons for they all serve
> and love and intend one God and they all live and work out of the
> free Spirit of God.[7]

So Ruusbroec shows how the ordinary way to God goes through
the One who called himself "the Way." He also emphasizes the
basic equality of the "good person" and the mystic, while indicating where they differ — in the degree of consciousness of their
common sonship. But how can a person move from the "active"
to the "inner life"?[8] In particular, what is the role of the Godman
in this crucial transition? Does the "good person" prescind from
Jesus in order to enter the mystical life?

In *The Spiritual Espousals*, Ruusbroec gives an extensive
description of what may happen to the person who has been living
the active life as perfectly as one possibly can and feels at the
verge of the inner life.[9] First,

---

[7] *Opera Omnia,* X, line 78-87: obviously, "faithful servants" is a quasi-syn-
onym for "good people."

[8] According to Ruusbroec, three main stages (usual but not necessary) can be
distinguished in the mystic's development: the "active life," the "inner life" or
the "life of yearning," and the "contemplative life." For present purposes it will
be enough to note that the "active life" refers to the pre-mystical condition that
characterizes the "good person": in order to pray and to practice the virtues one
employs all of one's faculties in the ordinary way, that is to say, without feeling
God's "working within." The "inner life" is tantamount to the "mystical life,"
where one's dynamic activity is replaced with passivity, and there is a feeling
that God is "working within." For more about the way in which Ruusbroec
orders the spiritual life, see *Mysticism Buddhist and Christian,* p. 144-155.

[9] *Opera Omnia,* III, a828-855.

> he will frequently be touched in his desire to see, to know, to under-
> stand who this Bridegroom, Christ, is: for his sake He became man
> and labored in love until death ... When a person considers (*aen siet*)
> this, he becomes overwhelmingly moved to see and to know Christ
> as He is in Himself; even though he knows Him in His works, that,
> he thinks, is not sufficient.

The two distinguishing marks of the good person still in the active
life are quite evident: spiritual practice is mainly a matter of "considering" (*aensien*); and the experience of God is restricted to the
Other's "works," that is, to the realm of the intermediaries. What
is new now, at the height of the active life, is the appearance of
"desire," and precisely of the desire to go beyond the intermediaries in order to attain to Christ "as He is in Himself." Such a person has reached the frontier and the question is, can such a person
do anything to enter into the land of mystical experience, into the
"inner life"? Ruusbroec indicates a twofold path. The first leads
upwards and is likely to cause some surprise for two reasons:
firstly, it consists in employing one's intellectual powers and far
from setting doctrine aside — in this case the twelve articles of the
Christian faith — it takes doctrine as the guide for this "desiring"
person to come nearer to God Himself. However, the outcome of
this ascent is equally unexpected from the author of a book enti-
tled *The Spiritual Espousals,* who has just shed light on a person's
longing for the perception of the Bridegroom. Ruusbroec presents
the "highest knowledge" as a disconcertingly apophatic experience — to "recognize, in the light of faith, that God is incomprehensible and unknowable." For him those who desire to see the
Man do not become enmeshed in the Humanity:

> Then he should do as the publican Zacchaeus did, who desired to
> see Jesus and who He was. He should run ahead of the whole
> crowd, that is, multiplicity of creatures; they make us little and
> short so that we cannot see God. And he should climb up the tree of

> faith which grows from above downwards, for its roots are in the Godhead. This tree has twelve branches, namely, the twelve articles. The lowest ones speak of God's humanity (*vander menscheit gods*) ... The top of this tree speaks of the divinity, of threeness of Persons and of oneness of God's nature. It is to this oneness that a person should hold fast on the top of the tree, for it is there that Christ must pass, with all his gifts.
>
> Here comes Jesus, and sees that man and addresses him in the light of faith: telling him that He, according to His divinity, is incommensurable and incomprehensible, and inaccessible and unfathomable, and surpassing all created light and all finite comprehension. This is the highest knowledge of God that a person may have in the active life: that he recognize, in the light of faith, that God is incomprehensible and unknowable.[10]

However, this cloud of unknowing that hovers over the peak of the active life is not where the spiritual life ends. At this point, Ruusbroec opens up a new vista. The "good person," who has climbed up the tree of faith as high as this, is ready to become an "inner person," a mystic, but on two conditions: first, one must go downwards now, in order to enter, or rather fall, into the Unfathomable; and one needs to acknowledge that desire is the true power of the human being, giving the ability to take the risk of such an irrational descent:

> In this light Christ speaks to that man's longing: 'Come down quickly, for today I must dwell in thy house.' This hasty descent is nothing other than a flowing-down with longing and with love in the abyss of the Godhead, which no understanding can reach in created light. But where intellect remains outside, there longing and love go in.

---

[10] *Opera Omnia,* III, a836-851 (paragraph divisions added). For the figure of Zacchaeus, see Luke 19,1-10.

From Humanity to Divinity in taking Communion

Many would have thought that for the mystic, who is supposed to enjoy immediacy, the Eucharist would be a special obstacle. If such intermediaries as "images" can appear to be a hindrance to mystical experience, are not the sacraments even more incompatible?[11] In their case the mediating sign is predominant as outward thing. At the moment of Communion one receives not only an image of Christ, but his Body as it really is, and, as we shall see soon,[12] the sacramental Body may produce an effect on the body and on the senses of the person receiving.

Given the reality of Christ as a man, Ruusbroec has no difficulty in ascribing to him what he considers to be the universally applicable structure of a human being.[13] Consequently, when Christ

---

[11] Ruusbroec actually came across people who, for contemplative reasons, rejected the sacraments as well as all intermediaries. (See chapter 5 of this study, note 74). In *A Mirror of Eternal Blessedness*, he presents the adepts of "natural contemplation" as "saying that they are elevated above all the sacraments of holy Church and that they have no need of those; nor do they want any of them ... Modelessness (*onwise*) they have found in themselves." These people come to "scorn God and his grace, holy Church and all its sacraments ... and say they live above all modes modeless" (*boven alle wise wiseloes*) (*Werken*, III, 191,5-16 and 193,7-10).

[12] The importance of the corporeal aspects of communion is not a novelty introduced by medieval mystics. Ever since the Church Fathers this point has been strongly emphasized. See my introduction to *A Mirror of Eternal Blessedness, Opera Omnia*, VIII, note 8 in 3.2.1.

[13] Obviously, Ruusbroec is not a psychologist, even if his description in *The Spiritual Espousals* and *A Mirror of Eternal Blessedness* of the psychosomatic aspects of mystical experience is remarkable. Nevertheless he makes use of a "picture of the soul" which he inherited from St. Augustine and, after Eckhart, developed himself. This enables him to locate aspects of the *extraordinary* phenomenon of mystic union in the *ordinary* structure of the human psyche. He is then able, so to speak, to make visible the different aspects of the experience. For a more extensive presentation of Ruusbroec's view of the human, see *Mysticism*

gives himself in Communion, he does so in a threefold way according to the tripartite division of the humanity he shares with everyone else: he offers his body, his spirit and his personality:

> He gives us His flesh and His blood and His bodily life, glorified, full of joy and sweetness. And He gives us His spirit with its higher faculties, full of glory and gifts, truth and justice. And He gives us His personality, with its divine clarity which raises His spirit and all enlightened spirits into the sublime enjoyable unity.[14]

Ruusbroec then goes on to describe how this gift, "which Christ has left in the holy Church as common to all good people,"[15] may be best received. The most striking feature is the great importance he attaches to the mental act of "observing and beholding." Naturally this priest, who throughout his life remained an upright member of the Church, accepted the doctrine current in his day as to the effectiveness of the sacraments: even if the person who

Buddhist and Christian, chapter 5: 'Profiling the Human'. Here it is enough to know that he sees the body-soul as consisting of three levels that are distinct but by no means separate. First there is the lower or outer level of the body and the senses (both exterior and interior), which has the "heart" as its centre. Next there is the level of the spiritual powers — memory, will and intelligence — which originate from the "unity of the spirit." Finally there is the "essence" (*wesen*), and this is the ontological core of the human being which is "suspended" in the divine Being. Ruusbroec also consistently uses the term "person" (*persoen*) or "personality" (*persoenlijcheit*), and applies it to the "unity of the spirit": "But all the faculties of the soul, however they act, have all their strength and their potency from their domain, that is, from the unity of the spirit, where it exists in its personal being" (*steet in sijn persoenlijcke wesen*) (*Opera Omnia,* III, b1446-1449). Psychologically speaking, "person" is the one source from which the different faculties draw their strength. From an ontological point of view, "person" is the essential capacity of the human being to exist independently. It is as "person" that Christ differs definitively from his fellow humans.

[14] *Opera Omnia,* III, b1152-1156. Ruusbroec wrote two extensive passages on the Eucharist, the first in *The Spiritual Espousals* (b1140-1207), the second in *A Mirror of Eternal Blessedness* (*Werken,* III, 149-197). Both will be discussed here.

[15] *Opera Omnia,* III, b1141-1142.

receives holy Communion ought to have faith in the sacrament, there is no need for him or her to experience any special feelings.[16] But if Ruusbroec does not intend to replace the Sacrament with some other, more "mystical" way of approaching God, he does want to show that it is possible to receive it in a fuller way. This may occur when, along with the sacramental union with Christ in Communion, one also has a "remembering" (*ghedincken*) of him. Ruusbroec here uses the verb "to remember" in the strong sense of "to represent": one does not just re-picture past events or things, but one makes oneself present to what is not perceptible at that moment. Thus "to remember" Christ is almost the same as to give personal attention to him or to meditate on him.[17] Briefly, the mystical author suggests that those who receive the Sacrament should do so as consciously as possible, with all their heart and mind. And he goes on to describe this spiritual exercise of "remembering" as a person's realization of the twofold movement that characterizes "meeting."[18]

On the one hand, the person who communes should "consider and behold" (*merken ende aensien*)[19] how Christ comes to him or her. In a passage from *The Spiritual Espousals*, Ruusbroec dwells

[16] "And Christ wishes us to receive Him sacramentally and spiritually ... Although a person may not have such feelings nor such desire, if he intends God's praise and His glory and his own growth and his blessedness, he may freely approach the table of our Lord, if he has a conscience pure of mortal sin" (*Opera Omnia*, III, b1203-1207).

[17] For the importance of "attention," see chapter 1 of this study, note 38.

[18] It is no surprise that "meeting" is prominent here: see chapter 5 of this study, where it was shown that "meeting" is a key notion for Ruusbroec.

[19] *Aensien,* "to behold," is an important word, for as a rule it figures in the description of the "inner life" and its starting point. See, for example, the first quotation corresponding to note 9. For our purpose the most interesting characteristic of this way of seeing is that it foments, or rather ignites, the beholder's desire thus evoking a felt, "burning" love.

on the first way of this coming, which concerns the level of the body and the senses.[20]

> Now observe how we should commemorate (*ghedincken*) Him. We should consider and behold (*aensien*) how Christ inclines towards us with loving affection and with great desire and with bodily lust, with heartfelt flowing-away into our bodily nature. For He gives us what He has received from our humanity, that is, flesh and blood, and His bodily nature. We should also consider and behold this precious body, tortured, transpierced and wounded through and through for very love and fidelity, for our sake. Herewith we are enriched and fed in the lower part of our humanity with Christ's glorious humanity.[21]

On the other hand, as "meeting" implies that the divine action provokes a human reaction, the person who takes Communion should go to "meet Christ in every way that Christ comes to him." At the level of the "heart," this may happen in the following way:

> He should raise himself up to receive Christ with his heart, with desire, with felt affection, with all his faculties, and with longing lust ... And this lust cannot be too great, for our nature receives its nature, that is, Christ's humanity, glorified, full of joy and dignity. Therefore, I want, in this receiving, a person to melt and flow away, for desire, for joy and for bliss. For he receives and is united with the most beautiful and the most gracious and the most lovable of all the sons of mankind.[22]

Ruusbroec continues with an account of the intense compassion that this person may feel for the "suffering body of Christ which he receives," and refers to the possibility that perhaps "much is

---

[20] For his remarks on the other two levels, see above, the text that corresponds to note 14.

[21] *The Spiritual Espousals*, in *Opera Omnia*, III, b1157-1165.

[22] *The Spiritual Espousals*, in *Opera Omnia*, III, b1174-1181.

shown" to him or her, and that stigmatisation may even occur.[23] And he concludes by remarking that "this is how we satisfy Christ with respect to the lower part of His humanity."

Like the Queen of Sheba

For Ruusbroec the person who receives holy Communion can extend his sacramental union with Christ in faith, in so far as such a person is enabled to "behold" this union as their mutual "meeting" and may then also feel it at the first, lower level of their common humanity. But for the next two steps on the way to the Divinity, this mystic has been sparing in details. Nevertheless, in *A Mirror of Eternal Blessedness,* he has inserted a treatise on the Eucharist that completes his former exposition.[24] Two passages deserve special attention here.

The first is part of the section that explains how Christ gives himself in the Sacrament, and Ruusbroec indicates a mystical level at once by addressing "whoever wants to become drunk with love." Yet here again, as in *The Spiritual Espousals,* he stresses the link between Communion and paying attention: one has to "look at and note and admire (*aensien ende merken ende verwonderen*)," and once more the communicant is supposed to become

---

[23] *The Spiritual Espousals,* b1190-1195. "This felt affection along with compassion and the intense imagination may be so great that a person might think that he felt the wounds and the lacerations of Christ in his heart and in all his members. And if any person could, in any way, really receive the signs of our Lord's wounds, it would be this person."

[24] This explanation of the Eucharist is quite long: *Werken,* III, p. 149-197 (the whole *Mirror* goes from p.129 to p. 219). For a detailed presentation of this major work of Ruusbroec, see my Introduction to *Opera Omnia,* VIII. For the first passage considered here see *Werken,* III, 158,20-161,4.

aware of the love Christ shows in giving his flesh and blood: "such a marvel of love was never heard of before." However, this time meditation is focused upon the "nature of love." This is the point where Ruusbroec smoothly introduces into the text on the Eucharist the essence of his mystical teaching: "Now, the nature of love is always: to give and take, love and be loved. And both of these are in anyone who loves." It is easy to recognize in this twofold movement the aspect of "union" which, in the mystic's being-one with God, goes together with "unity."[25] Ruusbroec then draws on his own mystical language to express the "nature of love" or "union" in the idiom of nourishment:

> Christ's love is voracious and generous: even though he gives us all that he has and all that he is, he also takes back all that we have and all that we are. And he demands of us more than we can accomplish. His hunger is great without measure: he consumes us thoroughly, for he is a voracious glutton who cannot stop eating: he consumes the marrow out of our bones ... If we could see the voracious lust Christ has for our blessedness, we would not be able to restrain ourselves from flying into his throat. Even though my words sound wondrous, those who love understand me well.[26]

[25] *Werken*, III, 158, 29-32 and see chapter 5 of this study, especially the text that corresponds to note 61.

[26] Is this a shocking image of Christ? Guido de Baere has an excellent answer to this question: see his "'Christus een ghieregh slockard' of de wansmaak van Ruusbroec," *Tegendraads genot: opstellen over de kwaliteit van middeleeuwse teksten*, eds. Karel Porteman, Werner Verbeke, Frank Willaert (Leuven: Peeters, 1996) 84-92. In any case, "hunger" as a metaphor for mystic union (even if one may question if this is just a metaphor) is quite prominent in Ruusbroec's descriptions: e.g., in *The Spiritual Espousals,* the divine "touching" (*gherinen*) in the "unity of the spirit" inspires the following reaction: "Here begins an eternal hunger which will never be filled. It is an inward avidity and craving on the part of the faculty of loving and of the created spirit for an uncreated good ... See, here begins an eternal voracity and insatiable craving in an eternal failing. These are the poorest people alive, for they are voracious and gluttonous and they have bulimia ... Here are great dishes of food and drink about which no one knows but

The coexistence of voracity and generosity is rephrased a little later: "Jesus' love is of such noble nature, that when it consumes, it wants to feed. Even though Jesus consumes us altogether in him, he gives us himself for this."

Ruusbroec next shifts from the lofty, mystical theme of hungering and feeding to that of taking holy Communion: "Christ gives to our spiritual hunger and our heartfelt affection his body as food." This implies that the mystic's inward craving after the invisible Other can focus immediately upon the specific, perceptible signs of bread and wine. In sacramental, as in spiritual, communion the same "meeting" takes place, but in an embodied way. The humanly concrete thing (and any sign is a thing), far from cheapening the mystic's high experience, serves to enhance its relevance:

> For all that they have inward in the spirit, they also receive outward in the holy Sacrament. And thus they are holy in the receiving, and still holier in the having, and most holy in having and receiving.[27]

Ruusbroec follows up this reflection with a brief repetition of what he has said in *The Spiritual Espousals*: Christ gives himself in his body and his soul, and "above all this he shows us and

the one who feels this" (*Opera Omnia*, III, b1314-1324). However, the most striking, highly mystical passage appears almost at the end of *A Mirror of Eternal Blessedness* , as in this sample: "And the Holy Spirit gives himself and visits us, and touches (*gherijnt*) the burning spark of our soul. And this is the beginning and the source of eternal love between us and God. Practice of love is free, and it is not ashamed of itself. Its nature is voracious and generous. It always wants to demand and offer, give and take. God's love is voracious. It demands of the soul all that it is, and all that it can do. And the soul is rich and generous, and wants to give everything to voracious love that it demands and desires; but it cannot fulfill it, for its createdness must last for ever ... Furthermore, the love of God is also fathomlessly generous. It offers and shows the soul all that it is, and it wants to give that to the soul all freely. Now the loving soul is particularly greedy and voracious, and yawns wide ... Behold, thus can love give and take" (*Werken*, III, 214,14-215,6).

[27] *Werken*, III, 171, 24-28.

promises us his Godhead in eternal enjoyment" (*ghebruken*). There is the threefold gift and the possibility for the communicant to attain to mystic union with the Divinity: "What wonder is it that they jubilate (*jubileren*) who savor and experience this?" (notice the term "jubilate"). But first Ruusbroec catches the reader's imagination by recalling the Queen of Sheba's meeting with King Solomon:

> When the queen of Eastland beheld (*aensach*) the richness, the honor and the glory of king Solomon, then her spirit gave out from great wondering and she fainted and fell into unconsciousness.[28]

[28] See 1 Kings 10,1-10. It seems to me that Ruusbroec borrowed this biblical illustration of mystical experience from Richard of Saint-Victor. It figures in Book V of the *Benjamin Major* where Richard describes the transition from "meditation" to "contemplation," which occurs through "ecstasy" (see chapter 3 of this study: "The Fallacy of Ecstasy," especially the texts corresponding to notes 47 and 48). The Queen is mentioned in chapter 12, and Richard gives the gist of the story as follows: "After seeing for a long time and marveling greatly, at long last on account of greatness of wonder she comes to the failure of her spirit." Richard's influential definition of wonder deserves to be quoted here: "Who does not know that wonder takes its beginning when we discern something beyond hope and above expectation? And so when something begins to be seen that it is scarcely possible to believe, the newness of a vision and of a thing that is scarcely believable is accustomed to lead to wonder of mind ... And, I ask, whence comes wonder, except from an unexpected and incredible manifestation?" (*Benjamin Major*, Book V, ch. 9). "Wonder" also plays a prominent role in Hadewijch's mystical writing; for example when she evokes in Vision 6 the moment of "fruition" (*ghebruken*) of the Divinity, she introduces that passage (see chapter 4 of this study, the first quotation after the one that corresponds to note 21) as follows: "But then wonder seized me because of all the riches I had seen in him, and through this wonder I came out of the spirit in which I had seen all that I sought." Hadewijch mentions the Queen of Sheba in *Poems in Couplets* 26, str. 3. On Richard's view of "wonder," his influence on Hadewijch, and the role of "wondering" in mystical experience, see Paul Mommaers, "Is Hadewijch emotioneel?," *Emoties in de Middeleeuwen*, eds. R.E.V. Stuip, C. Vellekoop, Utrechtse Bijdragen tot de Mediëvistiek 15 (Hilversum: Verloren, 1998) 145-151.

On receiving the Sacrament, something similar may happen. As long as the communicant considers and experiences the properly human aspects of the Godman, he or she certainly comes under his influence. However, this person remains basically human. The effect of Christ's corporeal and spiritual perfection extends the limits of consciousness without actually bursting them: one does grow, but in a measurable, conceivable manner. Thus the final stage for the communicant has not yet been reached. As communion is received, it may be possible, in addition, to "behold" Christ's Godhead and, then, be overwhelmed by the emotion of "wondering."[29] There comes a decisive fork in the mystic road — consciousness either collapses or reaches beyond itself:

> For even though we are able to receive all that belongs to his humanity and remain in quietness, when we behold (*aensien*) his Godhead that we have before us in the Sacrament, we wonder so much that we have to transcend ourselves (*onthooeghen ons-selven*) in the spirit in superessential love, or we would fall into unconsciousness through wonder and disquietness before the table of our Lord.

[29] It may come as a surprise to hear of Christ's "showing" his Godhead and the communicant's "beholding" it. In Ruusbroec's writings "to show" (*vertoenen*) is not a simple word, but no adequate semantic study of it is available. In any case, it does not mean in the first instance that something is made visible to someone. To be granted (and this is mostly a contemplative gift) a "showing" of God signifies that one senses or feels a Presence rather than sees a Something. Indeed it is precisely the invisible and incomprehensible that may be "shown." In *The Twelve Beguines,* Ruusbroec writes of God "showing" himself: "when the sun of God's grace enters the open, elevated heart ... all the soul's powers rejoice in this new feeling (*bevoelen*) of God's grace. For God shows (*vertoent*) himself to the elevated soul as he is in his nature, that is, bare and unimaged (*bloot ende onghebeelt*), formless and modeless (*formeloes ende wiseloes*), without measure and without ground (*sonder mate ende sonder gront*). This is how he is the object (*voerworp*) of the elevated desire and the emptied soul" (*Werken,* IV, 100,10-17). As for Christ "showing" his Godhead, one should certainly not think of the Humanity as somehow pointing at a Divinity appearing in some "beyond." It is Jesus the Man who presents in himself what is not representable.

Quite clearly Ruusbroec is not content simply with the way in which the "great wondering" affects the Queen of Sheba. Christ is not just a distant Solomon who makes the "beholder" faint. Through gradually sharing with the communicant the different aspects of his Humanity, the Godman makes such a person "wax great" as a human being, enabled to go beyond her or his own self and then attain to the highly mystical experience of "unity" (*eenecheit*):

> But with devotedness and heartfelt affection (*liefden*) we eat and consume the humanity of our Lord into our nature; for affection (*liefde*) draws into itself all that it loves. And with such an affection (*liefden*) our Lord consumes and draws our nature into him, and fills us with his grace. And then we wax great and transcend ourselves (*onthooeghen ons-selven*) in a divine affection (*liefde*) above reason. When we eat with our spirit and consume and aspire with bare love (*met blooeter minnen*) toward his Godhead, behold, we meet his Spirit, that is his love (*minne*) that is great without measure; that burns up and consumes our spirit and all its works, and draws them with it in unity (*eenecheit*) where we experience rest and blessedness.

And Ruusbroec concludes his exposition of the way in which the Sacrament may be consumed with a short sentence: "Behold, thus we shall always eat and be eaten, and go up and down with love (*met minnen*). And this is our life in eternity."[30]

---

[30] *Werken*, III, 160,35-161,1. The term *liefde* ("affection") can be defined as follows: "[It] expresses the sensitive and affective aspects of the experience of love. Depending on the object of this experience, it is given positive or negative value." *Minne* "is love in its orientation towards and in its meeting with another person, whether it be God or man." A passage from *The Spiritual Espousals* that expresses the unifying nature of *minne* in a Christ-centered way, and clearly distinguishes *minne* from *karitate* ("charity"), deserves to be quoted here: "We should also dwell in the unity of our spirit, and flow forth with expansive charity (*met wider karitaten*) in heaven and on earth, in clear discernment. And hereby we bear a likeness to Christ with respect to the spirit and give Him satisfaction. We should also, through Christ's personality, with one-fold intention and with

Different ways of experiencing Christ in receiving the Sacrament

A second passage from *A Mirror of Eternal Blessedness* is important; it is part of the lengthy section in which Ruusbroec describes the "difference among the persons who shall receive the holy Sacrament."[31] He distinguishes some ten "groups" of communicants, but here only the first three will be considered.

In describing the first group, Ruusbroec gives a summary of his earlier explanation of the communicant's union with the Godman at the level of the "heart," for the people he has in mind here are "so much moved in affection (*beweeght in liefden*) toward the human nature of our Lord." However, his focus now is on what may happen to those who are "tender-hearted by nature" and "of a weak complexion": they run the risk of getting stuck in this sensible experience. Clearly, Ruusbroec does not disapprove of affectionate union as such, but he is critical of the consequences of excessive sensitivity. First, he warns against the tendency to turn heartfelt love into some separate, self-sufficient feeling:

> And for this their practice is of the senses and desirous and altogether filled with images of our Lord's humanity (*verbeelt met der menscheit*). And they cannot feel nor understand how one can receive our Lord in the spirit, without the Sacrament. And this is the reason why they inwardly languish in longing and in the desire they have for our Lord.

enjoyable love (*met ghebrukelijcke minnen*), transcend ourselves and the createdness of Christ, and rest in our inheritance, that is, the divine essence, in eternity." (*Opera Omnia,* III, b1196-1201). For these definitions, see the "Explanation of Technical Terms" in *Opera Omnia,* II, p. 272.

[31] The whole section fills *Werken,* III, 175,5-197,31. It ends with the following conclusion: "Then we may receive our Lord whenever we wish in the Sacrament or, with love, in our spirit." The description of the first group runs from 175,12 to 177,27.

In short, these persons of feeling remain "unelevated and unenlightened in the spirit." However, Ruusbroec does not suggest that they desist from their affectionate experience. He wants them to relativize it, in the positive sense of relating it to a further form of consciousness. They should learn to climb up to the level of the spirit.

Once he has opened up a new spiritual perspective for the tender-hearted communicants, Ruusbroec goes on to discuss a psychological phenomenon that is bound to divert their sensibility away from the Lord. As their feeling for the Humanity springs from their sensitive nature, human nature may make itself felt, and their religious practice, which "is still of the senses and lives in flesh and blood," may kindle their "animal lust" and cause pleasurable sensation to fill their consciousness:

> Now these people are mostly of weak complexion and by nature subject to inclinations. And therefore, when they pray or want to devote themselves to the humanity of our Lord with desire and with affection (*met liefden*), then they sometimes are easily touched and moved to animal lust against their will, for their practice is still of the senses and lives in flesh and blood. And then, the more they look on themselves and on that bodily disordered movement, the more it waxes and the more it moves nature in disorder and in failing.

Ruusbroec reacts calmly to these carnal temptations of Christ's affectionate devotees. He does not suggest that they crush their disposition nor fly from it. Neither does he want them to focus self-consciously on "that bodily disordered movement," but rather to redirect their desirous attention to the One intended in the first place: "Thus they are imaged with him (*met Heme verbeelt*) in soul and in body, in heart and in senses." This mystic Master of "imageless" (*onverbeelt*) experience remains faithful to the "imaged" (*verbeelt*) One.

The second group of people who receive the Blessed Sacrament have a different disposition.[32] Being by nature "subtle and intelligent of spirit," their religious practice is not in the senses but in the spirit, and so they "choose a life turned inward."[33] Yet their intellectual gifts do not prevent their being subject to carnal motions, for they are "unchaste by nature."

The tenor of Ruusbroec's description — written for the most part with much feeling — is not to disparage these high spirituals suffering from base inclinations. On the contrary, he thinks they may well become true contemplatives:

> If it is the case that they believe, hope, and trust more in God than in their practice or in all their works, they are elevated above their reasonable understanding into divine light. Furthermore, if they remain there elevated in divine light ... they are free and know God and the truth and root of all virtue.[34]

Yet here also, as for the tender-hearted, there is a warning note intended to open up the possibility of a more complete religious experience: whereas the first group fails to function at the level of the spirit, the second neglects their sensibility. As soon as these spiritually gifted people feel their carnal nature reacting, they reject it strongly and overcome the temptations by turning inward:

> And when these people feel this in themselves and consider it, then they abandon and scorn in themselves all that is contrary to God and their spirit ... And then they abandon what is of the senses and flee

---

[32] *Werken,* III,177,30-180,11.

[33] These highly spiritual figures remind one of Hadewijch's "fighting cock," the schooled "champion" of the spiritual life, mentioned in chapter 4 of this study.

[34] For a similar appreciation of highly educated contemplatives who do "without grace" — "deft in natural knowledge, often quite mannerly with respect to the exterior life, idle (*leedich*) and elevated by natural contemplation," see *The Realm of Lovers, Werken,* I, 23,15-24,28.

> inward in the spirit before the countenance of our Lord ... 'For in weakness is strength made perfect' in all those who struggle and flee with prayer in their spirit before the presence of God.[35]

Ruusbroec does not find fault with this spiritual strategy. He even goes so far as to compare these people with the centurion who "was uncircumcised in nature."[36] This "pagan" petitioned the Lord for his "servant who lay in his house weak," and the servant — obviously representing the spiritual person's unruly sensibility — was healed. However what Ruusbroec criticizes is that this kind of healing does not integrate the body and the senses with religious experience. This "fleeing inward," however helpful, may suffer from a tendency to escapism or, to put it more positively, these spiritual people, remaining the body-soul humans they truly are, may fail to realize their full potential "in the spirit." There is a lack of real embodiment here, and this prevents such people from receiving holy Communion in its fullness:

> As long as these people feel in their nature unchaste inclinations and lust toward sins, their desire and affection for the humanity of our Lord (*lost ende liefde toe der menscheit*) are impeded and hindered, and their servant, namely bodily nature, is contrary to God and their spirit ... Behold, these people have no desirous longing (*begheerleken lost*) for the holy Sacrament as long as they thus struggle.

Ruusbroec suggests with great skill a prayer for this type of communicant, which expresses his view on the accomplished contemplative:

---

[35] According to Ruusbroec, this is what St. Paul did "when he was tempted in the flesh" (2 Corinthians 12,9). There is, in *The Spiritual Tabernacle,* a very striking description of Paul learning to accept that he was "powerless as to his body," although he had received the highest contemplative gifts (*Werken,* II, 247,18-248,9).

[36] See Matthew 8, 5-10.

'I shall cry and pray without cessation, until that time when your grace and my faith heal my servant; and then I shall praise you and serve you with soul and with body, and with the totality of my self (*met gheheelheiden mijns selfs*) and all my faculties.'

With Jesus on Mount Tabor

It has been seen that for Ruusbroec the Humanity plays a key role in different ways in attaining to the experience of the Divinity. In addition, he has shown that the sacramental Body is far from being a hampering intermediary; on receiving communion, one may excel the queen of Sheba and come to "transcend oneself." The Sacrament can enable both affectionate and intellectual characters to develop their partial experiences into one that covers the body-soul complex "in its totality." However, the question may still be raised if, in Ruusbroec's view, Jesus is more than the Way that secures the passage from ordinary to mystical awareness of God. In the final analysis, is he simply the Door that opens onto the Divine? In fact in a passage from *The Sparkling Stone*, Ruusbroec explains in unmistakable terms how Jesus remains at the heart of mystical experience even at its most advanced stage.

Ruusbroec makes use here of the scene in St. Mark's Gospel where Peter, James, and John follow Jesus up Mount Tabor.[37] As usual, before beginning his contemplative interpretation of the story, the mystical author reminds the reader of the "objective" cornerstone upon which the experience he has in mind ought to be founded:

The lamb of God, that is the humanity of our Lord (*de menscheit ons heeren*) has delivered himself up to death and opened the Book

---

[37] Marc 9, 2-8. *Opera Omnia*, X, 700-751.

of Life for us ... And therefore all knees bend before the name of Jesus, for he has fought for us, and won.[38]

Ruusbroec then shows the role of Jesus both in the mystic's reaching as well as "tasting" the being-one with God:

> Jesus leads us on to the mountain of our bare mind (*opden berch onser bloter ghedachten*) in a region barren and hidden and reveals himself to us glorified in divine brightness. And in his name his heavenly Father opens for us the living book of his eternal wisdom. And the wisdom of God enfolds our bare vision (*bloete ghesichte*) and the simplicity of our spirit in a modeless (*wiselosen*) simple taste of all that is good without distinction. For there is contemplation and knowledge, taste and feeling, existence and life, having and being ... And therefore, if we would always stay with Jesus on Tabor, that is on the mountain of our bare mind, we would always experience an increase of new light and new truth, for we would always hear the voice of the Father that would touch (*gherijnen*) us, whether it flows out in grace or draws us in in unity (*in eenicheiden*).

Ruusbroec then goes on to evoke the experience of this twofold divine movement, and one notices once more that the mystical being-one is essentially a compound reality: in terms familiar from Chapter 5, the accomplished oneness with God consists not only of "unity" (here, to undergo the "touch of God ... that draws in"), but of its interplay with "union" (here, to undergo the "outflowing touch"):

> The outflowing touch (*uutvloeyende gherijnen*) of God makes us alive in the spirit and fills us with grace: it enlightens our reason and teaches us to know the truth and discernment of virtues and it keeps us upright before God's presence with such great power that we are able to endure all the taste, all the feeling and all the gifts of God that flow out without failing in our spirit. But the touch of God that draws in (*intreckende gherijnen*) requires that we are one with

---

[38] *Opera Omnia,* X, 682-684 and 694-695.

God (*een te sine met gode*) and that we lose our spirit (*ontgheesten*) and die in bliss, that is in the one and only love that encompasses the Father and the Son in one enjoyment (*in een ghebruken*).[39]

Finally, Ruusbroec presents Jesus as the One with whom ("if we follow") and in whom ("one with God's Son," "elevated into our origin by the Son") the mystic is "drawn in." It is the Humanity that takes along the human ("we all") into that unity where "we are one being and one life and one bliss with God" — surely as daring an expression as one is likely to find in any mystical writing!

And therefore, when we have ascended with Jesus the mountain where our images cease (*opden berch onser onghebeeltheit*), if we follow him with onefold vision, with intimate pleasure and with joyful inclination (*met ghebrukelijcker neyghinghen*), we feel the strong heat of the Holy Spirit that makes us burn and melt into God's unity (*eenicheit gods*). For where, one with God's Son, we are brought lovingly back to our beginning, we hear the voice of the Father that touches us, drawing us in ... And therefore, when we are elevated into our origin by the Son ... there all our powers fail and we fall down headlong into our open vision and we all become one, and one all in the loving embrace of the unity of the three (*in dat minlijcke omhelsen der drier eenicheit*). Where we feel that unity we are one being and one life and one bliss with God (*een wesen ende een leven ende eene zalichede met gode*), and there all things are fulfilled and all things renewed.

[39] For a detailed discussion of this passage, see my Introduction to *The Sparkling Stone*, 3.2, "The Nucleus of Ruusbroec's Mystical Teaching," *Opera Omnia*, X, p. 24-29.

CHAPTER VII

RUUSBROEC:
RUUSBROEC: THE INNER AND THE OUTER —
THE HIGH AND THE LOW

The previous chapter ended with Ruusbroec's evocation of the person who attains through the Humanity to the height of mystic union. After the ascent of an inner Mount Tabor with Jesus, there comes about union with the Son and the feeling of that unity where "we are one being and one life and one bliss with God." That lofty image of the accomplished contemplative may make one wonder: what happens to the humble Humanity of Christ? Is it left behind, along with all the merely human, on the slope of mystical Mount Tabor? Moreover, what is one to make of Ruusbroec's interpretation of the Tabor story? It may seem that he is interested only in the best part of it, in the Jesus who "reveals himself to us glorified in divine brightness." Yet, according to Mark, the moment of shining exaltation was followed at once by a sobering descent into the worst aspects of the human condition: "on their way home," the apostles had to learn that the "Son of Man is to endure great suffering and be treated with contempt."[1]

---

[1] Mark 9,9-12. By inserting the Transfiguration into Jesus' earthly life, precisely at the moment when it is about to take a crucial turn, Mark vigorously addresses the problem of the ultimate value of the Humanity of Christ. What is the sense of his life before Easter, in the overwhelming light of the resurrection and glorification? Is there any lasting truth to be found in what he taught and did, and, most of all, in what he suffered? Was the scandalous Passion just a tragic accident? According to Mark, it is in the debasement of the Humanity that the

In addition there is another issue left over from chapter 6 of this study: apart from the first two groups of "persons who shall receive the holy Sacrament," what remains to be said of the third group mentioned by Ruusbroec, and how does his teaching about them complete his exposition of the mystic's reception of Communion?

In fact, Ruusbroec did not neglect the descent of Jesus from Mount Tabor. His account of the feeling experienced by the advanced mystic on being brought back down with Jesus allows him to develop a key issue of his teaching. A clear way to introduce this point is precisely by reference to the third group of communicants:[2]

> The third group ... are people turned inward who, through the grace of God, walk in their turning inward before God's countenance with free elevated spirit, drawing inward and following after: heart and senses, body and soul with all the bodily faculties. These people are in control of their spirit and their nature.[3]

Evidently, Ruusbroec presents this group as the model for contemplatives. They are the "highest who nobly approach the Sacrament," for they achieve what the first two groups do not. Being at once affectionate and spiritual, they realize what the others pray for: "to praise you and serve you ... with the totality of myself."[4] To start with, these perfect communicants appear blessed with psychological integration: the different levels of their psyche work

self-revelation of the Divinity takes place. The Tabor pericope shows a "Christology that does not try in any way to pass by or beyond the human existence of Jesus." See Paul Lamarche, "Transfiguration," *Dictionnaire de Spiritualité* XV (1991) 1148-1151.

[2] *Werken,* III, 180,14-184,33.

[3] *Werken,* III, 180,16-21.

[4] W*erken,* III, 179,33-34. See chapter 6 of this study, the conclusion to Ruusbroec's description of the second group.

in harmony. When they turn inward, the body and the senses are not left to themselves but they "follow after" the spirit. However, does this peaceful integration of the lower aspect of the human person imply its disappearance in the wake of the spirit's movement? Is it a case of one-way sublimation?[5]

Ruusbroec gives his answer when he goes on to clarify the nature of this well-balanced state. He shifts from a psychological to a spiritual point of view, and describes the way in which these full-fledged contemplatives experience union with God. As usual, he first reminds the reader of the ordinary foundation upon which their experience rests: believing in Jesus Christ, they "have true knowledge" of the Godman. It is this creed which they develop into experiential knowledge by "practising" their faith:

> In their turning inward with an unimaged spirit (*met onghebeelden gheeste*), they are elevated through bare love (*met blooeter minnen*) before the nature of the divinity; in their turning outward, they are imaged through heartfelt affection upon our Lord's humanity (*met herteleker liefden ghebeeldt toe der menscheit Ons Heeren*).[6]

This balanced and rich text must rank as the key passage in Ruusbroec regarding the position of the Humanity in mystical experience. The sentence hinges upon a contrast: "turning inward" in opposition to "turning outward,"[7] and each of these elements is further specified by a pair of expressions that correspond to each other: "through bare love" echoes "through heartfelt affection," and "the nature of the divinity" responds to "our Lord's humanity."

---

[5] In any case, these excellent contemplatives "may sometimes be moved in nature," as Ruusbroec notes a little further on, at 180,25.

[6] *Werken,* III, 180,29-33

[7] Such a literary device is not surprising in Ruusbroec: on the way in which he designs his sentences, see Mommaers and Van Bragt, *Mysticism Buddhist and Christian,* 142-144.

This third group certainly consists of contemplatives in the strict mystical sense. Ruusbroec consistently uses the expression "to turn inward" to indicate the psychological procedure employed by all types of contemplatives.[8] It is a practice that leads to a condition he calls *ledecheit,* an ambigous word, that can mean "emptiness" as well as "idleness." Such ambiguity is not unintentional. On the contrary, it rightly suggests that the consciousness of those who turn inward is stripped of every activity and of all content: they "empty themselves of images and of all works."[9] Persons belonging to the third group, no less than the adepts of the "natural" way, go all the way inward, but for them the inward movement is linked to a "turning outward," and this is where the main contemplative teaching of this passage comes. To express this specifically in terms familiar in this book, in the case of these contemplatives being "unimaged" is succeeded by being "imaged."

It should be perfectly clear now how Ruusbroec, writing as a mystical author, can account for the Christ-centered experience of the contemplative communicants he is discussing. There is common ground between the experience of the third group and that of the mystical being-one described in chapter 5 of this study. Both

---

[8] In almost all his works, Ruusbroec refers to what he calls "natural contemplation" (*natuerlijc scouwen*) and/or "to turn inward without grace" (*sonder gracie inkeeren*). Moreover, he shows his appreciation for this "natural" way and the experience to which it can lead, while also raising doubts about it. For a study of this theme, see *Mysticism Buddhist and Christian,* chapters 10 and 12. On his description and appreciation of the method of "turning inward" as such, see ibid., 220-229, where it is shown how Ruusbroec draws a parallel between his own method and that of the adepts of the "natural" way. Of course the term "method" should be used with caution in the case of the contemplative who turns inward "with grace" (see ibid., 227 n. 39), and note that in the key passage above, from *A Mirror*, "love" comes into play in the contemplative's turning inward, which is not the case when one turns inward "without grace."

[9] *Opera Omnia,* III, b1983.

are seen to be compound phenomena in which two contrasting aspects concur. So much so that the mystic's condition does not appear as a state but as a twofold movement. This feeling of a ceaseless to and fro is described at the end of a passage from *The Seven Rungs*, where Ruusbroec evokes being-one with God:

> So, too, we shall go outward into our sensitive life (*uutgaen tote in onse senleke leven*) and go inward with love and cling to God and remain one with God without moving.[10]

When Ruusbroec comes to write "incarnational" texts, he is able, as a "phenomenologist" of mysticism, to extrapolate in Christo-centric terms his general descriptions of mystic union. There is no need for him to bring into play any extra-mystical arguments (dogmatic, moral, or practical) to secure a position for Jesus. He simply shows what it actually means for the mystic, who has gone inward, to "go outward into his sensitive life," namely, to be "imaged upon our Lord's humanity."

With regard to the opposites that make up mystical oneness, the word "(God-)like" (*ghelijc*) shows most clearly the fundamental identity of the Christ-centered and the general descriptions of mystic union. As was seen in Chapter 5, "(God-)like" belongs to the same semantic chain as "union," "with intermediary," "working," and "otherness." All these quasi-synonyms refer to the active aspect of being-one which, as Ruusbroec points out again and again, "renews itself always."[12] Here is one among many passages where he indicates how in fact the "likeness" that originates from "unity," takes shape in the mystic's life:

[10] See, in chapter 5 of this study, the text that corresponds to note 72. For this passage, see *Werken,* III, 269,21-22.

[11] See note 61 in chapter 5 of this study.

> For the fruitful unity of God (*eenicheit gods*) maintains itself above the unification (*eeninghe*) of our faculties and always exacts from us likeness (*ghelijcheit*) in love and in virtues. And this is why we are touched, every moment anew, so that at every moment we may be newer and more (God-)like in virtues (*ghelijcker werden in doechden*).[12]

In this passage the phrases "likeness in virtues" and "more (God-)like in virtues" are clues to the reader that this is how the mystic as such comes to follow Jesus. This is, then, Ruusbroec's way of showing that the "humanity of our Lord" is part and parcel of mystic union in the strict sense.

But how is one to understand the concept of "being imaged"? Firstly, it is noticeable that in descriptive passages (like that quoted above) the term "image" (*beelde*) refers to some inner representation that allows the human person to become conscious of reality. The image as such is a natural "intermediary" or "means" (both concepts implied by the word *middel*), which occurs either at the level of the spirit, as an "intellectual image" (*vernufteghe beelde*) or at that of the senses, as a "sensible image" (*sinleke beelde*).[13] The mystic is supposed to change from being "imaged"

---

[12] *Opera Omnia,* III, b1837-1840.

[13] On the nature of "intellectual images" and their role in mystical experience, see *The Realm of Lovers* (*Werken,* I, 82,23-34 and 84,18-34), *The Spiritual Espousals* (*Opera Omnia,* III, b886-955 and b1728-1760), and *The Twelve Beguines* (*Werken,* IV, 19,31-22,25). In these passages Ruusbroec makes it perfectly clear that certain concepts reappear in the advanced mystic's consciousness, after being first "transcended." From having been the means that led the mystic to attain to mystic knowing they change into the expression of that experiential knowledge. Briefly, the mystic goes beyond the *vernufteghe beelden* only to encounter them again infused with divine presence. For him the image develops from "true" and "useful" to "real" and "enjoyable." In the passages from *Espousals* and *Beguines,* Ruusbroec shows what it means for the mystic to "speculate" (*speculeren*). For the expression *sinleke beelden,* see *The Spiritual Tabernacle* (*Werken,* II, 122,22).

(*verbeelt*), that is, filled with images, to being "image-less" (*onghebeelt*), that is, free of all images. The process of being "emptied" is called "to be stripped of images" (*ontbeelden*).

However wide the range of the term "image," it refers mainly to sensible representations. And it is interesting to note (keeping in mind that the contemplative is "imaged" upon the Humanity) that image and affection go together almost as cause and effect. One is "imaged" for being sensibly touched; the image reflects what has impressed itself upon the human heart. A fine passage from *The Sparkling Stone* helps to illustrate the affective import of the image: Ruusbroec is explaining in three points what is needed when a "good person wants to become an inward, spiritual person"; he suggests that in the first place the "heart should be free of images" (*onverbeeltheit van herten*), and then goes on to specify this:

> If his heart is to be free of images (*wie onverbeelt wilt sijn van herten*), he should not possess anything with affection (*met liefden*) ... For all relationship and all affection which is not purely for the honour of God bring images in the heart of man (*verbeelt des menschen herte*).

He then explains how liberation from the web of images may be brought about:

> He must forego all fleshly affection and cling to God alone with desire and affection (*met loste ende met liefden*) and possess him in this way. This will drive out all encumbrance from images and all disorderly affection for creatures. And if he possesses God with affection, man will be freed of images inside (*wert van binnen onverbeelt*), since God is a spirit and no man can make a proper image of him (*god ghebeelden*).[14]

---

[14] *Opera Omnia*, X, 25-38.

This account of the nature of the image (and of the way in which the human spirit can go beyond it) clarifies the sense of the mystic's being "imaged through hearfelt love (*met herteleker liefden*) upon the humanity of our Lord." This is not a matter of keeping the image of Jesus before one's eyes: in place of such an active, pictorial notion, a passive, sculptural one would be more helpful. On turning outward, people in the third group of communicants feel that they are being formed after the image of Jesus from within in their hearts. The "unimaged" contact with God exerts a transforming power that makes itself felt in the senses and the body. This is how these high contemplatives can become "God-like" in their very human way; they come to be like "God's humanity" (*menscheit gods*). This conformation to Jesus does not of course exclude thinking of him in an imaginative manner. As Ruusbroec puts it a little further on in *The Sparkling Stone,* "in his spiritual practice one should concentrate on good images (*goede beelden vore nemen*), such as the passion of our Lord."[15]

The experience of the third group of people who receive the Sacrament has been seen to consist of a twofold movement, namely, the going back and forth from the outer to the inner. But Ruusbroec adds another, vertical dimension to the mystical experience of being-one.[16] He begins with the comic figure of Zacchaeus

---

[15] *Opera Omnia,* X, 38-39. This is the text that provided the starting point in chapter 1 of this study (see note 2). It is also worth recalling how Richard of Saint-Victor describes the highest degree of contemplation or "passionate love": "the image of the humility of Christ is set before the eyes" (see chapter 3 of this study).

[16] The background to Ruusbroec's mystical use of the four dimensions is Ephesians 2,18: "May you be strong to grasp ... what is the breadth and length and height and depth of the love of Christ." He contrasts his conception of God with that of the adepts of "natural mysticism" as follows: "He is a living something (*een levende yet*) which is higher and deeper, longer and broader than all he has created or whatever he could make" (*The Twelve Beguines, Werken,* IV,

running ahead of the crowd and climbing a tree near where Jesus would pass, only to hear the Lord calling him: "Zacchaeus, come down quickly, for I must even today stay in thy house."[17] This time, however, Zacchaeus stands not for someone on the brink of the mystical life, but for a person at its height. The contemplative communicants of the third group "resemble this man" as follows:

> And through faith and love they climb into the highest level of their mind, where the spirit stands unassailed by images (*onverbeeldt*) and unimpeded in its freedom; there is Jesus seen, recognized and loved in his Godhead. For there is he always present to the free elevated spirits, who have transcended themselves (*hen-selven onthooeght sijn*) in love for him.

On the other hand, from that height they are sent back down:

> But he says to them all: 'Go down quickly, for high freedom of spirit cannot keep on standing except in lowly obedience of mind. For you must know me and love me, as God and man: highness above all, and brought low below all. And so you shall savour me: when I elevate you above all, and above yourselves in me; and you bring yourselves low below all, and below yourselves with me, for my sake; then I must come into your house and keep dwelling with you and in you, and you with me and in me.'

It is no surprise to discover here also the core of Ruusbroec's teaching: mystic union necessarily implies the reciprocity of

---

50,24-25). The four dimensions in God developed from the time of Augustine into an important speculative theme and already a century before Ruusbroec, Hadewijch transformed it into a mystical motif. See Paul Mommaers, "*Opgaen en nedergaen* in het werk van Jan van Ruusbroec," *Ons Geestelijk Erf* 69 (1995), 97-113; 193-215; 70 (1996), 216-239; 71 (1997), 3-40. For the speculative and mystical interpretation of the four dimensions in God, see the first article, p. 99-111, and the third, p. 217. In this chapter use will be made of some of the material gathered in "*Opgaen* en *nedergaen* ," I-IV.

[17] See chapter 6 of this study, the text that corresponds to note 10. For the present text, see *A Mirror of Eternal Blessedness, Werken,* III, 181,5-182,30.

"meeting." While the human climbs up, God comes down, so that a mutual indwelling takes place. The striking expression used here by Ruusbroec to suggest the divine presence in the human person is that God should speak of being "in your house." Since the God-man is the focus of the contemplative communicant's experience, the divine Other is such that he wants to come to the mystic not only with his Godhead but also with his Humanity. For such a mystic the only way to "taste" real oneness is by receiving God in the outer as well as in the inner, in the lowest as well as in the highest; one cannot possibly "know" the Man without being brought down with him "below all."

After this account of the twofold movement that constitutes the experience of these accomplished mystics, Ruusbroec returns to his earlier description — "turning inward/turning outward" — but only to suggest that both dimensions coincide:

> And therefore their life and their practice is turning inward (*inkeer*) to God and turning outward (*uutkeer*) to themselves. The turning inward is with elevated free spirit, in loving reverence toward God and in God. The turning outward to themselves is a displeasure and an annihilation of themselves (*vernieuten haers-selfs*)… They stand in themselves between looking inward and looking outward, always in self-control to practice either whenever they want.[18]

---

[18] *Werken*, III, 182,31-183,7. A little further Ruusbroec gives the following psychological description: "Their looking inward is sometimes with reason and with images and in modes (*ghebeelt ende in wisen*), sometimes above reason, without images and without mode (*beeldeloes ende sonder wise*)" (183,13-15). Here, there is another reference to the heart of Ruusbroec's teaching, namely "meeting." See chapter 5 of this study, note 49: the passage from *The Spiritual Espousals* mentioned there deserves to be quoted here in full: "Now Christ comes from above as a lord and a generous giver who can do all things; and we come from below as poor servants, unable to do anything of ourselves, but needing everything. Christ comes into us from within outwards, and we come to Him from without inwards. And therefore a spiritual meeting must take place here" (*Opera Omnia*, III, b1392-1396).

For the question raised in this book, the most telling element in Ruusbroec's description of the ideal contemplatives is the stress laid on the downward movement that seizes them so as to unite them with the humble Humanity. But it should not be forgotten that this descent happens to spiritually "elevated" persons, those enabled to "transcend themselves" (*hen-selven onthooeght sijn*).[19] It is precisely this interplay of upwards and downwards which interests Ruusbroec, to the point that he has developed it into a major theme of his mystical teaching and it has become his favourite way of clarifying the issue of the Humanity.

Before turning to Ruusbroec's further treatment of this theme, a general observation is appropriate here. Christianity frequently represents the ordinary way of life of the person who has responded to God's grace, as well as the contemplative path, as an ascent, and figurative terms — like a "mountain," a "tree," and a "ladder" — recur as stereotypes. In this it simply adopts the vertical view of the divine that seems to be ingrained in human consciousness. Human beings tend by nature to imagine the Ultimate as the "highest" and God as dwelling "on high"; they raise eyes and hands to the One who is "in heaven," whether in the visible heaven of cosmic religions or the spiritual heaven of acosmic religion.[20]

This feeling for the Most High and for the possible ascent of the human does not prevent Christianity from highlighting God's own descent. This unexpected movement of the divine has manifested itself in Christ. With regard to his Godhead he is "from above," as

---

[19] The Middle Dutch expression *ont-hooeght* suggests perfectly this elevation: the prefix *ont* indicates the movement away from one's normal condition, i.e., here, one's "height" (*hoochte*).

[20] "A man says: 'O God' and looks up to heaven. Now, it is this which can teach us the sense of the proposition that 'God lives on high'." Ludwig Wittgenstein, *Nachlass,* 1932-3, quoted by Fergus Kerr, in *Theology after Wittgenstein,* 150.

St. John's Gospel puts it more than once; yet according to St. Paul, he "did not count equality with God a thing to be grasped, but emptied himself."[21] With regard to his Humanity, "he humbled himself," going as far as to "accept even death — death on a cross." This absolute descent of the Godman is precisely the reason why he was granted the absolute ascent of resurrection and ascension. For, according to John, it is in the crucifixion that the exaltation takes place: "I shall draw all men to myself, when I am lifted up from the earth" (12,32; 8,28). And Paul continues the hymn in Philippians as follows: "Therefore God raised him to the heights and bestowed on him the name above all names." Thus from the outset the Christian tradition gives prominence to God's coming down, and therefore the person who wishes to come into touch with God should not begin by trying to lift himself up to the Most High, but lower himself so as to meet the One who made himself the Lowest. For a Christian, descent is the necessary preliminary for any truly religious ascent; the cross becomes the mountain, the tree, and the ladder.

As for Ruusbroec, he adopts the common view of the divine as being on high. So in *The Spiritual Espousals* the person who in the "life of yearning" experiences tender longing for the Beloved appears thus: "He casts his inward eyes upwards and contemplates the heavenly hall full of glory and joy, and his beloved crowned there,"[22] and often enough mystic union is designated as "elevation." However, this vertical trend is only part of Ruusbroec's notion of God. A three-dimensional image of God makes itself felt throughout his writings and he even shows a preference for seeing God as "depth."[23]

[21] For this and the next quotations from Paul, see Philippians 2, 7-9.

[22] *Opera Omnia,* III, b460-462. For the "inner life" or the "life of yearning," see chapter 6 of this study, note 8.

[23] See above, note 16.

"To be lifted up and brought down"

For a final clarification by Ruusbroec of the role of the Humanity, a useful starting point can be a passage from *The Twelve Beguines*. Here Ruusbroec describes the way in which grace moves the sinner who has repented and turned into a "good person":[24]

> If he goes upward (*op-gheet*) with the sun of God's grace, following it through virtues and holy exercises, he comes into full summer, that is, he clings to God through love without fear, and he is free and empty (*ledich*) of himself as well as all creatures. This is the highest virtue as for the ascent (*opganghe*). Next he goes with the sun of God's grace into the humble resignation of himself through all suffering and all that God wills for him and all creatures. So, of all this he is empty (*ledich*) and at peace. And in this way he finds in himself the ground (*gront*) of humility and meekness.

This passage chiefly shows how the two movements differ. By rising above oneself and all creatures, the human being becomes empty in the sense of detached, or "abstracted" from everything that is not God himself. This sublimating process allows the human to open, and, being now "free," to attain the divine. By going down through self-surrender in the vicissitudes of life, the same person discovers within a "ground" of depth.[25] However, these contrasting movements are seen to have a certain equality, for in either case it is the same term, "empty" (*ledich*), that indicates the outcome. Whether the emptiness on high is indeed the same as deep down will require further elucidation, but the

---

[24] See *Werken,* IV, 97, 8-26. For the "good person," see chapter 6 of this study. One has to remember especially that even the most advanced mystic has always to be such a "good person," for the mystic knows in feeling what the non-mystic knows in faith.

[25] As will be seen further on, this "ground" appears as an ever deepening depth, an interior "abyss."

meantime attention has to be given to the way in which Ruusbroec goes on to describe the experience of being one with God, which is made possible by this twofold emptiness:

> And the Holy Spirit dwells and reposes in him in the ground of his humble resignation; and we repose and dwell in him through lovingly clinging to him with free reverence.

Here the soul's contrasting movements are shown to complement each other. Together they bring about the mutual indwelling of the divine and the human. Whereas the ascent makes the human repose in God, the descent allows God to do so in the human. The main reason for Ruusbroec's preoccupation with this twofold movement now becomes clearer. He wants to show above all that the mutual "giving" must not be overshadowed by the "taking,"[26] to use one of his well-known expressions. Thus the reader, who once again has been reminded that the "nature of love is always to give and take," finds the passage in question concluding: "Thus the scales of love between God and man stand even and equal."[27] As the two scales represent reciprocal giving, attention is drawn to the need for the human giving to correspond to God's giving; alternatively, and here the downward movement appears, to let the Giver "take" (from) the human. Ruusbroec attaches such importance to this point that the downward movement may even seem to preponderate over the upward movement. But this is to anticipate, and we must first follow the mystic's descriptions.

---

[26] See chapter 6 of this study, the passage that corresponds to note 25 ("Now, the nature of love is always: to give and take, love and be loved. And both of these are in anyone who loves" [*Werken*, III, 158,29-32]) and the second quotation in note 26. For a passage where Ruusbroec explicitly identifies "taking" with the upward and "giving" with the downward movement, see chapter 6 of this study, note 30: "Behold, thus we shall always eat and be eaten, and go up and down with love. And this is our life in eternity" (*Werken*, III, 160,35-161,1).

[27] *Werken*, IV, 96,1 and 97,25-26.

From a later passage in *The Twelve Beguines*, it becomes clear that the soul's descent is not caused exclusively by the painful aspects of human life. Here Ruusbroec has recourse once more to the image — "an example and a figure," as he calls it — of the sun's course.[28] This time he not only describes what happens to the "good person" but he also evokes the experience of the "inner person": the contemplative's desire climbs up to God, resembling "the sun's ascending during the month of April, which makes for growing and flourishing." The account of this ascent soon ends with the curt remark: "But this is not our highest life." Yet, a little later Ruusbroec describes the ascending desire of the inner person: it becomes so intense that it turns into rage as "impetuousness and unquietness" take possession of this person. This reaches the point where he or she wants "to depart and be with Christ."[29] But the author intervenes once more: "(This desire) does not feel the highest of the grace of loving, for some of its own will is still alive in it." At this point the reader is suddenly confronted with the paradoxical interconnection of the upward and downward movements. It dawns on the yearning desire that it "cannot reach higher, it descends and says what Christ said: 'Lord, not as I will, but as thou wilt.' This is the highest of its life, and so it comes back into itself."[30] Ruusbroec summarizes:

> This is why for us to feel the very highest that love is capable of, we ought through grace and desire to elevate ourselves with all our powers to the very highest we can achieve, which is in Cancer, where all our powers fail for impetuousness and unquietness of

---

[28] *Werken*, IV, 99,7-102,19. The signs of the zodiac are used by Ruusbroec, especially in *The Twelve Beguines*, to characterize different aspects of the spiritual life; for example, in the present passage, the soul is represented as reaching first Cancer and then Leo.

[29] *Werken*, IV, 101,29-30. Philippians 1,23.

[30] *Werken*, IV, 102,3-6. Matthew 26,39.

love. There we ought to totally renounce ourselves for the highest spirit to flourish in us; and we shall say with Christ to our heavenly Father: "Lord, into thy hands I commit my spirit."[31]

It has been shown already how Ruusbroec, following in Hadewijch's footsteps, emphasizes again and again the phenomenon of the mystic's "failing" in the face of God. In order to be granted *ghebruken,* "fruition," one has to suffer *ghebreken,* "failing," for divine Abundance is such that it ceaselessly overwhelms all the powers of the human soul. In the present passage this uplifting "failure" is linked to the presence of the contemplative's will. However God-given and altruistic the upward movement of this person's desire may be, "some of its own will is still alive in it." Even the most well-intentioned ascent towards the Other does not alter the fact that through its will the human self lives on in this "taking," and therefore the mystic's liberating "failure" cannot develop into his or her enjoying the "highest spirit" — unless this "inner person" accepts to do at this stage what all "good persons" ought to do again and again, that is, "to renounce ourselves."

It is noticeable how in this passage the Godman appears as the reference point for the mystic's upward and downward movement. His or her desire rises so strongly that it wants "to depart and be with Christ." There is a note of escapism in the high flight of this longing. On feeling God's touch, this person is eager to be freed from the human in order to attain the divine. He or she cannot wait to overcome "otherness" (*anderheit*) and be absorbed in "unity" (*eenheyt*). However, the Godman appears not only as the exalted Christ but also as the humbled Jesus. This Man shows the mystic how to descend. It is precisely by giving up his own way of intending the Father on high (with "my will," "my spirit") that he

---

[31] *Werken,* IV, 102,10-18. Luke 23,46.

has reached "unity." This is a unity in which the Son allows the Father to dwell and repose in his selfless depth as the unalterably Different. Ruusbroec can display the "inner person" repeating the words of Jesus so as to adopt his attitude of mind. As has already been shown in chapter 6 of this study, further passages confirm that if this person grows up, he or she will experience not only the downward movement — following the example of Jesus — but also Jesus living this movement in him or her.

It is the desire of the "inner person" that lifts one up to God, for desire (*begherte*) is the dynamic aspect of love (*minne*). And, for Ruusbroec, the most valuable expression of this loving ascent is "to praise and honour God" (*gode loven ende eren*), as he regularly calls it. Moreover, he repeats that this person's "works" — putting the virtues into practice — are to be closely connected with the ascending words and feelings of praise: one should always give praise "with words and with works." Yet once more the mystic's upward movement is shown to go together with a "falling down." This appears most strikingly in *The Spiritual Espousals*: here it is said of the "inner person" that "to praise God is the most delightful and the most gladsome work of the loving heart," and nevertheless this joyful work causes pain as well, "a woe of the heart": "one is wanting in thanks, praise, in honor and in service of God."[32] Ruusbroec then illustrates and explains this:

When natural fire, by its warmth and its power has forced water or other liquids to boil — that is, its highest work — the water reverses and falls back again to the very bottom, and it is once more forced to the same work by virtue of the fire, so that the fire is always driving upwards and the water always boiling. The inward fire of the Holy Spirit works in like manner: it drives, stokes and spurs the

---

[32] See *Opera Omnia*, III, b272-297.

heart and all the faculties of the soul to a boil, that is, to thank God and to praise him in the manner that I mentioned before. And likewise, one falls back once more to the same ground where the spirit of God is burning, in such a way that the fire of love may always burn and the heart of that person may always give thanks and praise with words and with works and always remain in lowliness, so that he reckons as great that which he should do, and would gladly do; and what he does, he reckons as small.[33]

Once again, Ruusbroec is alive to the vivacity of God's action and also to the complex character of mystic union as a compound phenomenon.[34] Note the pointed repetition of the word "always"; there is an incessant drive to the divine vitality and it gives rise to a human experience in which the upward movement of praise and the lowliness of failure are continuously combined.

Ruusbroec, however, does not see the "inner person's" descent as merely an interior movement. The "woe of the heart" is also caused by the mystic being found wanting "in service of God"; one is supposed to "do works" with ever more fervor, even if brought down again and again; these "works" should appear in the outer world, for they are meant to touch God's creatures. Already in *The Realm of Lovers,* his first book, Ruusbroec makes this perfectly clear. Here the inner person, stirred by burning desire to "praise and honor" God, is compared to the fourth choir of angels, the Potestates (Powers). These are "always, without cease, oriented upwards (*opgherecht*) with all their powers through great

[33] *Opera Omnia,* III, b285-297.

[34] A typical passage from *The Spiritual Espousals* highlights this divine vivacity: it describes how the grace of God "is situated in the unity of our spirit like a fountain, and it wells in the same unity whence it arises, just like a living vein welling out of the living ground of God's richness" (*Opera Omnia,* III, b1266-1268).

desire, and they are in a position to contemplate the Trinity."[35] However, the inner person may be brought a step further. In this case, he or she comes to realize that "God is lacking much praise and honor and reverence."[36] At that moment, the mystic resembles the fifth angelic choir, the Princes (Principalities), who are "oriented upwards for God's greater praise (*opgherecht in meerderen love*)." However, this most lofty choir is not able to constantly give God enough praise, and this failure "makes them come down." But where does this descent lead them? To the world, to God's creatures:

> This makes them come down (*neder-keeren*) and look at the rational creatures who are made for God's praise and honour just as well as they themselves are ... Thus there appears in the angels great compassion and mercy ... These angels are the strong Kings, for they are oriented upwards to God (*opgherecht te Gode*) as well as bent down (*nedergheboecht*) to the creatures, and again lifted up (*op-ver-heven*) together with the creatures.[37]

To conclude the comparison of the inner person with the highest angelic choirs, Ruusbroec indicates the reason why the Princes (Principalities) of the fifth choir are above the Potestates (Powers) of the fourth. The reader is supposed to see at once that the full-fledged mystic must always come down from above into the human world: "For the Potestates are oriented upwards (*opghe-recht*), but they are not aware of this kind of coming down (*neder-keeren*), this is beyond them (*boven hem*)."[38] Not surprisingly Ruusbroec presents Christ thus:

> He was always oriented upwards (*opgherecht*) in freedom, honour-ing and praising his Father with great desire. And he was and

---

³⁵ *Werken,* I, 43,31-44,3.
³⁶ *Werken,* 1, 47,24-25.
³⁷ *Werken,* I, 49,19 and 49,25-50,1.
³⁸ *Werken,* I, 50,4-6.

always is oriented downwards (*nederghekeert*) to every need of the people and to all sinful people with great compassion and mercy and with heart-felt prayer to his Father for the need of all people.[39]

Another image preferred by Ruusbroec for the mystic is that of an eagle, because this is the bird that soars highest of all. For example, in *The Spiritual Tabernacle*, he compares to the eagle the adept of "natural contemplation" as well as the person who "contemplates with grace." However, these two differ in the result of their moving upward, for the first "nests and rests in his own essence," whereas the second "flies above himself in God, and that is where he nests." Another difference between them is that although both descend from their height, the "natural" mystic is "in his coming downward proud and deceitful, not able to stand up to suffering and using offensive language," while the other's "coming down is so amiable with works and words... And he is so gentle and humble of heart."[40] In *The Seven Enclosures*, Ruusbroec refers again to the eagle as he describes what happens to the person whose "intention and love soar above all virtues to the person whom he loves and has in view." The upwards moving person experiences union with God in this way:

> Therefore, he is just and flies up to where he loves and always back down again where he exercises himself in virtue and good works. Thus he goes forth and returns like lightning from heaven. His life and his nourishment consist in ascent and descent. And so does the eagle. In his highest flight, he spots the little fish in the sea by which he lives. And thus he flies upwards and downwards, and in both movements he is fed and nourished.[41]

[39] *Werken*, I, 51,32-52,4.

[40] *Werken*, II,336,16-29 and 337,2-15. See also Mommaers and Van Bragt, *Mysticism Buddhist and Christian*, 258-261.

[41] *Opera Omnia*, II, 728-735.

But is it possible to specify how the mystic's upward and downward movement are related to each other? Clearly Ruusbroec is not prepared to blur, let alone efface, the difference between them. Are these contrasting feelings to be seen as independent moments that alternate with each other, or as foreign elements that exist side by side? Ruusbroec would certainly disagree, as he makes clear in *The Spiritual Tabernacle*:

> For although humility and freedom are contrasted in their way of working, they are nonetheless always inseparable. For just as the mind ascends to God in freely given reverence and enters into eternal rest, so it also freely descends in humility, and sinks itself in God, in the same eternal rest. Here, then, to ascend and to descend are of equal nobility. For they both live and work out of one and the same ground of abandon *(doechsamheit)*.[42]

In the passage from *The Twelve Beguines* that formed the starting point for this section, Ruusbroec used the same term, "empty" *(ledich)*, to refer to the outcome of both the upward and the downward movement.[43] Thus, the person mentioned was said to be "free and empty" as well as "empty and at peace." But the same happens here to the person enjoying "eternal rest": once again, the contrasting movements appear to lead the mystic to one and the same ultimate state, and Ruusbroec's writings contain a series of elaborate explanations with regard to this final equivalence (too many to be explored here).[44] The few lines given above

---

[42] *Werken*, II, 60,28-61,3.

[43] See above the quotation corresponding to note 25, *Werken*, IV, 97,8-26.

[44] For example, there is the motif of being "annihilated through love" *(te nieute in minnen)* as opposed to being "annihilated through humility" *(te nieute in oetmoede)*. There is also the idea that the mystic's *opganc* ("ascent") turns into an *overganc* ("passing over") so as to resemble the *nederganc* ("descent"). In *The Sparkling Stone*, Ruusbroec defines the difference between the "secret friends" and "the hidden sons of God": "For the friends feel nothing inside but

show clearly enough the answer he has in mind. Firstly, the terms "freedom" and "free" deserve attention. Ruusbroec has a liking for this word family,[45] and generally he uses "free(dom)" in connection with the soul's upward movement, which detaches it from what remains below.[46] In this case he surprisingly, but no doubt

a loving, living ascending within certain ways (*eenen minlijken levenden opganc in wisen*), but beyond that the sons feel a simple, dying passing over, beyond all manner (*eenen eenvuldighen stervenden overganc in onwisen*) (*Opera Omnia*, X, 350-353). On these points, see Mommaers, "*Opgaen* en *nedergaen*," part IV, p. 4-8 and 8-11. In *The Twelve Beguines*, Ruusbroec describes the person who, in "fathomless blessedness," (*grondelose salicheit*) experiences "God's being" (*Gods wesen*): "He sees himself as depth and exalted into … God's being. There he finds himself a single, fathomless blessedness with God and all his saints … This is above everything and underneath everything; this is the empty foundation (*een ledich fundament*), that is, the fathomless support/subsistence (*grondelose onthout*) of God and everything created" (*Werken*, IV, 26,32-27,4). *Onthout* ("subsistence") is synonymous with *onderstant* ("support"); both correspond to the Latin terms *sustentaculum* and *suppositum*. Thus *onthout* signifies the supporting, subsistence-giving origin. For *onthout* in a christological context, see *Werken*, II, 110,14 and 114,24.

[45] See Mommaers, "*Opgaen* en *nedergaen* ," part IV, p. 12-15 the detailed excursus on "freedom" (*vriheit*).

[46] So, in *The Spiritual Tabernacle*, it is said in a general way that "we should freely orient upwards (*vrileke oprichten*) our free mind (*vri gemude*), with all the good works, in God's honour" (*Werken*, II, 70,24-25). As for the contemplative union with God, it is necessary that one is able to "freely" go upwards or inwards. Here, "inner freedom means that a person may raise himself up to God unhindered, free of all images" (*Opera Omnia*, X, 42-43), or "that a person could turn within himself, imageless and unhindered, as often as he wishes" (*Opera Omnia*, III, b131-132). See also above, the citation from *A Mirror* corresponding to note 18. And here is a striking, Christ-centred description from *The Spiritual Tabernacle*: "This is why we should imitate Christ and go upwards in freedom (*gaen-op in vriheiden*), and deliver ourselves up to God's free unity (*vrie enecheit Goeds*). Thus we die to ourselves every hour and possess an eternal free life in God (*vri leven in Gode*).This is what Christ did, according to his humanity, from the first moment his spirit was created, and he will be bent on this forever. We should also go downwards freely (*nedergaen vrileke*) and

deliberately, links "freely" with the person's descending in humility as well as ascending to God. The key to understanding this two-way sense of "freely" lies in the final word of the closing sentence: "abandon" (*doechsamheit*).

It may help here to reconsider how Ruusbroec has prepared the steps to a clearer insight into this basic abandon. He began by referring to something that is not difficult to understand, namely, that the mystics' descent into the human condition implies their abandoning themselves: one goes "into the humble resignation of oneself." On the other hand, however, the author elaborated on a phenomenon which is far from self-evident, namely that a person's ascent to God equally involves self-surrender: "one descends and says what Christ said: 'Lord, not as I will, but as thou wilt' — 'Lord, into thy hands I commit my spirit.'" In the passage now being considered, Ruusbroec joins these two threads and shows how both contrasting movements can be called "free": each of them springs from the same selfless source. Thus the "equal nobility" of ascent and descent becomes understandable. In being one with God, the soul deploys her activity — a re-action to divine action — in contrasting movements which are both permeated by the same passivity, as they originate from the same "ground of abandon."

Another significant passage (from *The Seven Rungs*) hinges upon the same contrast between "freedom" and "humility."[47] It is

renounce ourselves in every heaviness that comes our way. Thus we carry our cross and die to our nature, and once more we imitate Christ who for our sake went down (*neder-ghinc*) in every misery till he died on the cross. And with these two (movements), that is, with his going upwards and his going downwards in freedom (*met sinen opgane ende met sinen nederganc in vriheiden*) he has bought for us freedom in God (*vriheit in Gode*)" (*Werken*, II, 44,13-27).

[47] *Werken*, III, 234,17-33.

part of the description of the fourth rung of the "ladder of love" which shows how the "ground of humility" may appear in a person. This happens through God "touching us," so that "we surrender our own will to God's dearest will ... and God's will being free and freedom ... he makes us free." Thus one receives the spirit that "makes us cry with the Son: 'Abba, Father'."[48] A description follows of the experience of those who are united with the Son in this way:

> There we see ourselves lifted up to the height and lowered into ourselves, and full of gifts and graces in union with God. Here the highest freedom and the lowest humility are gathered together in one person (*in eenen persoon*). And the practice in lowliness and height which belongs to this (one state) is unknown to outsiders.[49]

In conclusion, a return can be made to *The Twelve Beguines*. In the final part of this work, Ruusbroec devotes several pages to describing "three modes of love that lift a person up to God."[50] Remarkably, this gradual ascent proves to be a threefold descent, and at each of these steps or modes Christ appears as the living focus. The first mode, which is "felt love," is already familiar. Obviously this love lifts the "inner person" up, for "it spurns (worldly) pleasure and taste." And yet, it also brings him or her down into a "humble lowliness." This descent into "displeasure with himself" is quite puzzling since felt love is a delightful gift of the Lord, as a result of which "pleasure and taste permeate" the whole person. The solution lies in the nature of the Giver who simply *is* Abundance, so much so that his divine giving always comes to the human receiver as an overflowing "flood of gifts."

48   Romans, 14-15.
49   *Werken*, III, 234,28-33.
50   *Werken*, IV, 196,16-198,35.

The only way for the limited human being to accept this profusion to the full is to "fail from wealth" and "fall down before God's majesty":

> The first mode is felt love towards God. It spurns pleasure and taste, and all other things which are inordinate in the practice that tends towards the love of God. And (this first mode) puts the person in a humble lowliness and displeasure with himself. It makes him cry out: "Lord, help me, so that I love you!" And the more he cries and desires, the more he loves ... Pleasure and taste permeate heart and sense, soul and body ... The more gifts he receives from God, the poorer he is, for all God's gifts demand a giving back... to receive and to give back is the beginning of love's way ... The flood of gifts is so great that it flows over the sensitive life. Such is the soul's wealth that the senses cannot bear it, but the loving heart wants to die for God's honour and the benefit of holy Christendom ... At this point the senses fail from wealth (*ghebreken*), feeling and pleasure, and fainting they fall down ... The rational soul forgets herself and all differentiated virtues and falls down before God's majesty.[51]

The second mode of love has not been mentioned so far. It exceeds the first mode because it implies a much deeper descent which allows for a much deeper mutual giving. In this case there is no end to the downward movement for it brings the person "underneath everything created." And the exchange of gifts is so radical that it involves the very self: "Give yourself to me as I give myself to you." In addition, Ruusbroec makes it clear that the mystic experiences this unimaginably deep descent only in order to be united with the Godman: "the humble lowliness in which Christ lived and we live with him."[52] He is the One who as Jesus

---

[51] *Werken,* IV, 196,19-197,19.

[52] The unfathomable lowliness of Christ who "humbled himself in our humanity below all creatures" (*Werken,* IV, 149,20-24) appears often in Ruusbroec's writings, for example, in the phrases "humbling himself below all people" and "coming down, yes falling down, under the feet of all sinners" (*Werken,*

descends into absolute lowliness, "underneath everything created," while as Christ he lives at "infinite height," "above all created-ness":

> Then God's Spirit speaks in the loving soul: "Give yourself to me, I give myself to you!" Then the soul herself falls down in a humble lowliness which is underneath everything created ... The humble lowliness is the dwelling place of God, with all his gifts. And he shows the loving soul his eternal height above all gifts and above all createdness. Whoever wants to live according to God's counsel beyond the commandments, needs to renounce himself and abandon himself below all creatures in the humble lowliness in which Christ lived and we live with him. Christ's life was and is humble lowliness. Whoever lives with him ... remains in his own ground, unmoved by joys and sorrows ... Christ dwells in him and therefore he (Christ) brings about great fruit of virtues, and shows this person the infinite height where he lives with Christ in God above all gifts and above all virtues and above all createdness of creatures ... For Christ lives in him with the spirit of his strength, and in the infinite height this person lives with Christ in God, and feels in himself an unmoved blessedness.[53]

Finally, through the third mode of love, "failure" impinges on the selfhood of the mystic — in Ruusbroec's own terms on his or her very "person" (*persoon*); its effect is to "annihilate"[54] the self and

III, 257,18 and 147,24-25). Thus Christ was "brought low below all" (see the quotation corresponding to note 18) and "voluntarily subject to the whole world" (*Werken*, II,112,23-24).

[53] *Werken*, IV, 197,24-198,19. There is another passage from *The Twelve Beguines* evoking the mystic's depth-experience: "Immersed and forever sinking away in the fathomless depth of God. Down there, there is nothing (*en is niet*). There, in our resigned lowliness, we are God's realm, in which he lives and reigns and we with him below all createdness of creatures" (*Werken*, IV, 111,19-23).

[54] See, for the meaning of "person" (*persoon*), Mommaers and Van Bragt, *Mysticism Buddhist and Christian,* chapter 5: "Profiling the human"; similarly, on "annihilation," see the same work, passim.

allow it to realize Christ's words, "Give yourself to me." In his description of this experience, Ruusbroec concentrates in masterly fashion on what has appeared as the core of his teaching: for the human person being one with God is a Christ-centred, essentially compound phenomenon:

> After this there follows the third mode of love which is hidden from all who are not annihilated by this practice of love. This is where the spirit of wisdom ... makes one feel what unity in love with Christ in God is, and what otherness with Christ standing before God in eternal reverence is. Unity in love cannot become otherness, and otherness cannot become unity; thus they are both divided in one spirit. Otherness is blessed in its standing before (God), looking at God with eternal reverence; unity in love with God is blessedness, resting and enjoying in eternity. This is the highest experience one can feel here in time through God's gift and grace.[55]

---

[55] *Werken*, IV, 198,22-34.

SELECT BIBLIOGRAPHY

ADNÈS, Pierre, "Visions," *Dictionnaire de spiritualité* XVI (1994) 949-1002.

ALVAREZ, Thomas, "Thérèse de Jésus (sainte)," *Dictionnaire de spiritualité* XV (1991) 616-618.

ANDRÉS MARTÍN, Melquiades, "Osuna (François de)," *Dictionnaire de spiritualité* XI (1982) 1037-1051.

BAERE, Guido de, "Het 'ghemeine leven' bij Ruusbroec en Geert Grote," *Ons Geestelijk Erf* 59 (1985) 172-183.

—, "'Christus een ghieregh slockard' of de wansmaak van Ruusbroec," *Tegendraads genot: opstellen over de kwaliteit van middeleeuwse teksten*, eds. Karel Porteman, Werner Verbeke, Frank Willaert, Leuven: Peeters, 1996, 83-92.

BALTHASAR, Hans Urs von, *Herrlichkeit: Eine Theologische Aesthetik*, III-2: *Theologie*, 1: *Alter Bund*, 2: *Neuer Bund*, Einsiedeln: Johannes Verlag, 1967-1969.

BAUMGARTNER, Charles, "Extase," *Dictionnaire de spiritualité* IV/2 (1961) 2045-2189.

BEIERWALTES, Werner, *Denken des Einen: Studien zur Neoplatonischen Philosophie und Ihre Wirkunsggeschichte*, Frankfurt am Main: Vittorio Klostermann, 1985.

BENVENISTE, Émile, *Problèmes de linguistique générale*, Paris: Gallimard, 1966.

BERNARD OF CLAIRVAUX, *Selected Works*, translation and foreword by G.R. Evans; introduction by Jean Leclercq, O.S.B., preface by Ewert H. Cousins, The Classics of Western Spirituality, New York: Paulist Press, 1987.

—, *Sermones super Cantica Canticorum 36-86*, eds. Jean Leclercq, C.H. Talbot, H.M. Rochais; preface by Christine Mohrmann, Sancti Bernardi Opera II, Roma: Editiones Cistercienses, 1958.

—, *The Works of Bernard of Clairvaux*, 4 volumes, Kalamazoo: Cistercian Publications, 1976-1981.

BONAVENTURE, *Itinéraire de l'esprit vers Dieu*, text by Quaracchi, introduction, translation and notes by Henry Duméry, Paris: J. Vrin, 1978.

—, *The Soul's Journey into God; The Tree of Life; The Life of St. Francis*, translation and introduction by Ewert Cousins; preface by Ignatius Brady,

O.F.M., *The Classics of Western Spirituality*, New York: Paulist Press, 1978.

BREMOND, Henri, *Histoire littéraire du sentiment religieux en France*, VI: *La conquête mystique*: *Marie de l'Incarnation*; *Turba magna*, Paris: Bloud et Gay, 1922.

CHÂTILLON, Jean, "Richard de Saint-Victor," *Dictionnaire de spiritualité* XIII (1988) 593-654.

CULLER, Jonathan D., *On Deconstruction: Theory and Criticism after Structuralism*, London: Routledge and Kegan Paul, 1983.

DANIÉLOU, Jean, "Mystique de la ténèbre chez Grégoire de Nysse," *Dictionnaire de spiritualité* II (1953) 1876-1885.

DEBLAERE, Albert, *De mystieke schrijfster Maria Petyt (1623-1677)*, Ghent: Secretarie der Academie, 1962.

DEBRAY, Régis, *Vie et mort de l'image*: *Une histoire du regard en Occident*, Bibliothèque des idées, Paris: Gallimard, 1992.

DESCARTES, René, *Philosophical Writings*, a selection translated and edited by Elizabeth Anscombe and Peter Thomas Geach with an introduction by Alexandre Koyré, Edinburgh: Nelson, 1959.

DUFFY, Eamon, *The Stripping of the Altars: Traditional Religion in England 1400-1580*, New Haven and London: Yale University Press, 1992.

EURIPIDES, *Ion; Hippolytus; Medea; Alcestis*, transl. Arthur S. Way, Loeb Classical Gallery 12, Euripides in Four Volumes 4, London: Heinemann, 1964.

FAESEN, Rob, *Begeerte in het werk van Hadewijch*, Leuven: Peeters, 2000.

FLIPO, Claude, "Regarder autrement: Images du ciel, images de la terre," *Christus* 181 (1999) 19-25.

FRANCIS OF ASSISI; CLARE OF ASSISI, *The Complete Works*, translated and introduced by Regis J. Armstong, O.F.M. Cap. and Ignatius Brady, O.F.M.; preface by John Vaughn, O.F.M., The Classics of Western Spirituality, New York: Paulist Press, 1982.

FRANCISCO DE OSUNA, *The Third Spiritual Alphabet,* translated and introduced by Mary E. Giles, Preface by Kieran Kavanaugh, The Classics of Western Spirituality, New York: Paulist Press, 1981.

GAGLIARDI, Achille, *Breve compendio di perfectione cristiana e "vita di Isabella Berinzaga,"* with an introduction and notes by Mario Bendiscioli, Florence: Libreria Editrice Fiorentina, 1952.

GERARDO GROOTE, *Il trattato "De quattuor generibus meditabilium,"* introduced, edited, translated and annotated by Ilario Tolomio, Publicazioni dell'Istituto di Storia della Filosofia e del Centro per Ricerche di Filosofia Medioevale: Nuova Serie 18, Padova: Editrice Antenore, 1975.

GILSON, Étienne, *La théologie mystique de saint Bernard*, Paris: J. Vrin, 1934.

GNILKA, Joachim, *Der Philipperbrief: Auslegung*, Herders theologischer Kommentar zum Neuen Testament X-3, Freiburg: Herder, 1968.

GREGORY OF NYSSA, *Commentarium in Canticum Canticorum*, Patrologia Graeca 44, 755-1120.

—, *The Life of Moses*, translation, introduction, notes by Abraham J. Malherbe and Everett Ferguson; preface by John Meyendorff, NewYork, Ramsey, Toronto: Paulist Press, 1978.

GRUNDMANN, Herbert, *Religiöse Bewegungen im Mittelalter*, Hildesheim: Georg Olms Verlagsbuchhandlung, 1961.

—, "Litteratus-Illiteratus: Der Wandel einer Bildungsnorm vom Altertum zum Mittelalter," *Ausgewählte Aufsätze*, III: *Bildung und Sprache*, Schriften der Monumenta Germaniae Historica 25/3, Stuttgart: Hiersemann, 1978.

GULLIK, Etta; Optat **DE VEGHEL**, "Herp (Henri de, Harpius)," *Dictionnaire de spiritualité* VII/1 (1969) 346-366.

HAAS, Alois, "La mystique comme théologie," *Revue des sciences religieuses* 72 (1998) 261-288.

HADEWIJCH, *The Complete Works,* translation and introduction by Mother Columba Hart preface by P. Mommaers, The Classics of Western Spirituality, New York: Paulist Press, 1980.

HADOT, Pierre, "Les niveaux de conscience dans les états mystiques selon Plotin," *Journal de psychologie* 23 (1980) 243-266.

HERCK, Walter Van, *Religie en metafoor: Over het relativisme van het figuurlijke* (Leuven: Peeters, 1999).

HUIZINGA, Johan, *Herfsttij der Middeleeuwen*, Baarn: H. D. Tjeenk Willink & Zoon, 1921².

JAN VAN RUUSBROEC, *Opera omnia, 1: Boecsken der verclaringhe*, edited by Guido de Baere; introduced by Paul Mommaers; translated by Philip Crowley and Helen Rolfson, Studiën en tekstuitgaven van Ons Geestelijk Erf 20, 1, Tielt: Lannoo; Leiden: E.J. Brill, 1981 (also published in the series Corpus Christianorum: Continuatio Mediaevalis 101, Tielt: Lannoo; Turnhout: Brepols, 1989).

—, *Opera omnia, 2: Vanden seven sloten*, introduced and edited by Guido de Baere; translated by Helen Rolfson, Studiën en tekstuitgaven van Ons Geestelijk Erf 20, 2, Tielt: Lannoo; Leiden: E.J. Brill, 1981 (also published in the series Corpus Christianorum: Continuatio Mediaevalis 102, Tielt: Lannoo; Turnhout: Brepols, 1989).

—, *Opera omnia, 3: Die geestelike brulocht*, edited by Joseph Alaerts; introduced by Paul Mommaers; translated by Helen Rolfson; directed by Guido de Baere, Studiën en tekstuitgaven van Ons Geestelijk Erf 20, 3, Tielt: Lannoo; Turnhout: Brepols, 1988 (also published in the series Corpus Christianorum: Continuatio Mediaevalis 103, Tielt: Lannoo; Turnhout: Brepols, 1988).

—, *Opera omnia, 10: Vanden blinkenden steen, Vanden vier becoringhen, Vanden kerstenen ghelove, Brieven*, edited by Guido de Baere, Thom Mertens and Hilde Noë; introduced by Paul Mommaers; translated into English by André Lefevere; Studiën en tekstuitgaven van Ons Geestelijk Erf 20, 10, Tielt: Lannoo; Leiden: E.J. Brill, 1991 (also published in the series Corpus Christianorum: Continuatio Mediaevalis 110, Tielt: Lannoo; Turnhout: Brepols, 1991).

—, *Werken*, naar het standaardhandschrift van Groenendaal uitgegeven door het Ruusbroecgenootschap te Antwerpen, I-IV, Tielt: Lannoo, 1944-1948[2].

JETTÉ, Fernand, "Extase, B: Mystique chrétienne, V: Tradition spirituelle du 13e au 17e siecle," *Dictionnaire de Spiritualité* IV/2 (1961) 2131-2151.

JULIAN OF NORWICH, *A Book of Showings to the Anchoress Julian of Norwich*, eds. Edmund Colledge O.S.A., James Walsh S.J., Pontifical Institute of Medieval Studies: Studies and Texts 35, Toronto: Pontifical Institute of Mediaeval Studies, 1978.

—, *The Revelations of Divine Love*, translated by Elizabeth Spearing; introduction and notes by A. C. Spearing, Harmondsworth: Penguin Books, 1998.

KERR, Fergus, *Theology after Wittgenstein*, Oxford: Basil Blackwell, 1986.

KIRCHMEIER, Jean, "Extase, II: Extase chez les Pères de l'Eglise," *Dictionnaire de spiritualité* IV/2 (1961) 2087-2113.

LAMARCHE, Paul, "Transfiguration," *Dictionnaire de Spiritualité* XV (1991) 1148-1151.

LANS, Johannes M. van der, *Religieuze ervaring en meditatie: Een godsdienstpsychologische studie*, Psychologische monografiën, Deventer: Van Loghum Slaterus, 1980.

L'image: Fonctions et usages des images dans l'Occident médiéval, Actes du 6e "International Workshop on Medieval Societies," Centre Ettore Majorana, Erice, Sicile, 17-23 octobre 1992, under the direction of J. Baschet and J.-Cl. Schmitt, Paris: Le Léopard d'Or, 1996.

MARGUERITE PORETE, *The Mirror of Simple Souls*, translated and introduced by Ellen L. Babinsky; preface by Robert E. Lerner, The Classics of Western Spirituality, New York: Paulist Press, 1993.

—, *Le Mirouer des Simples Ames*, ed. Romana Guarnieri, *Speculum simplicium animarum*, cura et studio Paul Verdeyen, Corpus Christianorum, Continuatio Medievalis 69, Turnhout: Brepols, 1986.

MARION, Jean-Luc, *Dieu sans l'être*, Paris: Fayard, 1982.

—, *L'idole et la distance*, Paris: Grasset, 1977.

—, *Prolégomènes à la charité*, Paris: Editions La Différence, 1986.

MARTIN, Melquiades Andrés, "Osuna (François de)," *Dictionnaire de spiritualité* XI (1982) 1050.

MEANY, M., *The Image of Christ in the Revelations of Divine Love by Julian of Norwich*, London: University Microfilms International, 1975.

MECHTILD OF MAGDEBURG, *Das flieszende Licht der Gottheit*, eingef. von Margot Schmidt mit einer Studie von Hans Urs von Balthasar, Menschen der Kirche in Zeugnis und Urkunde, N.F. 3, Einsiedeln: Benziger Verlag, 1955.

MEIER, John P., *A Marginal Jew: Rethinking the Historical Jesus*, 2: *Mentor, Message and Miracles*, Anchor Bible Reference Library, New York: Doubleday, 1994

MIQUEL, Pierre, "Icône, II: Théologie de l'icône," *Dictionnaire de spiritualité* VII/2 (1971) 1229-1239.

—, "Images (culte des)," *Dictionnaire de spiritualité* VII/2 (1971) 1503-1519.

MOMMAERS, Paul, "Gregorius van Nyssa (ca 335-395): De mens is nooit voltooid," *Denk-wijzen*, 4: *Een inleiding in het denken van Plato, Aristoteles, Plotinus, Gregorius van Nyssa*, red. Harry Berghs, Leuven: Acco, 1989, 93-120.

—, *Hadewijch: Schrijfster begijn mystica*, Averbode: Altiora, 1989.

—, "Internationale uitstraling van de Nederlandse mystieke literatuur," *Nederlands in culturele context*, Antwerpen: IVM, 1995, 133-151.

—, "Is Hadewijch emotioneel?" *Emoties in de Middeleeuwen*, eds. R.E.V. Stuip, C. Vellekoop, Utrechtse Bijdragen tot de Mediëvistiek 15, Hilversum: Verloren, 1998, 135-156.

—; Frank WILLAERT, "Mystisches Erlebnis und sprachliche Vermittlung in den Briefen Hadewijchs," *Religiöse Frauenbewegung und mystische Frömmigkeit im Mittelalter*, Cologne: Böhlau Verlag, 1988, 117-151.

—; Jan VAN BRAGT, *Mysticism Buddhist and Christian: Encounters with Jan van Ruusbroec*, Nanzan Studies in Religion and Culture, New York: Crossroad, 1995.

—, "*Opgaen* en *nedergaen* in het werk van Jan van Ruusbroec," *Ons Geestelijk Erf* 69 (1995), 97-113; 193-215; 70 (1996), 216-239; 71 (1997), 3-40.

—, "PaysBas; IV. Les XVIᵉ et XVIIᵉ siècles," *Dictionnaire de spiritualité* XII/1 (1984) 730-750.

—, "Une phrase clef des *Noces Spirituelles*," *Jan van Ruusbroec: The Sources, Contents and Sequels of his Mysticism*, edited by P. Mommaers, N. De Paepe, Medievalia Lovaniensia, series I, studia XII, Leuven: University Press, 1984.

—, "Union mystique et imitation de Jésus-Christ: Une controverse cruciale chez les capucins Flamands vers la fin du XVIᵉ siècle," *I Francescani in Europa tra Riforma e Contrariforma*, Perugia: Edizioni Scientifiche Italiane, 1987, 27-49.

MURDOCH, Iris, *Metaphysics as a Guide to Morals,* Harmondsworth: Penguin, 1993.

—, *The Sovereignty of Good*, London: Routledge and Kegan Paul, 1970.

MUSIL, Robert, *The Man Without Qualities: Three*, London: Picador Pan Books, 1979.

NEWMAN, Barbara, *From Virile Woman to Woman Christ: Studies in Medieval Religion and Literature*, Philadelphia: University of Pennsylvania Press, 1995.

PASCAL, Blaise, *Pensées*, translated with an introduction by A.J. Krailsheimer, Harmondsworth: Penguin Books, 1966.

PEERS, E. Allison: *The Complete Works of Saint Teresa of Jesus*, London: Sheed and Ward, 1946.

PLINIUS SECUNDUS CAIUS MAIOR, *Natural History*, translated by H. Rackham, Loeb Classical Gallery 394, Pliny in Ten Volumes 9, London: Heinemann, 1968.

PLOTINUS, *The Enneads*, translated by Stephen MacKenna, second edition revised by B. S. Page, with a foreword by professor E. R. Dodds and an introduction by professor P. Henry S.J., London: Faber and Faber, 1956.

—, *The Enneads*, translated by Stephen MacKenna, London: Faber and Faber, 1969.

—, *Traité 38 (VI,7)*, introduction, translation, commentary and notes by Pierre Hadot, Paris: Cerf, 1988.

POLANYI, Michael, *Personal Knowledge*, London: Routledge and Kegan Paul, 1958.

—, *The Tacit Dimension*, New York: Doubleday and Company, 1966.

—, *The Study of Man: The Lindsay Memorial Lectures 1958*, London: Routledge and Kegan Paul, 1959.

PSEUDO-DIONYSIUS, *The Complete Works*, translation by Colm Luibheid, The Classics of Western Spirituality, New York: Paulist Press, 1987.

QUIGNARD, Pascal, *Vie secrète*, Paris: Gallimard, 1998.

RAHNER, Karl, "Über Visionen und verwandte Erscheinungen," *Geist und Leben* 21 (1948) 179-213.

RICARD, Robert, "Laredo (Bernardin de)," *Dictionnaire de spiritualité* IX (1976) 277-281.

[RICHARD OF SAINT-VICTOR], *Ives: Epître à Séverin sur la charité; Richard de Saint-Victor: Les quatre degrés de la violente charité*, text-critical edition, introduced, translated and annotated by Gervais Dumeige, Paris: J. Vrin, 1955.

—, *Selected Writings on Contemplation*, translated with an introduction and notes by Clare Kirchberger, London: Faber and Faber, 1957.

—, *The Twelve Patriarchs; The Mystical Ark*; *Book Three of The Trinity*, translation and introduction by Grover A. Zinn, preface by Jean Châtillon, The Classics of Western Spirituality, New York: Paulist Press, 1979.

RICŒUR, Paul; André LACOCQUE, *Penser la Bible*, La couleur des idées, Paris: Seuil 1998.

ROQUES, René, "Contemplation, E: Contemplation, extase et ténèbre chez le Pseudo-Denys," *Dictionnaire de spiritualité* II (1953) 1885-1911.

ROS, Fidèle de, *Le Frère Bernardino de Laredo: Un inspirateur de Sainte Thérèse*, Paris: Vrin, 1948.

RUH, Kurt, "Zur Grundlegung einer Geschichte der franziskanische Mystik," *Vita seraphica* 61 (1980), 1-24.

SANDAEUS, Maximilianus, *Pro mystica theologia clavis*, Cologne: Gualteriana, 1640; facsimile Heverlee: Éditions de la Bibliothèque S.J, 1963.

SARTRE, Jean-Paul, *L'imaginaire*, Paris: Gallimard, 1986.

—, *Esquisse d'une théorie des émotions*, Paris: Hermann, 1960.

SOUTHERN, Richard William, *Medieval Humanism and Other Studies*, Oxford: Basil Blackwell, 1970.

STEINEN, Wolfram Von den, *Menschen im Mittelalter*, ed. Peter von Moos, Bern: Francke Verlag, 1967.

SZABÒ, Titus, "Extase, B: Mystique chrétienne, IV: Chez les théologiens du 13ᵉ siècle," *Dictionnaire de spiritualité* IV/2 (1961) 2120-2131.

TERESA DE JESÚS, SANTA, *Obras completas*, edited by Efrén de la Madre de Dios O.C.D.; Otger Steggink O.Carm., Madrid: La Editorial Catolica, 1972.

The Image and the Book: Iconic Cults, Aniconism, and the Rise of Book Religion in Israel and the Near East, ed. Karel van der Toorn, Leuven: Peeters, 1997.

The Cloud of Unknowing, edited, with an introduction by James Walsh, S.J.; preface by Simon Tugwell, O.P., The Classics of Western Spirituality, New York: Paulist Press, 1981.

TOMAS DE LA CRUZ, "Humanité du Christ, IV: L'école carmélitaine," *Dictionnaire de spiritualité* VII/1 (1969) 1096-1108.

VERNAY, R., "Attention," *Dictionnaire de spiritualité* I (1937) 1058-1077.

WEIL, Simone, *Cahiers* III, Paris: Plon, 1974.

—, *Waiting for God*, New York: Harper and Row, 1973.

WITTGENSTEIN, Ludwig, *Lectures: Cambridge, 1930-1932*, ed. Desmond Lee, Oxford: Blackwell, 1980.

—, *Philosophical Investigations*, transl. G.E.M. Anscombe, Oxford: Basil Blackwell, 1967.

—, *Remarks on the Philosophy of Psychology*, I, eds. G.E.M. Anscombe and G.H. von Wright, transl. G.E.M. Anscombe, Oxford: Basil Blackwell, 1980.

WOOLF, Virginia, *A Writer's Diary*, London: Triad Grafton Books, 1978.

PRINTED ON PERMANENT PAPER • IMPRIME SUR PAPIER PERMANENT • GEDRUKT OP DUURZAAM PAPIER - ISO 9706

N.V. PEETERS S.A., WAROTSTRAAT 50, B-3020 HERENT